50 Years of The Waitangi Tribunal

Whakamana i te Tiriti

EDITED BY
CARWYN JONES
AND MARIA BARGH

First published in 2025 by Huia Publishers and Te Tākupu, Te Wānanga o Raukawa

Te Tākupu, Te Wānanga o Raukawa
144 Tasman Road, PO Box 119
Ōtaki, Aotearoa New Zealand
www.tetakupu.wananga.com

Huia Publishers
39 Pipitea Street, PO Box 12280
Wellington, Aotearoa New Zealand
www.huia.co.nz

ISBN 978-1-77550-925-7

A catalogue record for this book is available from the National Library of New Zealand.

We acknowledge the support of the Arramat project, funded by the Canada Research Coordinating Committee's New Frontiers in Research Fund.

We also acknowledge and thank Ngā Pae o te Māramatanga for supporting this publication and/or presentation of this work through a **Whakaaweawe Impact and Transformation Grant.**

NPM
NGĀ PAE O TE MĀRAMATANGA

50 Years of The Waitangi Tribunal

Whakamana i te Tiriti

EDITED BY
CARWYN JONES
AND MARIA BARGH

HUIA

TE TĀKUPU
e rere e te kupu

Foreword
Chief Judge Dr Caren Fox
(Chairperson, Waitangi Tribunal)
vii

1 The Waitangi Tribunal and its Work
Carwyn Jones
3

2 I Te Tīmatanga ...
Hon Sir Edward Taihākurei Durie
(Chairperson, Waitangi Tribunal 1980–2004)
13

3 Historical Claims and District Inquiries
"The matter has been settled"?
Peter Meihana
23

4 Awa
Ngā Wai Honohono –
The Rivers that Join Us
Linda Te Aho
43

5 Wai me Te Taiao
"He pukenga wai, he nohonga tāngata,
he nohonga tāngata, he putanga kōrero" –
Steering the Constitutional Conversation
about Freshwater towards Rangatiratanga
Horiana Irwin-Easthope and Jacinta Ruru
61

6 Takutai Moana
Carried by Power, Unmitigated by Fairness
Wai 1071 The Report on the Crown's Foreshore and Seabed Policy 2004
Metiria Stanton Turei
85

7 Ika
Tai Ahu
109

8 Issues Relating to Treaty Settlements
The Most Dishonourable Process of Managed Chaos
Margaret Mutu
127

9 The Tribunal in the Settlement Era
Hon Justice Sir Joe Williams
(Waitangi Tribunal Acting and Deputy Chairperson 1999–2004, Chairperson 2004–2008)
145

10 Taonga
Te Reo Māori and Mātauranga Māori
Jayden Houghton
155

11 From Historical Claims to Kaupapa Inquiries
Judge Wilson Isaac
(Waitangi Tribunal Chairperson 2009–2023)
175

12 Toiora
Social Policy and Well-being
Carwyn Jones, Jacqueline Paul and Rhiannon Jones
183

13 Mana Wāhine
Ani Mikaere
205

14 Rangatiratanga
Constitutional Issues
Tracey Whare
223

15 Whakamana i te Tiriti
Carwyn Jones
243

Endnotes
253

Notes on Contributors
279

Index
283

Foreword
Chief Judge Dr Caren Fox

Me mihi ki a Ihoa, nāna te tīmatanga o ngā mea katoa, ā, kia whakahōnoretia tōna ingoa tapu. Kei ngā mate o te wā, hoki atu ki te Atua. Kei ngā reo, kei ngā mana, kei ngā kaituhi, kua kohi mai nei i ngā whakaaro nui i runga i te reo karanga o te wā, tēnā koutou katoa.

For the last fifty years, the Waitangi Tribunal's primary role has been to inquire into claims made by "any Māori" alleging that Crown actions, policies, regulations or statutes are inconsistent with the principles of the Treaty of Waitangi, resulting in prejudice to that claimant. Where it finds the claim well founded, the Tribunal may make recommendations to remove or mitigate that prejudice. It records these outcomes in reports.

The Waitangi Tribunal has a history marked by its commitment to in-depth hearings and reports. Its modus operandi has been to follow a steady programme of work, marked by some innovation, but focused on progressing as many claims as possible to completion through the release of its district historical, thematical/kaupapa and urgency reports.

Those reports have been embraced by most claimants. Some reports have resulted in improved Crown Treaty policy or genuine attempts to settle historical and contemporary injustices, even if the Tribunal's recommendations were not followed to the letter.

Other reports have recorded inconvenient findings and recommendations that have been negatively received by disaffected claimants or by a particular government. These reports may have languished, but they remain an inescapable record until picked up again by the parties to the Treaty.

These diametrically oppositional outcomes reflect the fact that the Tribunal must be courageous enough to make its findings and recommendations without fear or favour, affection or ill will. It does not act for the claimants or the Crown but rather remains the independent arbiter and inquisitor of the Crown–Māori relationship.

What is clear is that there is a need for greater public understanding and engagement with the Tribunal's reports. This book, written by experts and edited by Carwyn Jones and Maria Bargh, is an independent and honest appraisal of the work and reports of the Tribunal. Hard hitting and direct, the authors have not minced their words describing the toll its processes and inquiries take on claimants, the strengths and weaknesses of its reports and the impact of those reports on Crown actions, policy and legislation.

It highlights why the claimants come to the Waitangi Tribunal in pursuit of good government, fairness and access to justice. While the authors underscore the united calls for recognition of the essential exchange of the Treaty (kāwanatanga for rangatiratanga), there is a practical understanding that ultimately the two parties must talk and that the Crown–Māori relationship remains central to nation building in our country. This will become even more essential as the Waitangi Tribunal completes its hearing programme, as the Māori population grows and as we progress as a country towards the year 2040, 200 years after the signing of the Treaty of Waitangi.

Nō reira, kuhu mai e ngā tāngata o te īta, o te nōta, o te ēta, o te hauta, kuhu mai ki roto i te mahi o te Roopu Whakamana i te Tiriti o Waitangi.

Therefore, enter those from the east, north, west and from the south into the work of the Waitangi Tribunal.

Karanga rā, e Rata
Te hiku o te ika e
Whakaripo ake nei e

Tēnei a Tai
Whakamana te Tiriti e
Te ope nei e

Tainui e
E tama Rawiri
Paora e
Whakaterehia rā

Maranga mai
Te iwi oho ake rā
Tauiwi tahuri mai e

Whatungarongaro
Toitū te whenua e

The clarion voice of Rata calls
The movement in the tail of the fish responds

In our midst we now have Tai
Now is the time to give strength to the Treaty
Here too is the ope, all members of the Tribunal

Tainui
[Koro Wetere, Minister of Māori Affairs]
Rawiri
[David Lange, Prime Minister] and
Paora
[Paul Reeves, the Governor-General]
Through you, this fish can swim

Māori people rise and be vigilant
Tauiwi (Pākehā and others)
The time is now to face each other

As the light of the eye and the life of things living fade from sight, only the land is seen to remain, constant and enduring

Chapter 1

The Waitangi Tribunal and its Work

— Carwyn Jones

Composed by respected leader of Te Whānau-a-Apanui and Waitangi Tribunal member Sir Monita Delamere, "Karanga Rā", recalls the establishment of the Waitangi Tribunal and acknowledges the political and constitutional leadership of the time and some of those who contributed to shaping the Tribunal in its early years. Matiu Rata, Koro Wetere, David Lange, Paul Reeves and Edward Taihākurei Durie are all referenced in this waiata, which has been sung by Waitangi Tribunal members and staff at hearings since 1986. Now is the time to face each other and give strength to te Tiriti, its words proclaim. For half a century now, the Waitangi Tribunal has been empowering New Zealanders to do just that - to face each other and our history with clear eyes and to strengthen te Tiriti and the relationship it established between tino rangatiratanga and kāwanatanga.

This collection reflects on fifty years of the Waitangi Tribunal's work, the challenges it has faced and the contribution it has made to our understanding of the past, of the impacts of current law and policy, and of how we can strive for a more just future for Aotearoa.

The Waitangi Tribunal and the Treaty of Waitangi Act 1975

The establishment of the Waitangi Tribunal in 1975 was truly groundbreaking. It was a significant constitutional development for Aotearoa, providing statutory recognition of te Tiriti, albeit by means of Treaty principles. Having a membership comprised of Māori and Pākehā was a world-leading approach to the adjudication of indigenous rights and has proved to have been essential to the Tribunal's work.

The Waitangi Tribunal was established as a commission of inquiry by the Treaty of Waitangi Act, which came into force on 10 October 1975. The purpose of the Act is described in its long title:

> *An Act to provide for the observance, and confirmation, of the principles of the Treaty of Waitangi by establishing a Tribunal to make recommendations on claims relating to the practical application of the Treaty and to determine whether certain matters are inconsistent with the principles of the Treaty.*

Under the Act, the Tribunal's key functions are to inquire into claims of breaches of the principles of the Treaty, make findings as to whether Crown actions are consistent with the principles of the Treaty and make recommendations to the Crown for the practical application of those principles.

Parliament chose not to define in the Act what the principles of the Treaty are but, instead, for the purposes of the Act, gave the Waitangi Tribunal the "exclusive authority to determine the meaning and effect of the Treaty as embodied in the 2 texts and to decide issues raised by the differences between them". The Act requires the Tribunal to consider both the English text and Māori text of the Treaty in carrying out its functions. The requirement for the Tribunal to apply principles of the Treaty appears to be a direction from Parliament about the way in which the Tribunal should approach the interpretation and application of te Tiriti. That is, the Tribunal is directed to discern, through consideration of the text in light of the surrounding context, ideas that underpin the Treaty agreement and can be applied to modern circumstances. Principles that have been identified and applied by the Tribunal include partnership, active protection, equity, mutual benefit and equal treatment.

The Tribunal was established as a forum for Māori to bring claims based on te Tiriti. For a claim to be registered with the Tribunal, it must meet four criteria:

- The claim must be made by a Māori person (on behalf of themselves or a broader group).
- It must relate to some Crown action or omission.
- There must be an allegation that the Crown act or omission is in breach of the principles of the Treaty.
- The claim must allege that the claimant or claimant group is prejudicially affected by that breach.

There are some issues that the Tribunal is prohibited from inquiring into. It may not inquire into claims relating to private land (with some very limited exceptions) or matters that have already been settled by legislation. The Tribunal is also prohibited from inquiring into legislation that is before Parliament, unless a bill is, by resolution of the House of Representatives, specifically referred to the Tribunal for consideration. This has not occurred in the first fifty years of the Tribunal's existence.

When the Tribunal was first established, the Act provided that the Tribunal would have three members. The Chief Judge of the Māori Land Court was, ex officio, the chairperson of the Waitangi Tribunal. Two further members were to be appointed on the recommendation of the Minister of Māori Affairs and the Minister of Justice, respectively. Today, the Tribunal chairperson may be a judge or retired judge of the High Court or the Chief Judge of the Māori Land Court, and there is provision to appoint up to twenty other members. The chairperson and other members are appointed by the Governor-General on the recommendation of the Minister of Māori Affairs in consultation with the Minister of Justice. In considering the suitability of people to be appointed to the Tribunal, the Minister is directed to have regard to "the partnership between the 2 parties to the Treaty" and "not only to a person's personal attributes but also to a person's knowledge of and experience in the different matters likely to come before the Tribunal". Past and current members have had expertise in areas such as law, history, te ao Māori and public policy, amongst others. A panel of three to seven Tribunal members will be appointed by the chairperson to hear a particular claim or group of claims as an inquiry.

Many people are perhaps most familiar with the Tribunal's work in hearing historical claims. However, under its original legislation, the Tribunal did not have any historical jurisdiction. At that point, it could only hear claims relating to Crown action from 1975 onwards. In 1985, a legislative amendment meant that the Tribunal could inquire into matters as far back as the signing of te Tiriti in 1840. For around half of its fifty years of operation, historical claims became the main focus of the Tribunal's work.

In 2006, the Treaty of Waitangi Act was amended again so that from 2008 onwards the Tribunal could no longer receive any new claims that related to historical Crown action. Historical claims are defined as those claims that relate to Crown acts or omissions that took place before 21 September 1992. That date is chosen as effectively representing the beginning of the modern Treaty settlement process as it was the date on which Cabinet, in the context of the settlement of commercial fishing claims (in what became known as 'the Sealord deal'), approved principles for the settlement of historical claims. The Tribunal is still completing some of its historical inquiries, but its focus is now returning to its original jurisdiction of contemporary claims, which it is addressing through a programme of thematic or kaupapa inquiries.

Overview of this book

The fiftieth anniversary of the Waitangi Tribunal is a significant milestone and a logical point to take stock and reflect on the Tribunal's body of work and its role within New Zealand society. But how could we sensibly cover fifty years' worth of Waitangi Tribunal inquiries and reports and the associated historical research, legal analysis, findings and recommendations within a single book?

To answer that question, I sought the advice of my valued friend and colleague, and co-editor of this collection, Professor Maria Bargh. We discussed what this collection should look like and how it could contribute to the literature about the Waitangi Tribunal. We initially considered producing an update to the excellent collection of essays on the Waitangi Tribunal edited by Janine Hayward and Nicola Wheen and published in 2004. After all, twenty years had passed since the publication of that volume, and, in that time, the Tribunal had produced a number of significant reports on major historical claims as well as other urgent and groundbreaking inquiries. There was certainly plenty to update. However, the more we discussed the proposed collection, the more we thought that the major developments within the past twenty years ought to be considered in the context of the Tribunal's entire body of work. We also decided that we wanted this collection to be of real, practical use. That is, one of our objectives is to provide a resource to which people could refer to quickly identify issues that the Waitangi Tribunal has engaged with and recommendations the Tribunal has already made.

But we did not want the collection to only be a record of the Tribunal's findings. We thought that this collection could, and should, provide context and analysis of the Tribunal's work and identify challenges and future directions. We are very grateful to have been able to call on an amazing group of established and emerging Māori scholars as contributing authors to provide real subject-matter expertise and to also include the reflections of three former chairpersons of the Tribunal.

Following this introductory chapter, the collection begins with Hon Sir Edward Taihākurei Durie's account of the beginning and early days of the Waitangi Tribunal. His account not only provides insight into the formative years of the Tribunal but also recognises and acknowledges the people involved, their vision, leadership and other qualities they brought to this important kaupapa. Waitangi Tribunal members are appointed for both their knowledge and their personal qualities. The importance of having people of mana from Māori and Pākehā communities is one of the themes of this collection, particularly in the reflections of the former chairpersons. This is one of the features that makes the Tribunal work and supports its role in reconciliation and nation building.

The next set of chapters address the Tribunal's work in relation to lands, waters and the natural environment. The first of these is Peter Meihana's chapter on whenua and the Tribunal's historical inquiries. The large-scale land loss across the country and associated historical claims made up the bulk of the Tribunal's work through the 1990s and into the first decades of the 2000s, when the district inquiry programme was in full swing. The issues relating to historical land loss have already been the subject of considerable scholarship. Meihana, therefore, focuses on some of the more recent historical reports of the Tribunal to bring this scholarship up to date and to consider the Tribunal's engagement with history across the district inquiries.

The two chapters that follow are closely connected. Linda Te Aho's chapter examines the Tribunal's river reports. These reports cover both historical actions of the Crown as well as contemporary policy issues in relation to the health of our waterways. The Tribunal's findings and recommendations in these river reports laid a foundation for the river settlements that were subsequently negotiated. The chapter by Jacinta Ruru and Horiana Irwin-Easthope looks at the Tribunal's engagement with environmental issues, and it uses those particularly relating to freshwater as a case study to illustrate the way in which the Tribunal has approached these matters. These two chapters complement one another as each deals with different dimensions of the expression of tino rangatiratanga in water resources. Both identify the Tribunal's articulation of relevant Treaty principles as vital to the construction of current settlements and policy framing governance of, and relationships with, rivers and other water resources. They also draw out the constitutional dimensions of these issues, which is another thread that runs through this collection.

The chapters by Metiria Turei and Tai Ahu address claims that have their origin in historical breaches of te Tiriti but involve the Tribunal intervening in contemporary political controversies. Turei's chapter addresses the long-running issue of Māori rights in relation to the takutai moana or foreshore and seabed. Turei was a sitting MP when the Foreshore and Seabed Act was developed. She describes the controversy sparked by the Court of Appeal's *Ngāti Apa* decision, focusing on the Tribunal's analysis, which was scathing of the Crown's policy response and approach to this issue. Ahu's chapter explores the Tribunal's engagement with fisheries issues. In particular, Ahu explains how the Tribunal inquiries provided the foundation for the commercial fisheries settlement, the first of the modern Treaty settlements, and how the Tribunal's Treaty analysis is still playing into the implementation of that settlement today.

This leads directly into the settlement era and the Tribunal inquiries that have addressed the settlement process and issues of remedy. Margaret Mutu's chapter is focused on these issues. Mutu considers the way in which the Waitangi Tribunal has addressed claims relating to mandate, processes for dealing with overlapping interests, and other aspects of the settlement process. Mutu also addresses the Tribunal's limited binding jurisdiction to require that Crown forest licensed land or state-owned enterprise land be used to remedy well-founded claims. The issue of remedies also illustrates some of the interaction between litigation through the general courts and Tribunal inquiries and settlement negotiations. Justice Sir Joseph Williams was chairperson of the Waitangi Tribunal during the period in which the modern settlement process came to prominence, and, in his interview, he reflects on some of the ways that the Tribunal needed to adapt to deliver inquiries and reports that supported the objectives of reconciliation in that context.

In recent years, the Tribunal has transitioned from a focus on its historical, district inquiry programme to a kaupapa inquiry programme that concentrates on thematic claims that have broad impacts on Māori across the country. Jayden Houghton's chapter addresses some early and important forerunners to the kaupapa inquiry programme, the Te Reo Māori inquiry, claims related to the radio spectrum, and the Wai 262 inquiry, which dealt with a range of issues connected with mātauranga Māori and intellectual property and was described as the Tribunal's first whole-of-government inquiry. Houghton considers the influence of these inquiries and the factors that might have affected their impact on law and policy.

Judge Wilson Isaac was chairperson of the Waitangi Tribunal at the time the Tribunal formally shifted its focus to the kaupapa inquiry programme. In an interview, Judge Isaac reflects on the changes required by this shift in focus, noting that a different range of skills was required within the Tribunal membership to address the kaupapa claims. Also, he notes that there have been some adjustments in procedure to respond most effectively to the distinctive kaupapa that are the subject matter of the claims. The ability of the Tribunal to adjust to changing circumstances is a significant feature of the Tribunal's status as a standing commission of inquiry, and this flexibility is another theme that runs through this collection.

In the chapter that I co-authored with Jacqueline Paul and Rhiannon Jones, we consider some of the social policy issues that have been addressed, and are continuing to be addressed, through the kaupapa inquiry programme. In particular, we examine the Tribunal's findings and recommendations in relation to health, housing and the care and protection of tamariki Māori. Throughout these inquiries, the Tribunal has emphasised the importance of equity and tino rangatiratanga as Treaty principles that ought to frame social policy and the delivery of social services.

The final two substantive chapters analyse inquiries where the Tribunal has had to engage with issues of mana and rangatiratanga. Ani Mikaere provides an insightful examination of the Mana Wāhine Kaupapa Inquiry, its background and the issues it has addressed. This is an ongoing inquiry, and the Tribunal has not yet issued its report. Therefore, we do not yet know the nature of the Tribunal's findings and recommendations. Nevertheless, the Tribunal's engagement with the issues in this inquiry has already been significant in recognising the distinctive experiences of wāhine Māori and the particular prejudice that may arise from breaches of Treaty principles. Mikaere also points towards the constitutional dimension of the claims in the Mana Wāhine Kaupapa Inquiry.

Constitutional issues also form the central focus of Tracey Whare's chapter. Whare covers a number of inquiries that have an explicit constitutional aspect, including reform of the legislation governing the New Zealand Māori Council and the Crown's actions in entering into the Trans-Pacific Partnership Agreement – a multilateral free-trade agreement that eventually became the Comprehensive and Progressive Agreement for Trans-Pacific Partnership. Whare also touches on the nascent Constitutional Kaupapa Inquiry, which has already produced urgent reports on the Treaty Principles Bill and the review of Treaty principles in legislation.

The brief concluding chapter draws together some of the themes identified throughout the collection and considers some of the key threads that weave through the Tribunal's work over its first fifty years.

We hope that this collection will provide readers with some understanding of the breadth of the Tribunal's work, the challenges it has addressed, the immense contribution it has made to Aotearoa and the opportunities that lie ahead in strengthening te Tiriti and our foundational constitutional relationships.

“From its inauguration, the reconstituted Waitangi Tribunal would seek to blend the cultural preferences of both parties to the Treaty into its process and to initiate a bicultural jurisprudence.”

Chapter 2

I Te Tīmatanga …

— Hon Sir Edward Taihākurei Durie

The street protest that came with the 1960 All Blacks' tour of South Africa would be significant for the establishment of the Waitangi Tribunal. The traditional protest against the failed promises of the Treaty of Waitangi, led by the Kīngitanga, Kotahitanga, the Māori parliamentarians and Hāhi Rātana, had been profound but, eventually, was to little avail. The 1960 tour unleashed the power of street protest by Māori, now mainly urban, and Pākehā. Together, a new consciousness would form around national identity and social justice. The protest of 1960 would be the harbinger of reforms much larger than the composition of the All Blacks.

The protest on the tour began with a public meeting at the Wellington Town Hall, called by Whetu Tirikatene (as she was then), Dr Rolland O'Regan and Professor Whatarangi Winiata. From there, the Māori protest movement coalesced around land, language and Treaty to peak in the Land March of 1975, the year in which the Treaty of Waitangi Act was passed.

The traditional leadership, as formally recognised by statute, also reformed at this time, with the Treaty as a core remit. The Maori Community Development Act 1962 (initially called the Maori Welfare Act) added a national body, the New Zealand Māori Council, to the existing district councils. These were first provided for by the Maori Councils Act 1900 as proposed by the Kotahitanga leaders and Māori parliamentarians. The Māori Council system, devised by Māori but constrained by the requirement for parliamentary endorsement, remains the only form of Māori self-government specifically provided for by statute.

The approach of the New Zealand Māori Council was marked by the publication of a paper by an accountant, Henare Ngata (later Sir Henare), on statutes that contravene the Treaty. Some leaders, however, were persuaded by the prevalent view that the Treaty was not a legal document and could not be recognised in law. In refutation, Douglas Sinclair, a Hamilton medical practitioner, then led the Māori Council's case on the Treaty as a constitutional document and a source of legal principle. This would prepare the Māori Council for its later pathway of protest through the courts.

Ultimately, however, it was an Āpotoro Rēhita of Te Hāhi Rātana who secured official recognition of the Treaty. For this, Matiu Rata would hold the title of Piri Wiri Tua, a title previously held only by Rātana himself. At age twenty-eight, Matiu was the parliamentary representative for Northern Māori. After a long period in opposition, his party became the government in 1972, and for the next three years Matiu was Minister of Māori Affairs until National regained the government seats in the 1975 election.

During his three years as Minister, Hon Matiu Rata was responsible for significant legislation affecting Māori land and the Treaty, undoubtedly the two most prominent issues for the iwi of the day. In my view, his work in those areas, and on the recovery of Crown land that should previously have returned to Māori, was not equalled or surpassed by his successors in office. His land legislation of 1974 undid the Europeanising measures of the Maori Affairs Amendment Act 1967 and, for the first time, made the retention of Māori land by Māori and the improvement of Māori land titles the focus of Māori land law. Due to his efforts, that improvement continues to be the focus today.

He also introduced the Treaty as the yardstick for assessing Māori historic resource losses. Thus, he sought to counter the prevalent opinion that those losses had been settled with the endowment of tribal trust boards in line with the 1927 recommendations of the Sim Commission.

Initially, Matiu was only partly successful. At that time, his colleagues would not allow the Tribunal to reopen the historical claims. Matiu countered by appointing researchers to the District Māori Land Boards to report on specific land claims and to demonstrate how the task might be done. The first appointee was Professor Evelyn Stokes (later Dame Evelyn), a geographer from Waikato University, who began with a report to the Waikato District Māori Land Board on the Papamoa rifle range. In 1988, Dame Evelyn would be appointed to the Waitangi Tribunal when its jurisdiction was extended back to 1840. She had good Māori contacts, especially in Tauranga, and she set an exacting standard for researching Māori claims.

With regard to the Treaty itself, I think several things gave Matiu a sound political edge. He was committed to principle. The evidence for that is his journey on a protest yacht into the French nuclear testing zone at Mururoa in 1972.

He had faith in Māori capability. An example was his appointment of me as a Māori Land Court judge at age thirty-four to a place where no Māori had been before and where, until then, the average age had hovered in the sixties. He especially believed in the capacity of the law and the justice system to rectify a wrong. The evidence for that was his belief that only judges should chair the Waitangi Tribunal.

Most of all, Matiu was immensely affable, making many of his colleagues amenable to him. He could have you smiling and compliant even while shifting the ground from under your feet.

It has been said that the Treaty of Waitangi Act was drafted in response to the 1975 Land March. It may have been *enacted* in response to it, but I saw a draft that was near to final in August 1974. I was also informed that it was much watered down from the original, which provided for historical claims, and that support in the Cabinet was borderline. The Attorney-General, the highly regarded Martyn Finlay who was also a friend and advisor to Matiu, was said to be wavering in his support, and it was unlikely that it would pass through the Cabinet without his approval.

It was then that the protest movement kicked in once more, although who gave it the kick is speculative. It may be relevant that the protest march started from Te Hapua, just over the hill from where Matiu was born in the most northerly kāinga; but then a hīkoi from the tail of the fish to its head included more Māori communities. Through that show of widespread allegiance, like the large gatherings of warriors for the battle of Hingakaka, the Attorney-General was prompted to give his support, and Cabinet approval followed soon after.

So it was that on 10 October 1975, with royal assent, the Treaty was provided for in law and the Waitangi Tribunal was born. Later, Sir Monita Delamere would bestow a name more telling of its purpose – Te Rōpū Whakamana i te Tiriti o Waitangi.

Nonetheless, the Tribunal arrived just in the nick of time. In the 1975 Muldoon landslide election the following month, the government changed to one that was not entirely enamoured of the new law. There had not even been sufficient time to appoint the first Tribunal members.

For five years, the Tribunal barely got off the ground. Although there were initially just three members, with the Chief Judge of the Māori Land Court sitting by virtue of his office, for eighteen months the Muldoon Government deferred appointing the other two. It then appointed one Māori who would sit between two experienced litigators. One, the Chief Judge, Ken Scott, was a former Gisborne litigator with a formidable reputation amongst lawyers for his exacting standards. The other, Laurie Southwick, was a senior litigator, Queen's Counsel, president of the New Zealand Law Society and a visionary in legal planning. Graham Latimer (later Sir Graham) was the third chairperson of the New Zealand Māori Council but was better known to Prime Minister Muldoon as the president of the Māori section of the National Party. Muldoon and Latimer had shared a room together as junior party members. It would later be apparent that Sir Graham was not the compliant member his appointors may have thought him to be and that his appointors had misjudged his gait.

Unsurprisingly, given the founding membership, the Tribunal favoured a more legal approach to its inquiry, but it was not what the claimants had expected. With that and the chosen hearing venue – the chandeliered ballroom of the Intercontinental Hotel – many prospective claimants were disillusioned, and claims languished for want of prosecution. Only two went forward. These were Joe Hawke on Ngāti Whātua fishing rights in Waitematā Harbour, and Ted Kirkwood and others on the likely impact of the Waiau Pā power station on traditional fishing in Manukau Harbour.

When the membership was reconstituted in 1980, with the retirement of all but Sir Graham (knighted in that year), the next rōpū had an advantage. Prior to my appointment, I had visited North America to compare the less-successful operations of the United States Court of Claims managing American Indian claims by Western legal process, from 1924, with the blended-culture approach of the commission appointed in Canada under Justice Berger, in 1974, to inquire into the Mackenzie Valley Pipeline. This included consideration of the oil pipeline's impact on the native Inuit and Dene peoples. From its inauguration, the reconstituted Waitangi Tribunal would seek to blend the cultural preferences of both parties to the Treaty into its process and to initiate a bicultural jurisprudence. Hearings would also be on marae according to claimant preference.

The Tribunal for the first 1980s inquiry, on the industrialisation of the Waitara coast, would comprise Sir Graham, Max Willis (the former Stipendiary Magistrate for Gisborne) and me as the new Chief Judge. The claimants chose Owae Waitara marae as the venue. My appointment had been made by the then Minister of Māori Affairs, Hon Ben Riwai Couch. Hon Ben Couch was a former Māori Warden and a member of the Ikaroa District Māori Council. He was also a former All Black and one of those whose ancestry made him ineligible for the 1949 South African tour.

The report on the claim attracted wide publicity, involving, as it did, the government's Think Big industrial project, which was a major plank on which the government had been elected. The immediate and negative reaction of Prime Minister Muldoon served only to garner support for the report. There was much interest in the information on Māori fishing knowledge and practice, in the alignment of that with the objectives of a growing environmental movement, and the explanation of the Treaty and its application. There was then a sea-change in the government's response. Under the guidance of Hon Bill Birch (later Sir William) as Minister of Energy, significant changes were made, notwithstanding the need to renegotiate each of the overseas loans involved.

Sir Graham was a major contributor to the Tribunal, having an extensive knowledge of the many claims in many different areas and of the leading Māori for each area. He was also a natural negotiator. After the Lange Labour Government failed to renew his Tribunal warrant in 1984, Sir Graham, who continued to chair the New Zealand Māori Council, paved the way for the further development of the nascent Treaty law. Along with others, like Professor Whatarangi Winiata, he would lead the New Zealand Māori Council in a series of court actions against Labour's proposals to privatise Crown lands, forests, fisheries and broadcasting assets. These proposals threatened to divest the Crown of assets that could compensate Māori for their huge resource losses as a result of past Crown action that was contrary to the Treaty.

The engagement of the general courts was undoubtedly the most important step in building the law around the Treaty. This may not have happened were it not for some remarkable members of the legal profession: Martin Dawson, Sian Elias (now Dame Sian) and David Baragwanath (now Sir David). These three had a vision of justice for Māori and a better and more inclusive New Zealand. Unfortunately, Martin died in 2003. Dame Sian appeared for the first time in the Waitangi Tribunal as counsel for Nganeko Minhinnick and Carmen Kirkwood of the Huakina Trust in the 1984 Manukau hearings. The Tribunal was still in its infancy then, with Sir Graham, Paul Temm QC (later Justice Temm) and me as the panel.

Sian's natural instinct to mentor and inspire had her leave the conduct of the case to the people while drawing together the many threads of the inquiry to produce her customary stunning closings. She would go on to become Chief Justice, the first woman to hold that office in New Zealand, and to head the new Supreme Court that would replace the Privy Council as New Zealand's highest court.

Sir David appeared first as counsel for Matiu Rata, Sir Graham and others in the Muriwhenua inquiry soon after the extension of the Tribunal's jurisdiction and the expansion of the Tribunal's membership. I sat then with Bishop Manuhuia Bennett ONZ, Sir Monita Delamere, Georgina Te Heuheu (a lawyer and later Dame Georgina and Minister for Courts 2008–2011) and two other lawyers, Bill Wilson, who would become a judge of the Court of Appeal and a founding judge of the Supreme Court, and Joanne Morris.

In the course of that inquiry, in December 1986, Sir David raised with the Tribunal the imminent legislation for the alienation of Crown lands and its impact on the Muriwhenua people who had claims against those lands in their district. The Tribunal reported to the government the same day. By the insertion of what would become known as 'the treaty clause', government passed to the courts a decision on whether the legislation was contrary to the Treaty. The case, taken by Sir David and Dame Sian for the New Zealand Māori Council and the Muriwhenua Rūnanga, was decided in the Court of Appeal. There, it came before the likes of Sir Robin Cooke (later Lord Cooke) and Sir Ivor Richardson. The rest is history.

Sir David would go on to become a Court of Appeal judge and eventually, as a distinguished jurist, the president of the United Nations Special Tribunal for Lebanon.

For the Tribunal itself, the single most important step in its development during my tenure, to my mind, was the increase in the number of members in 1985. It came at the same time that the historical claims were brought within the Treaty's purview. The two members in addition to the Chief Judge would be increased to six members, at least four of whom were to be Māori. Each would then have a deputy in the event of illness, absence or conflict. The law on conflicts of interest was barely suited to a culture where one's mana to engage on an issue depended not on the absence of a relationship but on the existence of one.

The statutory amendment of 1985 provided a pool of at least eight Māori members. Amongst those appointed were members with significant life experiences as Māori with Māori as their mother tongue. These members were able to caucus on how tikanga might inform the way that hearings were held, evidence was viewed, conclusions were reached or recommendations were made. Their discussions led to clusters of witnesses appearing, feeding off each other. They led to kaumātua members chairing sessions when local kaumātua spoke and, for cultural reasons, the elucidation of evidence not by questions and answers but by sharing experiences.

The then Minister, Hon Koro Wetere, was a renowned Māori speaker with a long political experience, and the Māori world was well known to him. He made the statutory changes for the Tribunal to proceed further. He also made the necessary appointments for the task.

Those who were able to caucus and advise on the introduction of tikanga, in the first decade following the amendment, were Bishop Manuhuia Bennett ONZ, Sir Monita Delamere, Mac Temara, Ned Nathan, Lena Manuel, Turirangi Te Kani, Hepora Raharuhi Young, Keita Walker, Mac Taylor and Sir John Turei. Bishop Manuhuia and Sir Monita also led at several hearings.

From outside its members, the Tribunal also engaged with Dame Joan Metge, a leading social anthropologist with an acute eye for spotting the pattern in Māori social relationships – the essential thing in developing the jurisprudence or science of Māori law.

Appointed also in that formative decade were historians and academics in disciplines relevant to the Tribunal's work. They were, in order of their appointment, Professor Keith Sorrenson (Ngāti Pukenga), Professor Sir Hugh

Kawharu (Ngāti Whātua), Professor Dame Evelyn Stokes, Mary Boyd, senior lecturer in history, Dr Ngapare Hopa (Tainui, Ngāti Tūwharetoa), Dr Erihana Ryan (Ngāi Tahu), Pamela Ringwood and Dr Michael Bassett. Several other historians also supported the Tribunal's work including Professor Alan Ward of the University of Newcastle, who managed the Tribunal's Rangahaua Whānui research programme, and Dr Barry Rigby, who served as a staff member. He is the only one of that embryonic contingent still serving.

Keeping the Tribunal in contact with the rest of the country, and the political and commercial leadership of the country in contact with the work of the Tribunal, were John Kneebone, Sir John Ingram and lawyer Brian Corban. John Kneebone was a farmer, company director, local politician and past president of Federated Farmers. Sir John Ingram was an engineer and company director who was the first managing director of New Zealand Steel, with which the Tainui leadership had engaged in negotiations. He was also a trustee of the World Wildlife Fund.

Brian, a founder of the Corban Revell law firm, was a distinguished businessman, company chairman and director, and a community leader. He was also chairman of Television New Zealand and deputy chairman of the Broadcasting Corporation.

Giving legal effect to the Treaty required a strong legal team to ensure that the Tribunal's findings and recommendations were based on a sound interpretation of the Treaty principles and a robust analysis of the evidence. Professor Gordon Orr, former Secretary for Justice and Dean of the Victoria University Law Faculty, was a full-time Tribunal member. Others appointed were Sir Desmond Sullivan and Sir Peter Trapski, both formerly Chief Judges of the District Court, Bill Wilson QC and later a Supreme Court judge, Dame Georgina Te Heuheu, later Minister for Courts, and Joanne Morris who would also serve on the New Zealand Law Commission. Professor Orr, Sir Peter, Justice Wilson and Joanne Morris would also chair particular Tribunal inquiries.

The judges of the Māori Land Court were not Tribunal members but were appointed by the Tribunal chairperson to sit in the chairperson's place on particular inquiries. Those so appointed in the nascent period to 1995 were Judges Ashley (Chick) McHugh, Andrew Spencer, Heta Kenneth Hingston, Hoeroa Marumaru, Ross Russell and Glen Carter.

The old order began its transition to the new in 1995 and 1996, when eight new members were appointed. From that time also, it was increasingly apparent that the character of the Tribunal would change with the introduction of legal aid. Legal aid began in 1988 as part of the settlement of the New Zealand Māori Council proceedings on state-owned enterprises in the Court of Appeal. The original provision was unworkable, however, and matters had to wait until alternative legislation under the Legal Services Act 1991 could be brought into effect. I continued to chair to 2003, although I was also serving in the High Court by then.

In the final years of the century, it was clear that the old order of a single counsel representing a large Māori grouping was passing and that there would be many counsels representing a host of small claimant groups on legal aid. This would present new challenges and call for a different process.

Nonetheless, the waka was now afloat, and we should be grateful to the many, of diverse talents, who launched it.

"For New Zealanders, the term "calculated genocide" is difficult to comprehend, but for the people of Ngāti Whare the events discussed here are part of their oral histories."

Chapter 3

Historical Claims and District Inquiries

"The matter has been settled"?

— Peter Meihana

Established in 1975 under the Treaty of Waitangi Act, the Waitangi Tribunal has heard claims across a range of issues. Historic Treaty claims are defined in the Act as alleged breaches of Treaty principles that occurred before 21 September 1992. It was on this day that the Sealord deed was ratified by Cabinet, settling Māori commercial fisheries claims. It was on this day, writes David Williams, "as defined by Parliament, 'history' came to an end".[1] There are numerous registered claims yet to be covered in the Tribunals's thirty-seven district inquiry areas. There are also kaupapa, or thematic, claims that the Tribunal has heard. This chapter does not provide an extensive commentary on the Tribunal's establishment; this is discussed elsewhere. Instead, it discusses three reports that have been published since 2004. These have been selected because they highlight the various issues that the Tribunal has dealt with, including Crown purchases, confiscations, and the Native Land Court, which feature prominently across inquiries, as do cross-claims. The Mōhaka ki Ahuriri, Te Urewera, and Te Tau Ihu o te Waka a Māui (northern South Island) inquiries are discussed. The Ngāi Tahu Inquiry, one of the country's largest claims (in terms of land area) to be heard by the Tribunal, is touched on briefly. The chapter concludes with a discussion bringing together aspects of these claims that continue to inform the Tribunal's work. The chapter begins, however, with a discussion of Tribunal history and research. It draws on the work of historians who have been involved in Waitangi Tribunal work and history commissioned by the Tribunal.

The Tribunal, since its inception, has been an important source of Māori history. During the late 1950s to 1960s, disciplines other than history – economics, sociology, social anthropology – were used to explain the experiences of Māori. Academics, spurred on by the Hunn report, concentrated on issues faced by Māori who had moved to an urban environment. Debates taking place in the United States of America, South Africa and Britain also informed discussions about race relations in Aotearoa. Māori who entered universities and teacher training colleges were influenced by Māori historians such as Apirana Ngata and Pei Te Hurinui Jones. Their histories were whakapapa centred, and they too were committed to te reo Māori and culture.[2]

Pākehā historians at this time began to reposition New Zealand's history. From the late 1950s, historians drew heavily on the archival record. The focus on empire gave way to ideas about an emerging nation state with its own culture, heritage and identity. The national histories of Keith Sinclair and

W.H. Oliver did acknowledge and incorporate Māori and their relationship with Pākehā and the state.[3] In 1971, Sinclair argued that New Zealand's humanitarian foundations had created a society that, while not perfect, was better than in other settler colonies.[4] Soon after this, Alan Ward provided a general account of colonisation in his discussion of nineteenth-century Native policy, noting that "the colonisation of New Zealand, notwithstanding the Treaty of Waitangi and humanitarian idealism, was substantially an imperial subjugation of a native people".[5] Claudia Orange in her seminal work wrote that there has been an "overemphasis on humanitarian concern in the original Treaty negotiation, at the fair evaluation of the Treaty's role in serving British and settler interests".[6]

The Treaty of Waitangi was also considered in a new light at this time. In 1972, Ruth Ross presented her analysis of the Treaty documents at Victoria University of Wellington. The Treaty was, argued Ross, fundamentally a Māori document as it was the te reo Māori version that the overwhelming majority of rangatira had signed. Ross's analysis brought into question the role of missionaries in Treaty negotiations. Henry Williams's translation, in particular, came under scrutiny. By historicising the Treaty, Ross hoped to understand the intentions and motives of those involved at the time.[7] In 1972, the *New Zealand Journal of History* published a version of the paper.[8] Subsequently others, including Claudia Orange, built on Ross's analysis. Ranginui Walker remarked, it is the "most penetrating critique in recent times of the events surrounding the drafting and signing of the Treaty".[9] Most recently, Ned Fletcher has delved into how the English language draft of te Tiriti was prepared and argues that English and te reo Māori are reconcilable.[10]

History produced by the Waitangi Tribunal has contributed greatly to our understanding of the past. The nature and form of this history has been discussed by historians for some time. Keith Sorrenson argued in 1987 that the Tribunal was engaged in a radical revision of New Zealand history.[11] In 1990, Alan Ward discussed evidence presented before the Ngāi Tahu tribunal.[12] Historians have also discussed the differences between academic history and Tribunal history, it being argued that the latter is constrained by legal requirements and tested under cross-examination by lawyers; the former, however, typically follows a process that includes peer review and publication. In accordance with the Act, the Tribunal is required to investigate claims made by Māori that the Crown has acted in a way inconsistent with Treaty principles and that prejudicially has affected, or likely will affect, the claimant group.

A number of questions and issues arise here. Who has a right to claim? As is discussed below, cross-claims and overlapping interests are features of many Treaty claims. The Tribunal is invariably drawn into debates around custom while historians are pressured to present evidence on behalf of claimants that "assert control over neighbours and which impose artificial and expansive tribal boundaries".[13]

In 2001, W.H. Oliver instigated a more sustained discussion, describing the Tribunal's work as looking backwards towards a "retrospective utopia".[14] According to Belgrave, Oliver was not looking to"pen a critical obituary for Tribunal history, but raise questions".[15] Giselle Byrnes advanced Oliver's ideas further in 2004 by placing the Tribunal's reports in a much wider context of post-colonial, liberation or post-modernist history. She wrote that the Tribunal was "a noble but ultimately flawed experiment".[16] Others, including Jim McAloon, engaged in the debate. McAloon writes that Oliver and Byrnes share three main contentions: that the Tribunal "views the past entirely in the light of present concerns and agendas"; that the law and history are different disciplines "and the approach of one is therefore inimical to the other"; and lastly, that Māori and settler are cast within a binary of victim and villain that ignores "co-operation and interaction". According to McAloon, however, the Tribunal "is not so much imposing present agendas on the past as emphasizing arguments or perspectives that were evident in the nineteenth century and which were at the time marginalized".[17]

The Tribunal's reference to Treaty principles is also criticised by Oliver who argues they are the creation of "judicial activism" and are ahistorical. According to McAloon, "strictly speaking" the principles are a "legislative innovation"; moreover, the Tribunal, when judging the past, does so according to the context of the time. The "principle of active protection" has evolved and was "emphasized by the Court of Appeal in 1987", and something akin to "active protection" was implicit in Normanby's 1839 instructions to Lieutenant-Governor William Hobson. Commissioner William Spain, who was appointed to investigate the New Zealand Company's land claims, referred to "the spirit of the Treaty of Waitangi".[18]

With regard to evidence presented before the Tribunal, Oliver also states that the Tribunal privileges oral evidence over the documentary record. McAloon, citing the Ngāi Tahu claims, argues that this is not the case. Relying on the documentary evidence, the Tribunal found that the Ōtakou purchase did not include a promise of tenths. It was claimed that the signatories to Kemp's

Deed did not intend to sell land through to the West Coast but only as far as the foothills of the Southern Alps. This claim was dismissed. Furthermore, "more recent reports do not seem to privilege oral evidence to any greater extent". In the case of the Muriwhenua and Taranaki reports, oral evidence was used to "elucidate matters of custom and tradition" while it is "treated with the greatest caution" when it dealt with "strictly historical matters".[19]

In terms of history production, the Waitangi Tribunal not only reports on iwi and hapū claims. In 1993, it commissioned a series of reports that, as E.T. Durie writes, were "part of a strategic plan to manage a large workload within the restrictions of the Tribunal's legislation and resources".[20] It was recognised that the process, as it stood, "may unfairly advantage those cases first dealt with in the long claimant queue". A review was thus proposed that would group claims by district and "broad historical context". The research would be conducted using a standardised methodology and approach. The aim of the project was to report on resource loss and the causes of loss, and identify, in advance, any other issues that would typically emerge during a claim. While broad in scope, the reports would isolate specific issues that the various parties could focus on, "oppose, support or augment".[21]

The Rangahaua Whānui project produced district reports, thematic reports and a national overview.[22] A unit comprising Tribunal members with Māori cultural knowledge and the requisite historical and legal skills would be established to review the terms of the commissions. To maintain transparency, any proposed research would be made known to the Crown and claimant groups, and researchers would work with all parties involved. An invitation would be extended to the Crown Forestry Rental Trust, Treaty of Waitangi Policy Unit, Crown Law and "a representative of a national Maori body with iwi and hapu affiliations will be invited to join the mentor unit meetings".[23]

The various reports that were produced as part of the Rangahaua Whānui series culminated in the three volume *National Overview Report* compiled by Alan Ward. According to Chief Judge Durie "... these reports and Professor Ward's *National Overview* represent the most significant advance that has been made by the Tribunal to providing a planned approach to the management of Māori claims ... I think it is by far the most exciting and important development to have occurred since the historic claims process was started by Government in 1985".[24] The project was, in part, a response to the Crown's fiscal envelope policy. Both Alan Ward, who led Rangahaua Whānui, and Judge Durie had expressed concern that money was being deducted from the $1 billion allocated to settle all Treaty claims without a clear picture of the historical claims that were yet to be heard. Rangahaua Whānui was intended to streamline the process to settlement. The *Overview Report* influenced the way the Tribunal approached hearings, particularly with the introduction of the casebook method.[25]

Introduced in 1996, the casebook method was intended to "establish a more efficient procedure for bringing claims onto the Tribunal's hearing programme". Claims would be grouped together regionally, and research would be commissioned, culminating in a casebook that would be reviewed to ensure that the claims were "well founded". It was hoped that the casebook approach would help reduce the time between hearings.[26] Furthermore:

> *The casebook method aims to avoid the situation which sometimes occurred whereby the Tribunal had commenced its inquiry into claims when in fact they have only been partly ready for hearing and further research has been required. Such delays, which at times have been substantial, have increased the costs for all parties involved.*[27]

The first inquiry held under the casebook method was Mōhaka ki Ahuriri. The Mōhaka ki Ahuriri tribunal was formally constituted in 1996 at which time the inquiry included fifteen claims. The casebook, which comprised reports from earlier inquiries as well as reports prepared specifically for Mōhaka ki Ahuriri, was examined by Keith Sorrenson. At the end of 1996, he stated that "the reports address the principal issues, and are of sufficient quality to enable the Tribunal to proceed to hear the Mōhaka ki Ahuriri claims". However, he also noted that not all of the research had been completed. It was at this stage the casebook was distributed to the parties, including counsel for claimants, the Crown Law Office and the Tribunal. The decision to proceed, despite not having completed all the research, was due to a hesitancy to delay hearing the claims of groups that were ready to proceed.[28]

The twenty claims brought together under Wai 201 were heard between November 1996 and February 2000 and covered a geographical area that extended from "the Tutaekuri River to the south, Hawke's Bay to the east, the Waiau River to the north, and (mainly) the mountain ranges or the old Hawke's Bay provincial boundary to the west". The northern area is the traditional territory of Ngāti Pahauwera and subject to a whānau claim (Wai 731), a cross-claim by Ngāi Tane (Wai 436) and a comprehensive claim (Wai 216). To the south is the Ahuriri block, which was purchased by the

Crown in 1851 and was subject to a pan-hapū claim (Wai 400). Overlapping Ahuriri to the south is Waiohiki, which was covered by a hapū claim (Wai 168). The Mōhaka-Waikare confiscation lay at the centre and was subject to whānau and pan-hapū claims.[29]

The claims brought against the Crown during Wai 201 related to the pre-1865 purchases, land alienations following the introduction of the Native Land Court in 1865, military actions in 1866, the confiscations of 1867 and the 'return' in 1870 of the confiscated blocks. The Tribunal found that the Crown was not justified in confiscating land as there was no rebellion, and when land was returned, it was not returned to the rightful owners. The Native Land Court and the introduction of a new land-tenure system negatively impacted the claimants, destabilising Māori society. The land that was left in Māori hands was often isolated and unproductive, and the Crown failed to support Māori in developing. Consequently, Māori were unable to participate in the settler colonial economy.[30]

Prior to the close of claimant evidence in May 1999, Crown counsel requested for the boundary of the Mōhaka ki Ahuriri Inquiry to be defined. Again, there was some reluctance. The presiding officer, Judge Wilson Isaac, stated that it was "not appropriate to define with absolute certainty the claim boundaries of this inquiry district". At the time there were "no active neighbouring inquiries" and it was the Tribunal's preference to hear all claimant evidence as well the Crown's response. It was, then, at the completion of the hearings and the finalising of the report that the Tribunal was more "categorical" about the areas dealt with in its report. The Mōhaka ki Ahuriri tribunal did not address "the apparent interests in those lands of any claimant groups who did not appear before us". Similarly, interests in land claimed outside of the inquiry area by groups within it were not addressed. These issues would be dealt with by future tribunals.[31]

Te Urewera

The Te Urewera inquiry took place between 2003 and 2005, and at its completion comprised forty-five claims. The claims heard by the Tribunal were presented by Tūhoe, Ngāti Haka Patuheuheu, Ngāti Ruapani, Ngāti Whare, Ngāti Manawa, Ngāti Kahungunu, Ngāi Tamaterangi, Te Aitanga a Māhaki, and Te Whānau a Kai.[32] The first report, released in 2009, focused primarily on Tūhoe's constitutional claim, land confiscation and the military conflicts between 1869 and 1871. Many of the claimants spoke to the issue of authority

– mana motuhake. Tūhoe's Tamati Kruger stated, "My Tūhoe identity is my mana motuhake ... my mana motuhake, my Tūhoe identity is far greater than me ... it is a hidden treasure". Claimants considered that their ancestors did not sign the Treaty and had not ceded their sovereignty. The Tribunal found that the Crown's promises applied to all, regardless of whether or not they signed the Treaty.[33]

A central pillar of Tūhoe's grievances against the Crown concerned the confiscation of a large area of land in the eastern Bay of Plenty. The policy was intended to punish those Māori the Crown deemed to be in rebellion. The Tribunal found that Tūhoe took no part in the events used to justify the confiscation. At the time, the Crown acted outside of the law as it then stood, and its failure to return the land constituted a Treaty breach. The Crown conceded. Tūhoe and Ngāti Whare responded to the confiscations by lending their support to Te Kooti. The Crown's response was to send military expeditions to Te Urewera between 1869 and 1871, resulting in the death of eighty Māori.[34]

In the aftermath of war, Te Urewera was impacted by Crown purchases and the Native Land Court. In 1875, land south of Lake Waikaremoana came before the Native Land Court, placing pressure on Tūhoe and Ngāti Ruapani to alienate their interests. This marked the beginning of extensive land loss for communities of Waikaremoana. The Tribunal found that Crown purchasing and native land legislation were a breach of the Treaty, ultimately resulting in the loss of 85 per cent of their lands by 1930.

In its letters of transmittal, the Tribunal laid bare the impact of Crown actions in Te Urewera. For Tūhoe, in particular, the confiscation of land marked the "first substantial contact" with the Crown, and thus the Crown became regarded as an "enemy". In its pursuit of Te Kooti, "Crown forces acted mercilessly". People were "starved out of the region" as crops, shelter and taonga were destroyed. The Tribunal noted that "much of the evidence for these facts is to be found in dispatches and writings or memoirs of Crown officers". According to the Tribunal, there is "little for the Crown to be proud of" in its dealings with the people of Te Urewera; the feelings of "anguish and anger" have lingered to the present.[35]

The Te Urewera inquiry also brought into focus the issues that arise when dealing with historical evidence. In considering the Crown's actions during its 1869 campaign, the Tribunal found that they "went far beyond what was necessary or appropriate in depriving Te Kooti of a base, and were in breach of Treaty principles".[36] The decision to invade Te Urewera came following Te Kooti's attack on the Whakatāne district. To prevent further attacks and beat winter, James Richmond ordered an immediate assault on Te Urewera. In a letter written by H.T. Clarke, civil commissioner at Tauranga, Clarke describes a meeting at which Colonel Whitmore explains to Te Arawa and Whanganui military leaders his views and intentions. Whitmore began "by telling them of the great crimes and misdemeanours of the Urewera, that they had intermeddled with all the quarrels against the Pakeha, without any cause of provocation and now to crown all they were sheltering the scoundrel Te Kooti and had assisted him in his late raids". According to Clarke, Whitmore was "going to punish them, they must be exterminated".[37]

Te Harema pā was the site of the first engagement. Clarke, who was with the Crown forces, provides a graphic description of the attack in a letter to his sisters in which "the hauhaus lost five that we know of and thirty women and children". In a footnote, it was explained that "lost" had two meanings; "lost" in the sense that the men had been killed, and "lost" in that women and children had been taken prisoner. Clarke informed his sisters that "when Natives are excited they are more like demons" and that Te Arawa rangatira Te Pokiha gathered the women and children into one house over which he and his brother stood guard.[38]

Clarke also provided an account of events in his official report to the Native Department. Here he noted "all the men that bore arms and resisted were killed, four or five only making their escape; between thirty and forty women and children were taken prisoners". Whitmore, in his official report, stated that "The Hauhaus were scattered about the valley collecting their crops, so that all could not be killed ... Six men were shot, among whom was Matthew, a noted prophet and cannibal. It was unfortunate that some of the men were absent ambuscading another road, by which the column was expected, and others assisting Te Kooti. About fifty prisoners were taken, women and children, with much plunder and very large stores of provisions".[39]

In their submissions, the claimants stated that the Crown's actions at Te Harema "constituted the very worst of its exploits". Not only were they an "excess of intention", but "excess of action" also. Tuawhenua considered that Clarke's report "provides a description of a massacre of unarmed men". Whitmore's comment that "all could not be killed" was interpreted by Judith Binney as "evidence of his willingness to see as many 'Hauhau' as possible die". While the Tribunal agreed that Whitmore would have been "disappointed", it was unable to substantiate the claim that there was "a massacre of unarmed men".[40]

The treatment of Ngāti Whare (and likely Tūhoe) women during the attack on Te Harema pā was "one of the major claims against the Crown". Claimants spoke of the treatment of women by Te Arawa Crown forces, including "molestation and rape". Furthermore, the handing over of female prisoners was, according to Binney, a "calculated genocide", an attempt at exterminating their hapū.[41] The Crown rejected the claim of "genocide", placing particular emphasis on Clarke's letters written after the first expedition. It was the Crown's view they proved the invading forces "acted with the best intentions". He wrote, "I should have said that these chiefs suggested that I should write a letter to the husbands of these women telling them that their women would be properly kept and offered them a home if they should like to join their wives in Arawa country. This I thought very commendable."[42]

Claimants also spoke about the treatment of Ngāti Whare women at Ahikererū. They recalled the shame carried by women and how "those sordid stories were never told, were never revealed but kept secret, locked away in their hearts".[43] The Tribunal acknowledged that it faced difficulty in dealing with the evidence presented before it. In the first instance, it "involves serious allegations that have been a source of continuing grief". When Crown historian John Battersby was questioned, he could not refute categorically that rape and sexual violence had occurred, though he did state that "he was unaware of any documentary evidence to support such allegations". The issue that arises here, then, is reconciling oral traditions with official accounts that can be incomplete. In saying this, the Tribunal stated that it had "no reason to doubt the integrity of the claimants' oral histories".[44]

For New Zealanders, the term "calculated genocide" is difficult to comprehend, but for the people of Ngāti Whare the events discussed here are part of their oral histories. The Tribunal's findings on the Crown's action in Te Urewera highlight the way in which it deals with evidence. The Tribunal considered that events should be interpreted in the "broader context of Whitmore's strategy". The intent, as expressed in his correspondence, was to punish and "destroy" the hapū, which the Tribunal took to mean killing the men and leaving the women to be "absorbed into Te Arawa". With regard to the allegations of rape, the Tribunal could not "find conclusively for the claimants"; however, when the Tribunal considered Whitmore's instructions, Clarke's description of the expeditionary forces as excited "demons", that

Te Arawa and Ngāti Whare were enemies, and that the women and children needed protection following the attack, it found that "all the necessary conditions were in existence for such abuse to have occurred".[45]

Te Tau Ihu o te Waka a Māui

Te Tau Ihu o te Waka a Māui denotes the area north of the statutorily defined Ngāi Tahu takiwā. The inquiry district comprises eight iwi belonging to three waka. Ngāti Kuia, Rangitāne and Ngāti Apa ki te Rā Tō claim descent from Kurahaupō waka and were the tangata whenua at 1820. Ngāti Koata, Ngāti Toa Rangatira and Ngāti Rarua claim descent from Tainui waka. Ngāti Tama and Te Ātiawa claim descent from Tokomaru waka. In April 1989, Te Rūnanganui o te Tau Ihu o te Waka a Māui, a body representing the aforementioned iwi (as well as Ngāti Waikauri), registered a claim (Wai 102) with the Waitangi Tribunal. Wai 102 was submitted with the understanding that iwi would submit their own claims.[46] Many of these claims overlapped, both geographically and in terms of the impacts Crown actions had on Te Tau Ihu Māori. As per the Tribunal's casebook approach, the thirty-one claims were consolidated under the administrative number Wai 785, and claims would be heard concurrently.[47]

The Tribunal issued three reports. The first two preliminary reports were requested by claimants to assist in their negotiations, and the titles reflect key themes of the inquiry: *Customary Rights in the Northern South Island* (2007), *Customary Rights in Ngāi Tahu Takiwa* (2007) and *Te Tau Ihu* (2008), the final volume report.[48] The Tribunal found that the Crown commenced its purchase negotiations without determining who the owners were and the nature of customary rights. The Crown argued that the Waipounamu purchase rectified this omission. The Tribunal disagreed. Because the Crown had already granted land to settlers or "claimed that it had already bought it from others" it was impossible for "Māori to enter into fair, free, and informed transactions". The Tribunal also found that six iwi had "valid customary rights" inside the Ngāi Tahu takiwā.[49] In its Letter of Transmittal, the Te Tau Ihu tribunal stated that "historical breaches against Te Tau Ihu iwi continued into the twentieth century when the Crown chose to deal exclusively with Ngai Tahu within the takiwa, at the expense of Te Tau Ihu iwi that also had legitimate rights in the area".[50]

While the Tribunal was interested in custom and customary rights in Te Tau Ihu, it did not see its role as being the arbiter of such rights. Rather, claimants were encouraged to work towards an agreement amongst themselves as to where their respective rights and interests were located. However, in the Tribunal's words, these issues were in some instances "intractable". It was in this context that the Tribunal was asked "to make findings as to the rights held by each different group in the inquiry district". The Tribunal's task was not to be a "judge of customary rights per se" but to consider the treatment of those rights by the Crown in terms of its duties under the Treaty of Waitangi.[51]

Determining the date at which to judge when custom applied and how the Crown dealt with the rights of Te Tau Ihu iwi was one of the problems faced by the Tribunal. The year 1840 has been applied by the Native Land Court and the Crown. The Te Tau Ihu tribunal decided not to be "bound by that dictum" and took a more "flexible approach".[52] Here, the Tribunal looked to the Rēkohu inquiry for guidance. According to this Tribunal, "to freeze rights at that point prevented the natural emergence of rights as they would have otherwise evolved and was itself uncustomary".[53] The Te Tau Ihu tribunal also reiterated that if under custom defeated peoples retained rights, "we must ensure that we do not undervalue the rights of newer arrivals to whom raupatu had given the opportunity to develop their own rights and interests in the land".[54] This was the approach of the Rēkohu tribunal.

The Tribunal heard the claims of Te Tau Ihu Māori between 2000 and 2004; however, the claims were interrupted for fifteen months due to litigation over the Tribunal's jurisdiction to hear claims south of the Ngāi Tahu takiwā. It is not the purpose of this chapter to traverse the Ngāi Tahu claim; however, it is important to recognise that it did impact on the claims of Te Tau Ihu iwi. The Ngāi Tahu claim (Wai 27) was filed in August 1986 and heard between 1987 and 1991. The first hearing took place at Tuahiwi, beginning on 17 August 1987.[55] Two weeks prior to this, on 6 August, Kurahaupō-Rangitāne filed a claim with the Tribunal that included the area of the 1859 Kaikōura purchase that "lay to the north and east of the Clarence River and included the Awatere river valley from the coast to the headwaters, the inland Kaikoura range, and the coastline from White Bluffs to Cape Campbell to the Clarence river mouth, and all forests and fisheries adjacent thereto". On 10 August, Kurahaupō-Rangitāne filed a further claim extending their interests on the West Coast north of the Arahura River, that is to say, an area included in the 1860 Arahura purchase.[56]

The Kurahaupō-Rangitāne claim presented the Ngāi Tahu tribunal with some procedural issues that it attempted to resolve at Tuahiwi. However, it was apparent that Ngāi Tahu and Kurahaupō-Rangitāne "were at issue".

Ngāi Tahu made it clear that it did not want Kurahaupō-Rangitāne to be present or to participate in the Ngāi Tahu claim. The Tribunal requested that an affidavit be filed by Kurahaupō-Rangitāne "setting out the grounds upon which entitlement to claim was based". In September, written submissions were presented and were "strongly opposed" by Ngāi Tahu. In November, the Crown submitted that it was "important to have the boundary dispute resolved as it might place the Crown in double jeopardy".[57]

The Tribunal's decision was issued on 26 November. It found that boundaries needed to be determined and that the Māori Land Court was better qualified to resolve the issue. It also recommended legislative changes to enable the Tribunal to state a case to the Māori Appellate Court. Pending legislative change, the Tribunal decided to continue the claim. In 1988, section 6A of the Treaty of Waitangi Act was enacted, clearing the way for the Tribunal to refer the boundary dispute to the Māori Appellate Court. In February 1989, the question was put before the Māori Appellate Court, and in its 15 November 1990 decision it ruled that:

> ***The Ngai Tahu tribe according to customary law principles of 'take' and occupation or use had the sole rights of ownership in respect of the lands comprised in both the Arahura and Kaikoura Deeds of Purchase at the respective dates of those deeds.***

Section 6A was binding on the Ngāi Tahu tribunal and it was on this basis that the claim proceeded. In relation to the Arahura and Kaikōura purchases, the Tribunal found Ngāi Tahu's claims were well founded. It recommended that legislation giving effect to a tribal structure to negotiate a settlement with the Crown be enacted. The Te Runanga o Ngai Tahu Act 1996 and the Ngai Tahu Claims Settlement Act 1998 were the result.[58]

During the Te Tau Ihu inquiry, all iwi except Ngāti Koata claimed customary interests south of the statutorily defined Ngāi Tahu takiwā. Ngāti Kuia later abandoned its claim. Ngāti Apa ki te Rā Tō stated that it had customary interests "in the whole block of country from the southern bank lands of the Kawatiri (including Tauranga Bay) north to Kahurangi Point and inland of that coastline in an easterly direction to Nelson Lakes area. The Tainui-Taranaki claimed rights south of the Takiwa through conquest".[59]

Ngāi Tahu, to be expected, challenged the Te Tau Ihu tribunal's jurisdiction to hear claims within the statutorily defined Ngāi Tahu takiwā. The 1990 Appellate Court decision, the Te Runanga o Ngai Tahu Act 1996 and the Ngāi Tahu Claims Settlement Act 1998 were cited as evidence that Ngāi Tahu had an "exclusive entitlement". Moreover, the Appellate Court decision and section 6A(6) of the Treaty of Waitangi Act 1975 was "binding on all Tribunal panels". In October 2000, the Tribunal heard submissions from Ngāi Tahu, Te Tau Ihu iwi and the Crown. It found that neither the 1990 decision nor the legislation of 1996 and 1998 barred the Tribunal from hearing the claim. Ngāi Tahu subsequently sought a High Court review of the Tribunal's findings.[60] The Court, issuing its decision on 4 April 2001, agreed with the Tribunal.

In *Te Runanga o Ngai Tahu v Waitangi Tribunal* [2001] Justice McGechan found that section 6A of the Treaty of Waitangi Act did not bind future Tribunals. The Ngāi Tahu legislation was enacted to effect a settlement between Ngāi Tahu and the Crown, not other parties. As stated by Justice McGechan, this would "lead to absurdity. It would mean the Waitangi Tribunal, however constituted, is bound by a prior Māori Appellate Court determination in all future cases". Ngāi Tahu appealed the decision; however, the Court of Appeal agreed with the High Court and the Tribunal. In *Te Runanga o Ngai Tahu v Waitangi Tribunal* [2002], Justice Tipping concluded that "there is nothing in the legislation ... which prevents the tribunal from inquiring into the claims which Ngati Apa and other claimants have made". As far as the Tribunal was concerned regarding the issue of jurisdiction, "the matter has been settled".[61]

Conclusion

Waitangi Tribunal history has been subject to critique and criticism. In 2012, Tribunal member and former chief historian Grant Phillipson summarised and penned a response to these critiques. According to Phillipson, Oliver's "The Future Behind Us: the Waitangi Tribunal's retrospective utopia" was the "most influential critique of the Waitangi Tribunal ever written in its 37-year history", though if it had not been for Byrnes's 2004 book, *The Waitangi Tribunal and New Zealand History*, Oliver's interpretation "might not have become the predominant academic view of Tribunal history". Phillipson also notes, in particular, McAloon's "spirited defence of Tribunal reports as relatively orthodox empirical history". Oliver maintained his position that "colonialism was unavoidably bad and no Treaty or counterfactual thinking could make it otherwise".[62]

Phillipson observes that Oliver focused on the Taranaki and Muriwhenua reports while Byrnes, in her analysis, included reports up to 2000.

Belgrave suggested that since the 1990s, "the writing of Tribunal history had become more conventional anyway" and this was reflected in Te Whanganui a Tara/Wellington (2003), Turanga/Gisborne (2004), Tauranga Raupatu (2004), Kaipara (2006) and Hauraki (2006). This change in the way the Tribunal did history came about, in Belgrave's view, with the departure of Tribunal Chairperson Edward Durie in the 1990s. Nevertheless, the Tribunal still made findings according to Treaty principles.[63]

How influential was Oliver's 2001 critique 'inside the field of Treaty history'? According to Phillipson, the "Crown quickly adopted aspects of Oliver's critique". For instance, during the Turanga inquiry, Crown counsel quoted Oliver "extensively", though the Tribunal in its report did not "explicitly" engage with the Crown's arguments.[64] Where the Crown did engage with Oliver was in its 2006 Hauraki report. In evidence, Oliver suggested:

> *the responsibility of the state lies in the modes and the consequences of land acquisition; it is a responsibility which is not to be ignored because the colonisation and settlement of New Zealand, and of Hauraki, was in one way or another inevitable. It was a question of the way in which it was quite deliberately decided to act.*[65]

The Tribunal adopted Oliver's methodology, while also relying on the evidence of Belgrave:

> *In navigating through these perilous methodological straits one light in particular has helped us steer between the Scylla of "presentism" and the Charybdis of "historical inevitability", namely, whether an idea or concept had been voiced at the time, and was "in the public arena", to use a modern expression. If Maori, in particular, had spoken or written to Crown officials or politicians about their concerns, asked for remedy or sought support for a measure they thought beneficial; or if (as Dr Belgrave suggests) the Crown's own stated policy proposals included certain options, we think it entirely reasonable that such concerns and options be used as a measure of subsequent Crown action or inaction. We [the Hauraki Tribunal] have seen much evidence of this type ...*[66]

In Phillipson's assessment "the most important faultline running through Treaty history today" is an acceptance by historians "that colonisation could have been conducted more fairly than was actually the case". Historians today fall on either side of what he calls the "Martin-Fenton divide".[67] This would also apply to historians inside the Tribunal. In its Tauranga inquiry Tribunal member, Michael Bassett, produced a minority opinion stating that "the report goes too far". According to Bassett "the small three-clause document that constitutes the Treaty was not intended by the British Crown as requiring the erection of an all-powerful, regulatory, State apparatus that would govern every detail of Maori-Pakeha interaction". Moreover, "visiting the nineteenth century with 1960s and 1970s notions of the State's all-encompassing social responsibilities, and with some people's inflating views about the Crown's Treaty obligations, makes for bad history and indicates poor historical judgment".[68]

In 2014, David Williams discussed the aforementioned debates, what he termed "advocacy" or "juridical" history, the role of historians in the claims-settlement process, and the "ways and means that lawyers debate about time, law and history in the common law, and how the past is interpreted by legal reasoning to suit presentist purposes".[69] Noting Phillipson's summation, he comments that "there are indeed options other than one side or the opposite in a polarizing debate on historiography between contextualists and presentists". Williams also noted that "there are respectable academic arguments for a presentist perspective on history. On the other hand, it should not be assumed that the presentist brush (pejoratively understood) taints all evidence submitted to the Waitangi Tribunal and the Office of Treaty Settlements".[70]

While the Tribunal did not explicitly mention presentism or refer to Oliver in its 2007 and 2008 Te Tau Ihu reports, the influence of the Hauraki report is discernible. Before considering the Crown's purchasing of land in the northern South Island and the way in which it dealt with the Spain Commission and the New Zealand Company purchases, the Tribunal needed to establish "the foundations of the Crown's Treaty duty and the standards appropriate at the time".[71] It did this by posing a series of questions drawing on the Treaty of Waitangi, instructions to governors, statements in Parliament, policies and early Crown purchases. The failure to provide sufficient reserves had been criticised by both Māori and Crown officials at the time. The Tribunal also took this into account.[72]

The approach taken by the Tribunal in its Te Tau Ihu inquiry was informed by earlier inquiries. The Te Tau Ihu inquiry area was framed to the south by the statutorily defined Ngāi Tahu takiwā and was conducted according to casebook method. While first applied in Mōhaka ki Ahuriri the casebook method also came in the wake of the Ngāi Tahu inquiry. As Belgrave observes, it was "the first large iwi to have its claim heard before the tribunal in such a comprehensive manner, Ngāi Tahu was in the privileged position of being able to present its view of its history first"; but "it did have the capacity to open a parallel enquiry". Nor did the Tribunal expect to deal with issues of custom or customary disputes. The Māori Appellate Court in its 1990 decision found in favour of Ngāi Tahu. According to Belgrave, the Court created a "master historical narrative", citing Norman Smith's mid-twentieth century work, and did not seek any "historical or anthropological advice on the nature of Māori custom, or get advice from Māori academics with an interest in tikanga".[73]

The Ngāi Tahu inquiry generated a large quantity of research. Crown counsel submitted reports by historians Donald Loveridge, David Alexander, Tony Walzl and David Armstrong, all of whom would go on to write reports for iwi claimants. Michael Belgrave submitted evidence for the Registrar of the Tribunal, later entering academia, but he too continued to write reports for claimant groups. Alan Ward was commissioned by the Ngāi Tahu tribunal to "file independent historical reports on major points of contention" and, as discussed earlier, would make a "huge contribution" to the Rangahaua Whānui project.[74] The Mōhaka ki Ahuriri, Te Tau Ihu, and Te Urewera tribunals all benefitted from Rangahaua Whānui.

In *Te Urewera* report, the Tribunal acknowledged the kōrero and histories that tangata whenua shared, stating these histories "belong to the hapu and iwi of Te Urewera" and it was not the Tribunal's "role to retell them in detail; nor do we try to smooth those histories into a single historical narrative".[75] The Tribunal, in dealing with conflicting narratives, was not, according to Belgrave "attempting to wash its hands completely of these questions", rather, it "restricted examining these questions only where essential to exercising its jurisdiction".[76] A similar approach has been taken in the Porirua ki Manawatū Inquiry. In the concluding chapter of the *Horowhenua: The Muaūpoko Priority Report,* the Tribunal stated that iwi have their own interpretation of events and there might be "conflict at certain points":

> *It is not the Tribunal's task to choose between narratives or decide that one group's version is right and another group's version is wrong. Rather, our task is to examine the acts of the Crown to determine whether, by action or inaction, the Crown has breached the principles of the Treaty of Waitangi. In order to do so, it is necessary to set out each tribe's view of their relationships and customary interests in the contested lands of our inquiry.*[77]

The approach taken in Porirua ki Manawatū highlights continuities with previous inquires, but also some divergences. The inquiry area was established in 2009, "severing it from the Taihape district". The inquiry focuses on the claims of Ngāti Raukawa, Te Ātiawa/Ngāti Awa ki Kāpiti, and Muaūpoko. Ngāti Toa, Rangitāne, and Ngāti Apa, having already had their claims heard, were not part of the inquiry. Notably, there was a mandate dispute within Muaūpoko in 2013–2014. In June 2014, the Tribunal requested submissions "as to whether Muaūpoko claims should be prioritised and proceed to hearings in advance of other iwi or claimant groups". After considering submissions, and with parties neither supporting nor opposing the proposal, the Tribunal "granted priority to Muaūpoko claims".[78] The Tribunal issued its report on the Muaūpoko claims in 2017 with claims still to be heard. It remains to be seen how the Tribunal negotiates these complex and complicated histories.

“The Tribunal’s river reports take us deep into river communities, providing a glimpse into a world where rivers were everything.”

Chapter 4

Awa

Ngā Wai Honohono – The Rivers that Join Us

— Linda Te Aho

Rivers are noble and unifying forces.[1] Thanks to the Waitangi Tribunal, we have access to repositories of first-hand evidence that tell of the vital role of rivers in the lives of iwi and hapū. As a standing commission of inquiry, the Waitangi Tribunal investigates claims that the principles of the Treaty of Waitangi have been breached. The Tribunal is required to examine the Māori text of te Tiriti and the English text of the Treaty and determine how those principles should be applied.[2] In investigating alleged Crown breaches in relation to rivers, the Tribunal reports, themselves, have become taonga.[3] The river reports take us deep into river communities, providing a glimpse into a world where rivers were the life force. They recount stories of how particular rivers are formed and named and tribal perceptions of the significance of river systems. Many of the traditional knowledge holders who have proffered evidence have long since passed, making the information shared even more precious. Without exception, the river reports deal with loss of rangatiratanga and degradation of waterways. This chapter revisits some of the Tribunal's early findings and recommendations, including powerful statements about the nature of taonga, rangatiratanga, ownership and governance. This has created a whakapapa to be drawn on by later tribunals, and ultimately claimants and the Crown, for ensuing Treaty settlements. While the Tribunal reports are deep wells of wisdom, their effectiveness is undermined by the Crown's unwillingness to implement key recommendations. In the context of shifting political and legal landscapes,[4] despite fundamental flaws, Treaty settlements have proven to be a most effective mechanism for actively restoring and protecting the holistic well-being of rivers and the rights and responsibilities of kaitiaki.

The River Reports

Whāia te arawai – follow the river path

At the heart of this chapter are the early Tribunal reports that focus on river-related claims. Some claims are explicitly river focused, such as in the cases of Kaituna, Mōhaka, Ika Whenua Rivers and Whanganui. Others form a fundamental part of wider claims, such as in the cases of the Manukau Harbour and Pouakani, which involve the Waikato River; Motunui-Waitara, encompassing the Waitara River; and the Tūrangi township, where claims embrace the Tongariro and Tokaanu rivers.

In celebrating the contributions of the Waitangi Tribunal, it is important to remember that in fulfilling its role the Tribunal is the specialist body that has investigated claimed breaches of te Tiriti o Waitangi, such as loss of rangatiratanga or impacts on "taonga" and breaches of the Treaty or its "principles", both of which are legislatively undefined terms. In the early river reports, claimant voices are most prominent. Iwi and hapū representatives went to great lengths to persuade the Tribunal that rivers and river systems are taonga. Rivers are not explicitly mentioned in the words of either text, although fisheries are specifically included in the English text. Because of this, reports are rich with tikanga evidence of fisheries and traditional fishing practices, which, in turn, demonstrate the mana and mauri of river systems and river relationships.[5] In writing this chapter, I was reminded of the wealth of knowledge embedded in the Tribunal reports. Traditional knowledge is at the core of our indigenous identity, culture, language, heritage and livelihoods, and in the spirit of keeping that knowledge alive, I share excerpts here.

In this chapter, I identify representative claims relating to the loss or undermining of rangatiratanga in respect of rivers, mostly through the assumption of authority and control by the Crown or its agents. I also highlight aspects of the early debates relating to interpretation of key terms and the Tribunal's contributions to distilling Treaty "principles".

The final part explores the impact of the Tribunal's legacy. The Tribunal's deliberations and its recommendations for compensation and redress and for the Crown, claimants and communities to work together in the spirit of partnership have informed Treaty settlements. These, in turn, have transformed national models for wider resource governance and management. Legal and political landscapes are constantly changing. A review of the role and scope of the Waitangi Tribunal is on the horizon, and further changes to the Resource Management Act and the National Policy Statement for Freshwater Management are in train.[6] Even so, successive governments have been consistent in their promises to uphold Treaty settlements.[7] On this basis, I argue that Treaty settlements, though flawed,[8] are proving to be the strongest mechanisms for protecting and restoring rights and responsibilities in respect of rivers and for ensuring that communities work together towards that shared purpose.

Ō rātou taonga katoa – rivers as taonga, "precious and prized"[9]

The Tribunal's river reports take us deep into river communities, providing a glimpse into a world where rivers were everything. Rivers were (and in many cases still are) sources of spiritual and physical sustenance, highways and beloved ancestors. The reports invariably relate to the impacts on the mana and mauri of rivers and river systems and the associated loss or undermining of rangatiratanga.

On the question of whether rivers are taonga within the meaning of te Tiriti, the Tribunal in *Motunui-Waitara*[10] set out an early exposition of the important differences between the Māori text of te Tiriti and the English text of the Treaty. As the Tribunal reminded us in *Motunui*, the English text specifically refers to "fisheries":

> *Her Majesty the Queen of England confirms and guarantees to the Chiefs and Tribes of New Zealand and to the respective families and individuals thereof the full exclusive and undisturbed possession of their Lands and Estates Forests Fisheries and other properties which they may collectively or individually possess so long as it is their wish and desire to retain the same in their possession ...*

In the Māori text, however, there is no specific reference to fisheries but rather to "tino rangatiratanga" in respect of:

> *o ratou wenua (their lands), o ratou kainga (their habitations), me o ratou taonga katoa (and all their treasured things).*[11]

The Tribunal accepted the approach of iwi claimants, Te Ātiawa, that the general word "taonga" embraces all things treasured by their ancestors and includes the treasures of the forests and fisheries. The Tribunal recognised that tribal fishing grounds and specific areas that were renowned as sources of food were regarded as part and parcel of tribal treasure-troves. So began the jural recognition of rivers and whole river systems (and not just the fisheries) as taonga within the meaning of te Tiriti.

Knowledge holders have been poetic in their telling of why rivers represent the spiritual and physical mana of their iwi and hapū and are therefore treasures. Ramon Joe expressed the significance of the Mōhaka River in this way: [12]

> *As old Father Thames is to the Londoner*
> *As the Ganges is sacred to the Indian*
> *As the Jordan is spiritual to the Palestines*
> *So is the Mohaka all these things to Ngati Pahauwera*

The importance of taonga food species is a strategic focus of river reports, as is the metaphysical nature of rivers, including taniwha and kaitiaki stories.[13] The report on the Manukau Harbour claim provides classic examples. The holistic discussion of the impacts of industry on the harbour included the Waikato River. The Tribunal noted that the river offered much more than a network for intertribal travel and communication:

> *The river, its swamps and tributaries, provided food – eel, freshwater crayfish, whitebait, mullet, flounder, shellfish, waterfowl and wild vegetables. It provided irrigation for kumara, taro and hue. Whitebait has particular importance.*

As to spiritual and metaphysical dimensions, the Tribunal went on to say:

> *It is difficult to over-estimate the importance of the Waikato River to the Tainui tribes. It is a symbol of the tribes' existence. The river is deeply embedded in tribal and individual consciousness ... [T]here is a taniwha at each bend. The river has its own spirit. It is addressed in prayer and oratory as having a life force of its own. The spirits of ancestors are said to mingle and move with its currents.*
>
> *When Waikato people are sick, uncertain or about to undertake a journey or new venture they seek the blessing of the water and protection of their ancestors by immersion or sprinkling. Its curative and healing powers were claimed by several witnesses from personal experiences.*[14]

In the *Manukau Report*, the Tribunal agreed that taonga means more than objects of tangible value, and that a river may be a taonga as a valuable resource. Its mauri or life force is another taonga.[15]

A poignant example of the multifaceted nature of rivers and their treasure-troves being taonga is contained in the evidence of Bill Asher in the *Turangi Township Report*. There, the Tribunal examined the impact and disruption caused by the creation of a new township and extensive diversion of rivers for dam construction and power generation:

> *Effectively, the river has been destroyed as a place of harvest for us. Many species, most of them native, have disappeared altogether. These include inanga, toitoi, kokopu and morehana. You never see them shoaling any more, where once they were present in large numbers. It is still possible to take koura in some places, but in vastly reduced numbers. Watercress, too, has become a rarity ... With the passing of the natural features of our rohe has passed a*

> *way of life for our people. The taking of koura in particular was full of significance and ceremony. There were certain families which had the job of gathering particular caterpillars (called 'mounu') from the fields. They would sew the caterpillar onto threads, and they would be used as bait. The families who gathered them would distribute them to the people who went out to do the harvesting at selected days in the year, and at selected places. All that has gone now, although the practices were still in place right up to the time the project came to Turangi. It is a real loss to me that I cannot share with my mokopuna the way of life I once knew.*[16]

Another example of Tribunal reports as repositories of traditional river knowledge is found in the *Kaituna River Report*. The Tribunal captured the experience of Mrs Emily Schuster, a prominent weaver, who gave evidence as to the importance of river flora to weaving traditions. Mrs Schuster shared her knowledge of raw materials gathered from the riverbanks, which is recounted by the Tribunal as follows:

> *"In the Rotorua area," she said quite sadly, "we have progressed so much that the only place I can take the women is along the Kaituna River. The kiekie is essential and has to be specially treated. To get the true whiteness out of the kiekie it must be soaked in running water and the only place we can do this is the Kaituna" ... She told us that she "would lay down her life to save the Kaituna."*[17]

By the time the Tribunal heard the Mōhaka claim in 1983, there was no debate as to whether rivers were taonga. The claim concerned te tino rangatiratanga o Ngāti Pahauwera over the Mōhaka River, and the Tribunal found that the Crown, through legislation, in particular the Water and Soil Conservation Act 1967, failed to recognise and give effect to Ngāti Pahauwera rangatiratanga over the Mōhaka River.

As is common practice, the Tribunal had travelled to Mōhaka to hear the claimants present their evidence on their marae, to see their river and listen to stories of ancestral relationships with lands and waters. Much of the oral evidence related to mahinga kai.[18] Kahawai was often spoken of as being the most highly prized, sought-after and succulent of fish. Witnesses gave graphic accounts of various types of fishing along the river, and one witness gave a demonstration of how to catch kahawai with a reti board, a fishing aid peculiar to Ngāti Pahauwera. The report is rich with stories, whakapapa and ways the river is personified and glorified in the oral traditions, in chants, in waiata, in whakataukī and in other ways.[19] The sense that a taonga is passed to the present generation from those gone before, and will be passed on to the following generations, was stressed by many of the witnesses. The Tribunal was clear that this is an essential characteristic of a taonga, and it applies not just to the river itself but to the many benefits that the river provides the tribe because those benefits come from the river.

Of special significance to Ngāti Pahauwera were hāngi stones obtained from the river. Flooding dislodges the stones so that they periodically become available. Different types of hāngi stones were known and used by Ngāti Pahauwera, and they were named in the report:

- *taupunga – a greyish type also used as sinkers;*
- *opunga – a whitish, trachyte rock also used for weapons and sinkers;*
- *poutama – a pink type, obtained mainly from the top of the Mohaka river; and*
- *kowhaturi/kowhatumakauri – a black/blue type.*

The report goes on to explain that the whakataukī "Mohakaharara, taupunga, opunga" refers to the different types of hāngi stones that do not break when fired – a symbolic reference to unity within Ngāti Pahauwera, notwithstanding differences between iwi and hapū. This whakataukī, then, explains the origins of the river's name, Mohakaharara, as well as the significance of the river as "a unifying force". In the words of the late Canon Wi Te Tau Huata, "in the end it is the river, it is the river which joins us".[20]

Mana, tino rangatiratanga me ngā mātāpono o te Tiriti

E tou matou matua i te rangi, kia tapu tou ingoa,
tukua mai tou rangatiratanga,
kia meatia tou hiahia ki te 'wenua me tou hiahia i te rangi …[21]

Society was collectively organised with whakapapa being the backbone of a framework of descent groups led by rangatira who signed He Whakaputanga in the 1830s, declaring "Ko matou ko nga tino Rangatira."[22] The text of te Tiriti o Waitangi guaranteed tino rangatiratanga in respect of taonga, and as illustrated above, the Tribunal has agreed with claimants from the outset that rivers are taonga. The early river reports also provide formative statements about tino rangatiratanga. A constant theme in every river report is the loss or undermining of rangatiratanga. Claimants have raised the failure of the Crown to respect the mana of tāngata whenua by assuming control, such as via the Public Works Act takings for new townships and prioritising foreign species in the *Turangi Township Report*; dam construction to produce hydro-electricity in *Ika Whenua*; the assumption of control leading to the removal of gravel and hāngi stones in *Mōhaka*; offensive extraction, merging and discharge of water in *Manukau*; and the discharge of waste into precious waterways in *Kaituna* and *Motunui–Waitara*. The Tribunal grapples with the complexities of reconciling the differences in language used in the Māori and English texts and with other terms that could have been used, such as mana, and with the newly framed concept of kāwanatanga. In doing so, the Tribunal begins to breathe life into the meaning of the Treaty principles as part of its statutory mandate. The Tribunal also considers claims of river ownership.

The *Motunui–Waitara Report* presents an illuminating discussion about rangatiratanga. There, the Tribunal dwelled on evidence relating to the spread of Christianity among Māori communities and the close relationships formed with missionaries. Māori had quickly learned to recite large passages of scripture by rote. The missionaries played a major role in presenting and explaining the Treaty. According to the Tribunal, it would have been apparent that te Tiriti was written in "Missionary Maori".[23] The vast majority of rangatira who signed te Tiriti (rather than the Treaty) would have been in no doubt that they and the missionaries were agreed on what "rangatiratanga" meant. The term was well known to both parties for its use in scripture and prayer, as in "kia tae mai tōu rangatiratanga"(thy kingdom come) in the well-known version of the Lord's Prayer. In other words, and this is the salient point, the translation adopted by the missionaries equates rangatiratanga to God's will in respect of heaven and earth.

The Tribunal goes on to discuss the relationship between rangatiratanga and mana, explaining that rangatiratanga denotes the mana not only to possess what is yours but to control and manage it in accordance with your own preferences.[24] As the Tribunal points out, te Tiriti clearly advances that view, and the English text, referring to a "full exclusive and undisturbed possession" also permits of it. There is further support for that view in both preambles:[25]

> ***Ko Wikitoria te Kuini o Ingarangi i tana mahara atawai ki nga Rangatiratanga me nga Hapu o Nu Tirani i tana hiahia hoki kia tohungia ki a ratou o ratou rangatiratanga …***

and

> *Her Majesty ... regarding with Her Royal Favour the Native Chiefs and Tribes of New Zealand and anxious to protect their just Rights and Property ...*

In the *Kaituna River Report*, when discussing rangatiratanga, Sir Hugh Kawharu provides his insight into rangatiratanga:

> *It is totally against the run of evidence to imagine that [chiefs] would wittingly have divested themselves of all their spiritually sanctioned powers—most of which powers indeed they wanted protected. They would have believed they were retaining their rangatiratanga intact apart from a licence to kill or inflict material hurt on others, retaining all their customary rights and duties as trustees for their tribal groups ...*[26]

A short distance from Kaituna are the rivers that are discussed in *Te Ika Whenua Rivers Report*. In that report, the Tribunal addressed claims relating to the impact of the Crown reserving sole and exclusive rights to waterways to construct dams for power generation. Claimant evidence clearly established that the middle reaches of the Rangitaiki and the Whirinaki and Wheao rivers were taonga over which the hapū of Te Ika Whenua had mana and rangatiratanga. The following historical example of the recognition of Te Ika Whenua's tino rangatiratanga over the rivers was given by claimant researchers. When Ngāti Manawa returned to Karamuramu after fleeing to Rotorua, they found that the "Native Contingent under Captain Preece" was catching eels in the Ngātamawahine Stream. They asked Preece to cease eeling. He did. This, in the Tribunal's view, demonstrated that Preece recognised Ngāti Manawa's mana over the rivers.[27]

Ownership

The early river reports laid foundations for ongoing debate and discussion about the meaning of the words used in te Tiriti and the Treaty. The Tribunal makes it clear that rangatiratanga refers to authority that existed prior to, and was affirmed and guaranteed in, te Tiriti o Waitangi. Yet, the Crown has assumed ownership of freshwater in regulating its use and allowing commercial interests to profit. This Crown assumption is inconsistent with te Tiriti o Waitangi. In bringing inconsistencies such as this to the attention of the Waitangi

Tribunal and the courts, claimant groups have framed their claims in different ways. Having been forcibly removed from their homelands and waterways and excluded from the franchise and other forms of decision-making, some claimant groups have claimed ownership in water to restore rangatiratanga, and, in the face of increasing degradation, to be more meaningfully involved in the rehabilitation and protection of the health and well-being of waterways that go to the core of identity and sense of responsibility. In doing so, claimants have been forced to try and make sense of competing (and complex) English common law doctrines and their own tikanga understandings. Acknowledging that a range of opinions exists goes a long way to helping to understand some of the problems associated with ownership.[28] The legacy of conflict has brought ownership to the fore as a premise for rangatiratanga.

In assessing whether any part of the Mōhaka River had been sold, the Tribunal's discussion is an example of the confusion that occurs when a river is used as a border in attempts for iwi and hapū to create arrangements for shared occupation of an area. The legal recognition of the prior property interests of iwi and hapū as the indigenous peoples of the land, or "native title", was recognised in New Zealand courts as early as 1847.[29] The common law principle espoused in *Embrey v Owen* is that there is no ownership in naturally flowing water.[30] But, by the common law, ownership of land adjoining a river gives rise to the presumption that title in the riverbed extends to the middle line (*ad medium filum aquae*). It is a rebuttable presumption, and one that iwi and hapū had no idea about when entering into these arrangements. The *contra proferentem* rule is a doctrine that dictates how ambiguous clauses in contracts are to be interpreted in a way that does not favour the party who originally drafted the words in the agreement.[31] State law differs as to the applicability of common law doctrines in respect of rivers that are "navigable" and those that are "non-navigable". In some instances, the Crown legislated for ownership of riverbeds.[32] It is no surprise that the Tribunal would later admit in *The Pouakani Report* that the law relating to ownership in these respects is "confused and confusing".[33]

With crystal clarity the Tribunal found that the Whanganui River was owned by the hapū:

> *The conceptual understanding of a river as a tupuna or ancestor emphasises the Maori thought that the river exists as a single and undivided entity or essence. Rendering the native title in its own terms, then, what Atihaunui owned was a river, not a bed, and a*

river entire, not dissected into parts ... What they possessed is equated with ownership for the purposes of English or New Zealand law.

In Kaituna, the claim related to a proposal for a nutrient pipeline from the Rotorua Wastewater Treatment Plant to the Kaituna River, which did not call for the Tribunal to delve into debates about ownership. The claims were intended to stop the proposed scheme and promote suitable land-based disposal. However, the Tribunal, by appending the evidence of tohunga Irirangi Tiakiawa directly following its recommendations, literally gives him the last word in relation to the awa:[34]

We own this river, we have always owned it, we have never really surrendered ownership that authorities do as they please.

In *Mōhaka*, the Tribunal found that the Treaty's promise to protect Ngāti Pahauwera's rangatiratanga has a special application to the Mōhaka River.[35] The river was so central to their existence as a river people that the river would have been seen as the cornerstone of the Treaty's guarantee of their tribal identity. The Tribunal concluded that statutory provisions that assumed that the Crown owned the riverbed and waters, or appropriated such ownership to the Crown or conferred exclusive control over the waters on central and/or local government, were in breach of the letter of the Treaty and the principle that the Crown must actively protect the property of Māori to the fullest extent practicable.[36]

In this chapter, I have focused on the early river reports, which feature claimant voices and stress the autonomous authority embodied in rangatiratanga. But over time, the Tribunal has wavered on issues of ownership, rangatiratanga and sovereignty.[37] Successive governments have generally refused to recognise Māori claims of ownership and proprietary rights in water but have been willing to return title to associated lands such as riverbeds and lake-beds and to acknowledge rights to culture, such as kaitiakitanga.[38] Its inclusion in the Resource Management Act 1991 has seen kaitiakitanga come to mean something less than ownership, contrary to the depth of meaning of being a kaitiaki according to tikanga, which has kaitiakitanga as one of the manifestations of ownership.[39]

Most commonly, rangatiratanga in respect of water is framed as something more than the right to co-manage and much more than the narrow interpretation of kaitiakitanga that has gained traction. Some iwi and hapū have claimed ownership to entire waterways. Others have moved beyond the Tribunal claims and secured Treaty settlement redress mechanisms for the overarching and urgent purpose of restoring and protecting the health and well-being of waterways for present and future generations. Claimants are adamant that redress mechanisms be upheld and honoured and not undermined by legislative reforms. By Crown design, Treaty settlements intentionally avoid or defer issues of ownership and allocation. For example, Waikato-Tainui and the Crown explicitly agreed to defer any conversation about ownership.[40]

The position of Ngāi Tahu currently is to claim rangatiratanga over the Ngāi Tahu takiwā and is seeking co-governance of publicly owned assets.[41] In these processes, it is argued or assumed by claimant groups that ownership, or customary title, has not been ceded or sold to the Crown. There has been a level of discussion about unextinguished customary title, both as to the beds of waterways and to water itself.

There have been shifts of Waitangi Tribunal findings in relation to rivers and other water bodies, from ownership as at 1840 but subsequently being shared resources, to ownership continuing unextinguished to the present time. A test case on ownership based on unextinguished customary title has been opened by the Waitangi Tribunal as part of the claims relating to The National Freshwater and Geothermal Resources Inquiry (Wai 2358). The inquiry will continue into the impact of legislative and policy reforms or reform options on "Māori rights and interests" in specific freshwater resources, as identified by the Tribunal.[42] At the time of writing, issues of allocation and proprietary rights remain unresolved.

Ngā Hua Kua Puta – Restoring and Protecting Kaitiaki Rights and Responsibilities

While the Tribunal reports are wellsprings of wisdom, their effectiveness is largely undermined by the Crown's unwillingness to implement key recommendations. In the context of contemporary political and legal landscapes seen as "anti-Māori"[43] and a "war on nature",[44] it is important to remember that there has been some progress in honouring the promises of te Tiriti and the Treaty in respect of intergenerational rights and responsibilities, particularly in Treaty settlements that successive governments have promised to uphold. Certain settlements have embedded the primacy of health and well-being of rivers and other waterbodies in legislation and motivated mana motuhake outcomes at place, with reclamation and restoration of taonga food species and practices around them being a tangible example.

Tai timu, tai pari, tai ao – different ways of viewing the world

The Waitangi Tribunal has played a pivotal role in explaining the interconnectedness that is the essence of a Māori world view sourced in creation narratives. In the *Kaituna River Report*, the Tribunal explained how the lakes, rivers and estuary, in that case, were to be seen as a whole water system, and not in isolation, which was a view reiterated in the *Motunui–Waitara Report*. *Motunui* predominantly dealt with claimed impacts on ocean reefs, but the Tribunal agreed with claimants that the investigation needed to include the impact on river systems as well. The Tribunal also noted its discomfort in severing the water issues from the land issues, seeing them as indivisible, but acknowledging the practical need to make recommendations in respect of the urgent matter at hand, which was the impact of the outfall on water taonga. Similarly, in *Manukau*, the Tribunal found it impossible to consider the impacts of Crown breaches on the harbour alone, preferring instead to consider the history of the Waikato river and its relationship to the harbour.

The Tribunal has consistently promoted the cultural preference for land-based disposal systems rather than mixing waters contaminated by human waste with waters used for gathering food,[45] and other practices that cause spiritual or cultural offence.[46] In *Manukau*, the Tribunal was clear that Māori values are not contrary to development. Rather, the holistic world view recognised in the Tribunal reports emphasises the primacy of nature and the need for humans to tread carefully when interfering with natural laws and processes.[47] The difference is one of emphasis. The *Manukau Report* predated the 1985 extension of the Tribunal's jurisdiction to allow for historical claims. However, the Tribunal noted that the enormous losses sustained by the iwi and hapū of the Manukau needed to be examined, although it was beyond the Tribunal's jurisdiction to examine in any detail. In the Tribunal's view, the policies that led to the land wars and confiscations in the 1860s are the primary source of grievance although they occurred last century, and it was the continuation of similar policies that prevented past wounds from healing.[48]

Te mana o te awa – prioritising the health and well-being of rivers

The river reports exemplify a holistic approach to resource management that increasingly became the norm. The discussions and findings of the Manukau tribunal flowed into the 2010 Waikato River settlement. The Waikato River settlement ushered in a new era of co-management. It compelled local authorities across the catchment to meet regularly and work with mandated representatives of iwi and hapū towards the overarching purpose – to restore and protect the health and well-being of the Waikato River for future generations.[49] Significant cultural shifts have occurred as a result of joint management committees and stronger commitment shown by local authorities to work collaboratively with iwi and hapū. A recent example is the partnership between mana whenua groups and local authorities to create the Cambridge Wastewater Treatment Plant adopting a Matariki Framework.[50]

The Waikato River settlement embeds Te Ture Whaimana, the vision and strategy for the river's holistic restoration, as the primary direction-setting document for decision-making and coined the phrase "te mana o te awa" (the spiritual authority, protective power and prestige of the Waikato River). The settlement recognises that respect for te mana o te awa is at the heart of the relationship between the iwi and hapū and their ancestral river.[51] This concept was later reframed for national application to "Te Mana o te Wai".[52] Despite current plans to remove Te Mana o te Wai from resource consent processes and to "rebalance" the hierarchy of considerations in the National Policy Statement for Freshwater Management, the provisions of the Waikato River settlement and te mana o te awa continue to apply in accordance with the settlement.[53] So too do the provisions of other settlements, such as Whanganui. On this basis, it is fair to argue that Treaty settlements are proving to be the strongest tools for restoring and protecting the health and well-being of rivers for present and future generations.

In the colossal report on the Whanganui River, the Tribunal found that the Crown had breached the principles of the Treaty in many respects. There are moving accounts in respect of the relationship between the river and its people. The Tribunal's findings in relation to customary interests and title to foreshore and seabed and the river in its entirety are bold and forthright. The Tribunal found that the river was a single and indivisible entity, inclusive of the water; that Whanganui iwi possessed and held rangatiratanga over the river and never sold those interests; and that acts of removing possession and control from iwi were and are contrary to Treaty principles. The Tribunal recommended, among other things, that the river in its entirety be vested in an ancestor or ancestors of the iwi.[54] The Whanganui River settlement does not fully adopt the Waitangi Tribunal's recommendations set out in its 1999 report. Nevertheless, the uncompromising clarity of the Tribunal's findings and forward-thinking proposals laid the foundations for the settlement, which has attracted international attention for its according of legal personality and voice to the Whanganui River.[55] This mechanism provides an opportunity for more effective recognition of the rights and interests of the river to be healthy and well. The legal status of the river combined with stronger rights of kaitiaki when applying the Resource Management Act provides the strongest opportunity for effective participation by iwi and hapū in planning processes.[56] The Te Awa Tupua (Whanganui River Claims Settlement) Act recognises Te Awa Tupua as an indivisible and living whole, comprising the Whanganui River from the mountains to the sea, incorporating all its physical and metaphysical elements.[57] Te Awa Tupua also gifts us the famous saying ko au te awa, ko te awa ko au – I am the river, and the river is me, which is the epitome of a world view based on interconnectedness.[58]

Kaitiakitanga and kai sovereignty

Throughout the river reports, the Crown accepted that rivers once supported abundant resources, which have been seriously depleted and adversely affected. In *Motunui-Waitara*, the Tribunal identified the clear link between the gross pollution from industrial and farm waste and significant health effects experienced in the 1940s and 1950s, such as dysentery and boils.[59] Matters of biodiversity loss and indigenous peoples' health and well-being are often considered separately, but they are linked in many ways. The river reports describe extensive ecosystem changes and the dramatic decline of taonga species as healthy food sources.

New threats appear on the horizon. Proposals for law and policy reform ease restrictions on farmers regarding intensive practices that are known to cause major damage to waterways, and plans to remove Te Mana o te Wai as a primary factor in resource management decision-making will undermine decades of collaborative and visionary work. New pest species, such as *Corbicula fluminea* (invasive gold clams), join established pests, such as koi carp, causing havoc to native species in our rivers and streams. There is a reduced ability to counter them with biosecurity budgetary challenges.

Recognising that pathways to Māori wellness are through responsibility for and kinship with the land, the Tribunal was also later to recommend the establishment of a Māori health authority. In the Tribunal's *Hauora* report, the parties accepted that Māori health inequities are influenced by the cumulative effects of colonisation. The Tribunal's report on Hauora led to the establishment of Te Aka Whai Ora, the Māori Health Authority. While the authority was short lived, there is wider recognition of the need to address health disparities, with one of the solutions being to restore and protect the health and well-being of waterways, including traditional food sources, as a link to healthier lifestyles and rangatiratanga in practice. The Tribunal reports contain easily accessible repositories of information to support restoration efforts.

Treaty settlements, having drawn heavily from Tribunal reports, have led to shifts in policy and kaitiaki practice. Many river settlement entities have established and funded clean-up and restoration projects. These projects have resulted in restored habitat, relearned techniques and mana motuhake outcomes evident at significant tribal events. Poukai are examples of tikanga-immersed events that celebrate the Kīngitanga. They provide iwi and hapū with the opportunity to showcase taonga species such as kōkī (dried shark), whitebait and tuna. The Waikato River Authority has funded bio-blitz and holiday programme activities for tamariki that reconnect younger generations to these practices, for culture, language, identity and the promotion of healthier lifestyles. Whenua returned or purchased through Treaty settlements is being used to teach and learn gardening of taonga species, on whenua and in streams and rivers. As a result of this work, it has been inspirational to hear rangatahi speaking about kai sovereignty being an integral part of mana motuhake,[60] and reminding us that our taonga species are something that connect us through time:

> *Kai is the vehicle to our future. We are able to be enacted in whatever our journey is past this point through the kai that we are consuming and surrounded in and the kinds of environments that our kai can create for us for our flourishing futures.*[61]

Kohikohia ngā maramara[62]

The Waitangi Tribunal river reports embody ongoing efforts to address historical injustices and work towards a more equitable and sustainable future for iwi and hapū and the natural environment. For almost two centuries, conflicts have arisen between the signatories to te Tiriti and the Treaty due to differences in world views and the systems of law and governance that ensue. The nature of obligations under te Tiriti has been at the centre of those controversies, exemplified by the river claims. The legacy of the fact that prior to colonisation Aotearoa and Te Waipounamu were inhabited by autonomous sovereign nations adds layers of complexity. While there is unity in respect of water and the environment generally as taonga, and in regard to rangatiratanga as an enduring system of governance, it has proven difficult to reconcile the contradictory views that iwi and hapū have regarding ownership of water.[63]

The Tribunal led the way in determining that rivers, and the many benefits that rivers provide to iwi and hapū, are taonga within the meaning of te Tiriti. It is an essential characteristic that taonga are passed through generations. The river reports themselves, rich with evidence and reasoning, share the essential characteristic of taonga. They have contributed to watershed settlements that have attracted worldwide attention.

The river settlements provide mechanisms that guarantee more effective participation in planning processes and enable iwi and hapū to reclaim and restore traditional knowledge relating to river taonga. Although river settlements do not go as far as some of the river reports in the recognition of rangatiratanga, they represent significant progress.[64] Te Maire Tau observes that Treaty settlements have "fallen short of addressing the ownership of water, but that they do not necessarily negate provisions for ownership".[65]

The basis of every river claim is te Tiriti o Waitangi. On the cover of the early Tribunal reports, the design by artist Cliff Whiting invokes the signing of te Tiriti as an unending spiral that reflects the consequent interwoven development of Māori and Pākehā history as it continuously unfolds in a pattern not yet completely known. Within the pages, the Tribunal has carefully deliberated and delivered reports that provide ways forward for tāngata whenua and tāngata tiriti to live together in communities, and as a nation.

Ngā Wai Honohono – The Rivers that Join Us

The inspiration for the title of this chapter comes from the name of Te Arikinui Kuini Nga wai hono i te po; a name that celebrates an enduring relationship between two majestic rivers, Whanganui and Waikato. These rivers, and many others, together with the iwi and hapū who stand as their kaitiaki, have drawn strength and healing from the judicious deliberations of the Waitangi Tribunal. Te Arikinui succeeded to her father in September 2024. A legacy of the late Kīngi Tuheitia Potatau Te Wherowhero is the series of gatherings in 2024 that promoted kotahitanga – strength in unity. This mantra applies both in terms of iwi and hapū and of tāngata whenua and tāngata tiriti coming together to address complex challenges, including those at the heart of the Tribunal's river reports.

"Water bodies are a source of survival and providers of life, and from the beginning, Māori have lived on, around and in tune with their waterways."

Chapter 5

Wai me Te Taiao

"He pukenga wai, he nohonga tāngata, he nohonga tāngata, he putanga kōrero" – Steering the Constitutional Conversation about Freshwater towards Rangatiratanga

— Horiana Irwin-Easthope and Jacinta Ruru

Hapū and iwi have been maintaining their whakapapa connection, and related obligations, to wai (freshwater) for generations. Māori creation narratives emphasise the multifaceted relationship with wai. The relationship manifests in the present day through the various ways in which hapū and iwi connect with their respective waterways; through pepeha, exercising kaitiakitanga and the continuing assertion of rangatiratanga. The extent to which hapū and iwi can truly exercise rangatiratanga in relation to wai is often restricted by the exercise of kāwanatanga by the Crown. The constitutional question of how tino rangatiratanga is exercised generally in Aotearoa New Zealand is legally unresolved, including in relation to freshwater. Successive governments have continued to 'kick the can down the road'. But the call from hapū to uphold the tino rangatiratanga guarantees in te Tiriti o Waitangi are getting louder. This is particularly the case for wai, with hapū and iwi using a range of different avenues, including the Waitangi Tribunal and the courts, to emphasise their connection to wai and the responsibility to exercise rangatiratanga over their taonga.

This chapter explores the Waitangi Tribunal's extensive contribution to both the recording of hapū and iwi kōrero tuku iho about their connection to wai and the consequent findings and recommendations that have contributed to, and we say will continue to contribute to, a broader constitutional conversation about the way in which those connections to wai should be legally recognised in Aotearoa New Zealand.

Ko Wai a te Waitangi Tribunal – Hononga ki te Wai

The Waitangi Tribunal has heard extensive evidence about Māori connections to the environment and wai. It has documented this kōrero tuku iho in their reports over the years: "He pukenga wai, he nōhanga tangata, he nōhanga tangata, he pūkenga kōrero – Where the rivers meet, people come together; when people come together, there is discussion and sharing of knowledge."[1] As a result of this documentation process, the Tribunal itself has been a site of waters coming together and sharing of knowledge about connections with, and obligations to, wai. As Linda Te Aho has noted in her chapter,[2] the early Waitangi Tribunal reports in relation to rivers contain extensive references to evidence of kōrero tuku iho as the claimants in those cases were, in part, seeking to persuade the Waitangi Tribunal that the rivers and river systems were taonga. Therefore, while the Tribunal was considering potential Crown breaches of te Tiriti o Waitangi, the Waitangi Tribunal reports are an important and beautifully rich repository of hapū and iwi narratives that describe the connection of hapū and iwi to their atua, their natural environment and their wai. The value of the Tribunal's reports for this purpose alone cannot be overstated.

The Tribunal has also reported extensively about hapū and iwi connection to their respective wai and specific waterways.[3] As Linda Te Aho noted in 2012, "Water is at the heart of the earliest Waitangi Tribunal reports".[4] There are likely a range of reasons for this, including the whakapapa connection hapū and iwi have to wai, its importance to Māori generally and the jurisdictional reality that for the first ten years of the Tribunal's life, its jurisdiction was prospective. The very early reports were responding to the current issues of the period 1975–1985. The pollution of waterways, particularly the impact of proposed infrastructure generally on fishing, was a feature of the early reports. We have drawn on some of these earlier reports to frame this chapter. We then move on to more recent reports that focus on present-day management of freshwater, and we examine the Tribunal's recommendations in the context of the rangatiratanga guarantee in te Tiriti o Waitangi.

Ko Wai, Ko Ahau – the Tribunal's Recording of Our Whakapapa Relationship with Wai[5]

The starting point for the relationship that Māori have to water is the way in which Māori relate to their environment more broadly. We see ourselves not as masters of the environment but as members of it.[6] To us, the environment is holistic and interconnected. Inherent in this view of the world is not only reciprocity between descendants and ancestors, but also an obligation to pass the environment on and preserve it for future generations so that they may enjoy a relationship with the resource.[7]

This intrinsic relationship with wai stems from whakapapa, a genealogical connection linking Māori with all natural resources and the atua. The creation of the environment finds its origins in the union of Ranginui (the Sky Father) and Papatūānuku (the Earth Mother) and their children, who are key deities of various domains of the natural world. We can trace our origins to these atua through our whakapapa.[8] This means that we consider all forms of life and natural resources, including animals, plants, mountains and freshwater expanses such as rivers and lakes, as being kin, ancestors or parents. We have a whanaungatanga obligation of kinship. *Ko Aotearoa Tēnei*,[9] the Tribunal's Wai 262 report, detailed the Māori relationship with the environment.[10] The Tribunal describes the concept of kaitiakitanga as a foundational principle for the relationship between Māori and natural resources, including freshwater.[11] The mauri of wai is essential to the health of both the natural environment and the identity of Māori, being deeply intertwined with whakapapa and whanaungatanga.[12] The Tribunal acknowledges that prior to the arrival of settlers, Māori were kaitiaki of rivers, lakes and waterways, ensuring that their mauri was preserved through sustainable use and spiritual care.[13] Williams J, the presiding officer of the Wai 262 inquiry,[14] has described whanaungatanga as "the glue that held, and still holds, the system together; the idea that makes the whole system make sense – including *legal* sense"[15] and "the infrastructure around which the Māori values and legal system hung".[16] Whakapapa and whanaungatanga provide a framework for Māori to make sense of the world as they describe the relationships, and corresponding obligations, between us and the natural world.

The Tribunal, in *He Maunga Rongo*,[17] recorded the following evidence on behalf of Ngāti Mākino describing the original narrative of Ranginui and Papatūānuku:[18]

> *Water [wai] originates from the separation of Ranginui and Papatuanuku, and whichever form it takes on, [during] its descent from the realms of the sky father it is recognised by Māori as the everlasting regrets, longing and loss felt in the separation of the parents and their expansive and undying love for each other. So the sense in which water has its first importance is in that relationship between Rangi and Papa. The tears that fall from the sky become the nourishment of the land itself, on which all current existence depends. Wai sustains and is sustained by Papatuanuku. As the whenua [land] is nurtured by the wai-ahuru that protects the life within the placenta so the wai acts as a shelter for the human form that is nourished by the whenua. As Ngā Roimata a Ranginui descend to settle on Papatuanuku, they gather in the many rivulets of her form, flowing through her and over her, bathing and nourishing the lover that Rangi continues to yearn for.*

Consistent with the holistic way in which we view the natural world, Hōhepa Kereopa describes the interconnectedness of waters as reported by the Tribunal in *The Stage 1 Report on the National Freshwater and Geothermal Resources Claim* (Freshwater Report):[19]

> *Upon its descent through the warmth of Papatuanuku, the mists will begin to elevate. When it is nightfall the dew begins to fall on the surface of the earth, which are the land winds. All the rivers converge together from the valleys which follows the descent of the waterfalls forming into the mina or the cleansing waters whose role it is to gather all the impurities together and carry them to the river mouth. As a cleansing for the children of Tangaroa, the crest of the moon is lifted creating the mist and clouds, allowing the process to begin again.*

Water bodies are a source of survival and providers of life, and from the beginning, Māori have lived on, around and in tune with their waterways.[20] Cletus Maanu Paul gave evidence to the Tribunal in 1993 that his Moewhare people of Ngāti Manawa used their river "as a source for survival" and, to them, "the river was a provider of life – he tino taonga (a very precious gift)" that "provided water as well as food – eels".[21]

Waterways and waterbodies have mauri, or a vital essence – the spark of life kindled at the conception of all things.[22] The preservation of mauri is of paramount importance and the presence of mauri in all things entrusts an obligation to appreciate and respect that resource. The link between kaitiaki and mauri is explained by Tamati Cairns in his evidence for the Waitangi Tribunal in the Freshwater Report:[23]

> *As kaitiaki of the Waikato River (or the section in their domain), the Pouakani people have an obligation to maintain the mauri of the river. The mauri is the life force of the river. This includes taking care of the physical and spiritual health of the river.*

Maintaining mauri has both physical and spiritual elements. For the Pouakani people the physical dimension of maintaining mauri includes using the river responsibly so that it remains for future generations.[24] The spiritual aspect was ensuring that tikanga was followed.

This is but a snapshot of how the Tribunal, through some of its reports, has documented Māori relationships to wai. There are many more examples.

He Taonga te Wai: Tribunal Recognition of Wai as a Taonga

Through the evidence the Waitangi Tribunal has heard over the decades, the Tribunal has repeatedly accepted that waterways and water bodies, including streams, rivers, lakes and geothermal resources, are taonga of claimant hapū and iwi groups.[25] The Tribunal has found that water bodies are highly prized taonga because they are a significant resource to tangata whenua.[26] Different iwi, hapū and whānau groups each have their own specific stories and accounts explaining their particular association with their water bodies and why they are a taonga to them. Two consistent themes arise: the physical and metaphysical value of waterways are intrinsically important. As acknowledged by the Waitangi Tribunal in the *Te Ika Whenua Rivers Report*:[27]

> *Conceptually, a river is a taonga, a valuable food resource to those who possess it, which carries its own separate mauri (life force) and is guarded by the taniwha that inhabit it. The physical cannot be divorced from the metaphysical; the two are inseparable.*

As recorded by the Tribunal in *The Mohaka River Report*:[28]

> *Ngā maunga and ngā awa are regarded as being taonga representing the spiritual and physical mana of the iwi and for food resources providing for the sustenance of the iwi.*

The Waitangi Tribunal has also repeatedly confirmed that Māori have proprietary rights and interests in their freshwater bodies. For example, in the course of addressing whether a proposed pipeline to the Kaituna River was inconsistent with the Treaty of Waitangi, the Waitangi Tribunal, in the *Kaituna River Report* 1984, found that Ngāti Pikiao and Te Arawa owned the Kaituna River in 1849 and had done so for many generations.[29] In coming to this view, the Waitangi Tribunal relied particularly on the evidence of Te Irirangi Cairo Tiakiawa who recited the whakapapa, history and territorial authority of Ngāti Pikiao, which established them as the owners of these lakes and the river in question.[30] The Tribunal recommended that the pipeline scheme should be abandoned and an alternative option pursued.[31] This recommendation was adopted by the Crown.

In *The Mohaka River Report* (1992), the Waitangi Tribunal found that rangatiratanga as applied to the Mōhaka River and Ngāti Pāhauwera:[32]

> *… denotes something more than ownership or guardianship of the river but something less than the right of exclusive use. It means that*

the iwi and hapū of the rohe through which the river flows should retain an effective degree of control over the river and its resources as long as they wish to do so.

In both the *Te Ika Whenua Rivers Report* and *The Whanganui River Report,* the Waitangi Tribunal found that Māori have customary rights, sometimes equivalent to English proprietary rights, in the Rangitaiki River, Whirinaki River, Whēao River and Whanganui River (and its tributaries) and that the Crown breached the Treaty in respect of those river rights.[33]

The Waitangi Tribunal in the *Te Ika Whenua Rivers Report* found that the three Te Ika Whenua rivers (Rangitaiki, Whēao and Whirinaki) are awa and living taonga of the hapū of Te Ika Whenua. The rivers were indivisible and could be 'owned' in Māori terms as a taonga, a valuable food resource to those who possess it, that carries its own separate mauri (life force) and is guarded by the taniwha that inhabit it.[34] The rivers, therefore, provide material and spiritual sustenance and a strong continuing bond:[35] "The people belong to the river and the river belongs to the people".[36] The Tribunal found that while tino rangatiratanga should not be confused with modern-day 'ownership' Te Ika Whenua's customary rights entitled them to full use and control of their rivers and enabled them to enlarge and develop uses as time and circumstances dictated. The Tribunal went on to find that this full exclusive use and control of their taonga, their rivers, means that at 1840 they were entitled to have conferred on them a proprietary interest in the rivers that could be practically encapsulated within the legal notion of ownership of the waters thereof. The Tribunal went on to say that while the interest was akin to ownership in 1840 the Treaty anticipated a sharing of resources on which settlement depended, such as rivers.[37]

The Tribunal therefore found that while the claimants had shared their rivers for non-commercial uses it was "quite unacceptable that commercial property can be made from Te Ika Whenua interest in the rivers without any form of compensation or payment".[38] In particular, the Tribunal held that Te Ika Whenua are entitled to payment for the use of their interest in the rivers for power generation and recommended that the Crown consult and negotiate with Te Ika Whenua over past use and ascertain a suitable formula for payment for future use.[39]

In the *He Maunga Rongo* report (2008), the Tribunal found that Lake Taupō waters and fisheries were taonga that were exclusively possessed by

Ngāti Tūwharetoa.[40] This exclusive possession together with authority over a cultural and spiritual relationship and a responsibility to care for taonga were elements of the tino rangatiratanga that Tūwharetoa exercised.[41]

The Tribunal in its Freshwater Report accepted that the evidence presented to it demonstrated that water bodies are a taonga.[42] Poroti Springs was examined as a case study by the Waitangi Tribunal in its Freshwater Report. The Tribunal reported that the Poroti Springs are a taonga of great spiritual significance to Te Uriroroi, Te Parawhau and Te Māhurehure and to the whole of Ngā Puhi.[43] The springs were and are a highly prized resource; the waters were used for healing (rongoā) and also for ritual, and they provide physical sustenance in the form of watercress, eels and kēwai.[44] In 1896, the Māori Land Court vested Poroti Springs, in the Whangārei region, in six Māori owners. Then, in 1960, the Governor-General designated the springs and surrounding land as a Māori Reservation for the purpose of water supply for the common use and benefit of the local hapū. The Whaitiri Māori Reserves Trust is the body that administers the reservation. The Whaitiri Māori Reserves Trust has sought recognition of its ownership rights in the waters of Poroti Springs through the Waitangi Tribunal.[45] The Tribunal in the Freshwater Stage One Report, however, declined to make findings or recommendations about specific grievances and water bodies and instead considered that there were other avenues for redress for these specific claims.[46] In the case of Poroti Springs, the Trust claim is included in a district inquiry that is still to conclude.

"Te tino rangatiratanga ... ō rātou taonga katoa": Tribunal Approaches

Te Tiriti o Waitangi is Aotearoa New Zealand's founding constitutional document. Interpretation of te Tiriti is informed by He Whakaputanga o Ngā Rangatiratanga o Niu Tireni, also referred to as the Declaration of Independence.[47] Article 2 of te Tiriti o Waitangi provides:

> *Ko te Kuini o Ingarani ka wakarite ka wakaae ki nga Rangatira ki nga hapū – ki nga tangata katoa o Nu Tirani te tino rangatiratanga o o ratou wenua o ratou kainga me o ratou taonga katoa. Otiia ko nga Rangatira o te wakaminenga me nga Rangatira katoa atu ka tuku ki te Kuini te hokonga o era wahi wenua e pai ai te tangata nona te Wenua – ki te ritenga o te utu e wakaritea ai e ratou ko te kai hoko e meatia nei e te Kuini hei kai hoko mona.*

Without needing to examine textual differences that have been well traversed, it is sufficient to note that the Māori text guaranteed to Māori rangatira "te tino rangatiratanga" over their "taonga", or as Sir Hugh Kawharu translated, "unqualified exercise of their chieftainship" over their "treasures".[48] The claims to the Tribunal about freshwater have largely been framed through the whakapapa connection to wai and grounded in this tino rangatiratanga guarantee.

There have been differing approaches by different Tribunals to the tino rangatiratanga guarantee with respect to wai. The Tribunal in *Ko Aotearoa Tēnei* found that te Tiriti guaranteed Māori tino rangatiratanga over their taonga, including waterways, but previous legislation ignored these obligations and did not provide appropriate forms of recognition of Māori interests with issues regarding the environment.[49] The Tribunal in *Ko Aotearoa Tēnei* placed primary emphasis on kaitiakitanga as a flow on from tino rangatiratanga. The Tribunal describes the emphasis as follows:[50]

> *Kaitiakitanga is the obligation, arising from the kin relationship, to nurture or care for a person or thing ... Kaitiaki can be spiritual guardians existing in non-human form ... But people can (indeed, must) also be kaitiaki ... Mana and kaitiakitanga go together as right and responsibility, and that kaitiaki responsibility can be understood not only as cultural principle but as a system of law.*

Shortly after *Ko Aotearoa Tēnei* was released, Carwyn Jones commented on the emphasis the Tribunal placed on kaitiakitanga rather than tino rangatiratanga:[51]

> *No doubt many people will be disappointed that the Tribunal has stated that it may no longer be possible to deliver full-autonomy to Māori in all circumstances where Māori interests are at stake. But it seems to me that the report suggests that the constitutional Treaty guarantee of tino rangatiratanga requires that the default position ought to be that full decision making authority sits with the kaitiaki. This is a powerful starting point. Nevertheless, where other interests are sufficiently strong, these may need to be balanced against the protected Treaty interest, which may in turn lead to some form of shared decision-making. And in the rare cases where shared decision-making is not possible, the Tribunal notes that it must always be open to Māori to influence decisions that affect their taonga.*

The later Tribunal on freshwater in 2019, reporting on the Wai 2357 and 2358 claims (discussed in more detail in the next section of this chapter), grounded its analysis in the tino rangatiratanga Article 2 guarantee. In that regard, the Tribunal found that:[52]

> *As we see it, the Crown's guarantees to Māori in the Treaty, including the guarantee of tino rangatiratanga, require the use of partnership mechanisms for the joint governance and management of freshwater taonga – for example, through the use of section 33 of the RMA. For the most part, however, the presence of other interests in New Zealand's water bodies requires a co-governance/ co-management partnership between Māori and councils for the control and management of freshwater taonga. That is the Treaty standard for freshwater management.*

However, the Tribunal in its stage one Freshwater Report in 2012 acknowledges its agreement with the Tribunal's approach in Wai 262 as follows:[53]

> *The Tribunal found that kaitiaki rights exist on a sliding scale. At one end of the scale, full kaitiaki control of the taonga will be appropriate. In the middle of the scale, a partnership arrangement for joint control with the Crown or another entity will be the correct expression of the degree and nature of Māori interest in the taonga (as balanced against other interests). At the other end of the scale, kaitiaki should have influence in decision-making but not be either the sole decision-makers or joint decision-makers, reflecting a lower level of Māori interest in the taonga when balanced against the interests of the environment, the health of the taonga, and the weight of competing interests.*
>
> *This scheme is not incompatible with Māori having residual proprietary interests in – or, indeed, full ownership of – water bodies that are taonga. Rather, that would be a factor to be considered in terms of the weight accorded the kaitiaki interest vis-à-vis other interests in the resource.*

The Tribunal goes onto conclude in the stage two Freshwater Report, noting these approaches, that:[54]

> *Having heard the evidence of the claimants and interested parties in both stage 1 and stage 2 of this inquiry, our view is that the Māori Treaty right in the management of most freshwater taonga is at the co-governance / co-management part of the scale. Freshwater taonga*

are central to tribal identity and to the spiritual and cultural well-being of iwi and hapū, and traditionally played a crucial role in the economic life and survival of the tribe. The Crown's guarantees to Māori in the Treaty, including the guarantee of tino rangatiratanga, require the use of partnership mechanisms for the joint governance and management of freshwater taonga. The exception to co-governance and co-management is that, in some cases, the strength of the Māori interest in a particular freshwater taonga may be such that it requires Māori governance of that taonga. Our view was that the presence of other interests in New Zealand's water bodies will more often require a co-governance/ co-management partnership between Māori and councils for the control and management of freshwater taonga; that is the Treaty standard for freshwater management.

The Tribunal in its stage two Freshwater Report specifically acknowledges that, "In making this finding ... we were not departing from the Wai 262 findings but rather specifying the Treaty standard for one particular resource out of the many that come under the RMA".[55]

A later Tribunal, considering proposed regional planning committees, found that tino rangatiratanga, as guaranteed under Article 2, demands that Māori retain their ability to govern themselves, their lands and taonga.[56] The same Tribunal relied on fundamental Treaty principles, including partnership, active protection, equal treatment, Māori autonomy and the Article 2 guarantee of tino rangatiratanga.[57] These principles guided the Tribunal's investigation of the obligations owed by the Crown in creating a resource management system that respects and upholds Māori rights.[58]

The differences in approaches between these Tribunals as to the emphasis on tino rangatiratanga and kaitiakitanga have a bearing in the analysis, but the Tribunals land in similar places with respect to their recommendations. The Tribunal in *Ko Aotearoa Tēnei* stressed the need to have strengthened mechanisms within the Resource Management Act 1991 (the RMA) for Māori involvement in the management of freshwater;[59] this is very similar to the recommendation of the Tribunal in the freshwater inquiry, recommending that partnership and delegation mechanisms in the RMA are required.[60] Ultimately, all Tribunals considering the rights and interests of Māori to freshwater are aligned in their findings that (1) freshwater is a taonga, (2) Māori have rights akin to ownership and (3) the current system to manage freshwater needs to be reformed to appropriately recognise Māori rights and responsibilities.

The Freshwater Inquiry and Reports

In March 2012, the Tribunal granted an application for an urgent hearing into two claims about Māori proprietary rights in freshwater bodies and geothermal resources:[61]

- The Sale of Power Generating State-Owned Enterprises (Wai 2357) claim is about the Crown's policy to privatise four state-owned enterprises (power companies) without first protecting or providing for Māori rights in the water resources used by the companies.
- The National Water and Geothermal (Wai 2358) claim is about the Crown's resource management reforms, which the claimants said were proceeding without a plan to recognise and provide for Māori rights and interests in water.

The inquiry was divided into stages. Māori rights and interests in freshwater and the potential impact of the imminent sale of shares in one of the four state-owned power companies was heard as stage one. The focus in stage two was on the Crown's freshwater management regime and its reforms. Stage three of the inquiry is extant and proceeding currently, considering Māori rights and interests in geothermal resources.

To date, the Tribunal on freshwater has released two reports:

- The stage one Freshwater Report considered the claim in the specific context of the Crown's proposal to sell shares in certain state-owned enterprises. The Tribunal reported back in 2012.[62]
- The stage two Freshwater Report considered the Crown's freshwater management regime and its reforms.[63] The Tribunal reported back in 2019.[64]

Stage one Freshwater Report

The Tribunal emphasised the scope of this stage of the inquiry was limited and that it was "to determine the *nature* of Māori rights at 1840, not *who had the rights*".[65] The Tribunal defined tino rangatiratanga as "authority" and "political authority".[66] It stated: "We heard tribal histories of long occupation of territory, in which tino rangatiratanga (authority) was exercised over rivers and other waters, controlling access for travel and other uses".[67] The Tribunal confirmed that "te tino rangatiratanga was more than ownership: it encompassed the autonomy of hapū to arrange and manage their own affairs in partnership with the Crown".[68] The Tribunal agreed that both Treaty texts support a finding of ownership at 1840 and tino rangatiratanga was the closest cultural expression of full-blown ownership in 1840.[69] The Tribunal added that tino rangatiratanga is "a standing qualification of the Crown's kawanatanga".[70] The Tribunal emphasised its findings were generic in nature because:[71]

> *It is likely that all iwi and hapū in New Zealand would be able to demonstrate some or all of the 'indicia' set out by the claimants in respect of their particular water bodies. It is a matter common to all Waitangi Tribunal reports that Māori exercised tino rangatiratanga over their territories in 1840. Surely no Māori group would dispute that. As such, the nature and extent of their rights will be similar. But the question of whether a particular water body is taonga is a matter for case-by-case inquiry. Again, we doubt anyone would dispute that point.*

The Tribunal recorded that the claimants believed the Treaty protected their ownership and rangatiratanga over their taonga including water bodies.[72] The Tribunal set out a twelve-point "indicia of ownership" for water as follows:[73]

- the water resource has been relied upon as a source of food;
- the water resource has been relied upon as a source of textiles or other materials;
- the water resource has been relied upon for travel or trade;
- the water resource has been used in the rituals central to the spiritual life of the hapū;
- the water resource has a mauri;
- the water resource is celebrated or referred to in waiata;
- the water resource is celebrated or referred to in whakataukī;
- the people have identified taniwha as residing in the water resource;
- the people have exercised kaitiakitanga over the water resource;
- the people have exercised mana or rangatiratanga over the water resource;
- whakapapa identifies a cosmological connection with the water resource; and
- there is a continuing recognised claim to land or territory in which the resource is situated, and title has been maintained to 'some, if not all, of the land on (or below) which the water resource sits'.

The principal finding in the stage one Freshwater Report is that Māori did have rights and interests in their freshwater bodies for which, in 1840, the closest English equivalent was legal ownership. Those rights were then agreed on, guaranteed, and protected by the Treaty of Waitangi. Furthermore, the nature and extent of the proprietary rights Māori had were the exclusive rights of iwi and hapū to control access to and use of the water while it was in their rohe (region).[74] In that regard, the Tribunal agreed with the claimants, with its report concluding that the claimants' "evidence demonstrates that their water bodies were taonga over which hapū or iwi exercised te tino rangatiratanga and customary rights in 1840, and with which they had a physical and metaphysical relationship under tikanga Māori (Māori law)".[75]

The Tribunal recognised that the Treaty changed the relationship of Māori with water in three ways:[76]

1. the Treaty enabled non-Māori settlement in New Zealand; therefore, Māori consented to settlers having access to and use of New Zealand's waters;
2. the Treaty gave the Crown a right to govern, which entails balancing interests of the nation and environment, but Treaty rights cannot "be balanced out of existence"; and
3. "the Treaty conferred a development right on Māori as part of the quid pro quo for accepting settlement".

The Tribunal found that "the present law in respect of fresh water is not consistent with Treaty principles. Many Tribunal panels have found the Resource Management Act 1991 (RMA) to be in breach of the Treaty, including the Wai 262 Tribunal, but very few of the recommendations made in previous Tribunals reports have been implemented".[77] The Tribunal found that the RMA was in breach of Treaty principles as the Crown refused to recognise Māori proprietary rights when developing the RMA.[78]

Stage two Freshwater Report

The Tribunal, in this 2019 Report, recorded the claimants' position that "Māori want to be decision makers in the management of their freshwater resources ... they want to be at the table, to be decision makers for the resources over which they exercise tino rangatiratanga and kaitiakitanga".[79]

The Tribunal concluded that Māori rights to freshwater have been inadequately recognised, especially under Part Two of the RMA. The Tribunal agreed with the claimants that there are key weaknesses in the operation of the RMA Part Two[80] – more specifically, the weakness of the Treaty clause (section 8) and the potential for both Māori interests and the environment to be 'balanced out' in the hierarchy of matters to be considered by decision makers under sections 6–8 of the RMA.[81] The Tribunal agreed with previous Tribunal reports that section 8 is not adequate for the degree of protection and recognition of Māori interests as established under te Tiriti.[82] The Tribunal also found that sections 6–8 introduced tikanga requirements for the first time into statute law for freshwater management compared to prior legislation where Māori interests in water bodies had been excluded from decision-making and found that participation mechanisms were considered ineffective due to historical barriers.[83]

The Tribunal also considered Te Mana o te Wai and its connection to the then National Policy Statement for Freshwater Management (NPS-FM). The Tribunal emphasised that Te Mana o te Wai must be strengthened in the NPS-FM and incorporated as a matter of national importance in the RMA. The health of freshwater bodies must take precedence in freshwater management decisions, a perspective that needs to be embedded in legislation and policy.[84]

The Tribunal found that the RMA's allocation system, which follows a first-in, first-served approach, is one-sided, particularly for Māori. Māori have been disadvantaged by the allocation system, which often led to over-allocation and environmental degradation without proper consideration of Māori interests.[85] The Tribunal found further that the RMA and its allocation regime are not consistent with Treaty principles. They found that Māori have been prejudiced by not only the ongoing omission to recognise their proprietary rights but also the barriers that have prevented their participation in specifically the first-in, first-served allocation system and the lack of partnership in decision-making.[86]

The Tribunal deemed co-governance and co-management mechanisms as essential to ensuring the involvement of Māori in decision-making, particularly where Māori have strong interests in specific freshwater taonga. This is a Treaty standard for freshwater management.[87]

Recommendations of the Waitangi Tribunal: Freshwater

Waitangi Tribunal recommendations are generally non-binding.[88] That is the case with recommendations regarding freshwater. Often, Tribunal recommendations are ignored by those governments, and iterations of the Crown, that receive the recommendations. However, as discussed in the next section, Tribunal recommendations have been considered by governments and policymakers after the fact. Sometimes it takes quite some time for governments to consider Waitangi Tribunal recommendations.[89] But the benefit of having Waitangi Tribunal findings and recommendations available for hapū and iwi to use to continue to advocate for their rights and obligations to be recognised is a powerful tool. This remains the case even if some Tribunal recommendations are not accepted; they remain a tool for debate and advocacy for recognition.

The Tribunal's recommendations on wai have been well traversed by a variety of authors.[90] However, we have recorded some of those recommendations below as it is useful to remind ourselves of the breadth of the Tribunal's work. These recommendations remain largely extant.[91]

Wai 262 recommendations:

- Iwi management plans should identify iwi priorities for iwi resource management priorities and opportunities for delegation of control to kaitiaki or establishment of partnerships.[92]
- Local authorities should be required to regularly review their use of sections 33 and 36B of the Act, specifically for water governance, and report annually to the Parliamentary Commissioner for the Environment on why delegations were or were not made.[93]
- The Ministry for the Environment (MfE) should commit to building Māori capacity to participate in RMA processes and in the management of taonga. This commitment should include providing resources to help assist kaitiaki with the development of iwi resource management plans, and to provide further help in assisting kaitiaki to develop the resources or technical skills which are required to exercise their roles as kaitiaki.[94]
- MfE should develop guidelines for iwi participation in water governance, emphasising kaitiaki control, partnership, and influence on environmental decision-making.[95]

Wai 2358 (stage two) recommendations

- Amend section 6 of the RMA to include Te Mana o te Wai as a national importance that must be recognised and provided for by decision-makers.[96]
- Amend section 8 to state that the duties on the Crown in terms of the Treaty principles are imposed on all those persons who have exercising powers and functions under the RMA.[97]

- Establish a national co-governance body with 50/50 Māori and Crown representation to ensure the incorporation of Treaty principles and Māori values, rights and interests in freshwater policy and management.[98] The co-governance body should also assess whether a separate Water Act is necessary.[99]
- Amend sections 33 and 36B of the RMA to remove the statutory barriers and provide incentives or compulsion for the transfer of powers and joint management agreements, ensuring Māori involvement in freshwater management.[100]
- Amend the Mana Whakahono ā Rohe provisions to make co-management and co-governance compulsory for all matters concerning freshwater bodies that must be discussed and agreed by the parties.[101]
- Strengthen provisions for iwi management plans to have greater legal weight in both planning and consenting processes.[102]
- The Crown should offer co-governance/co-management for freshwater bodies in all future Treaty settlements.[103]
- The Crown should continue its approach of co-design of policy options, and this should be a regular feature of government where Māori interests are concerned.[104]
- The Crown should take action under urgency to ensure that under-sourcing no longer prevents iwi and hapū from participating effectively in RMA processes, including freshwater management and decisions regarding freshwater.[105]
- Water policy should be decided by or in conjunction with the national co-governance body, with details to be arranged between the Treaty partners.[106]
- The Crown and the co-governance body should consider retaining the Te Mana o te Wai Fund as a long-term fund for the restoration of degraded freshwater taonga.[107]
- The allocation regime should be urgently reformed to recognise and provide for Te Mana o te Wai.[108]
- Reform the water allocation system to ensure Māori are allocated water based on both catchment needs and regional circumstances. Provide iwi and hapū with a percentage-based allocation, ensuring that the allocation is renewable and non-negotiable.[109]

- Investigate other possible mechanisms for proprietary redress, such as compensation or royalties, to acknowledge Māori economic interests in freshwater.[110]
- Replace the first-in, first-served system with a fairer allocation model that takes Māori values, rights and interests into account, potentially through a percentage-based allocation system for iwi according to a regional, catchment-based scheme.[111]
- Provide an allocation of water for the development of Māori land (including land returned in Treaty settlements), where such an allocation is sustainable.[112]
- Amend the NPS-FM, including to:
  - specify that iwi and hapū must be directly involved in freshwater decision-making;[113] and
  - strengthen Te Mana o te Wai, implement national bottom lines for key attributes like sediment and make Māori values, rights and interests, including Te Mana o te Wai, compulsory within the National Objectives Framework.[114]
- Introduce national stock exclusion regulations and more effective measures for freshwater quality protection.[115]
- The Crown should provide urgent assistance, including funding and expertise, for water infrastructure and the provision of clean, safe drinking water to marae and papakāinga.[116]

The Tribunal in its stage two Freshwater Report also noted that "it may not be necessary for a test case to be brought before the Courts on whether native title in freshwater (as a component of an indivisible freshwater taonga) exists as a matter of New Zealand common law and has not been extinguished".[117] Such a recommendation flows into the next section as to the influence of the Tribunal on the broader constitutional conversation about rights and obligations to wai.

Influence on the Broader Constitutional Conversation

Regardless of government positions over the years, the Tribunal recommendations undeniably have had an influence on the broader constitutional conversation about the recognition of hapū and iwi rights and obligations in freshwater. This influence can be seen, including through the courts and policy development, over time.

The stage one Freshwater Report was considered by the Supreme Court in *New Zealand Māori Council v Attorney General*.[118] The Court considered whether the Crown's decision to sell a 49 per cent share in Mighty River Power could materially impair the Crown's ability to comply with the Treaty principles or meet its obligations under the Treaty.

The recommendation made by the Tribunal was to delay the share sale to negotiate its proposed solution, such as the "share plus" idea. The Tribunal was of the view that this idea would give Māori additional rights or powers tied to the shares, reflecting their guaranteed Treaty principle of tino rangatiratanga. The Court acknowledged the recommendation made by the Tribunal (i.e., the "share plus" idea) but ultimately concluded that the Crown's response in rejecting that idea was a reasonable decision as the Crown had proposed alternative ways to address Māori interests.[119]

The Court recognised the Tribunal's interim stage one Freshwater Report findings that Māori did have "exclusive right to control access to and use of water" in their rohe during 1840.[120] The Court also acknowledged that the Tribunal found Māori claims of Treaty breach regarding wai to be well founded.[121] However, the Court noted that rushing significant issues raised by the Tribunal was not the best approach to finding long-term, sustainable solutions.[122] It concluded that the proposed sale was consistent with Treaty principles even though it would preclude the Crown from providing Māori with shares in the generating company that had enhanced rights of control ("share plus"). It found the Crown would continue to have the capacity to provide equivalent and meaningful redress even after the sale. The Court viewed the Tribunal's ongoing freshwater inquiry as part of the evolving process for addressing Māori interests, while acknowledging that the recognition of Māori interests in freshwater bodies remains "a work in progress".[123]

The Deputy Prime Minister at the time, the Right Honourable Bill English, provided a range of assurances to the Tribunal including that:[124]

> *The Crown acknowledges that Māori have rights and interests in water and geothermal resources. The Crown made this position clear in the course of stage one of the Waitangi Tribunal inquiry into the Freshwater and Geothermal Claim. In addition to the ongoing Waitangi Tribunal Inquiry, these issues are being addressed through a number of parallel mechanisms. The recognition of rights and interests in freshwater and geothermal resources must, by definition, involve mechanisms that relate to the on-going use of those resources, and may include decision-making roles in relation to*

care, protection, use, access and allocation, and/or charges or rentals for use. Currently the Ministry for the Environment has responsibility for progressing policy development around these issues.

It appears that the Deputy Prime Minister's undertaking to the Supreme Court that the Crown acknowledges that Māori have rights and interests in water and geothermal resources and that work is ongoing with respect to recognition of those rights provided the Court with some comfort about the Crown's intentions.[125]

In reaching its decision, the Supreme Court did not engage with the Tribunal's discussion of the concept of rangatiratanga in any detail. This is something that the Court will not be able to avoid in the context of Ngāi Tahu's claim to freshwater, which was heard in February 2025.

As part of the dialogue, the Tribunal in its stage two Freshwater Report noted the Crown's assurances to the Supreme Court and, in particular, the Crown's confirmation that it was "open to discussing the possibility of Māori proprietary rights short of full ownership".[126]

While Tribunal recommendations are not often swiftly picked up by governments, they do continue to influence policy development over time. This is particularly the case in the environmental context, although often Tribunal recommendations are only part-implemented (representing a 'middle-ground' type approach to the Crown). The Crown is required to report annually on the "progress made in the implementation of recommendations made to the Crown by the Tribunal".[127] These section 8I reports can be a helpful indicator of how, if at all, the Crown is responding to Tribunal recommendations. However, in the authors' view, some of the reporting lacks specificity against individual recommendations.

In terms of the Tribunal's freshwater recommendations, the Labour-led Government undertook a review of the RMA. The timing of the initial review coincided with the release of the Tribunal's stage two Freshwater Report in 2019, and the government reported that the review was at least in part responding to the stage two Freshwater Report. That government ultimately passed the Natural and Built Environment Act 2023 and the Spatial Planning Act 2023. These Acts attempted to address a range of issues with the RMA, including criticisms made by the Tribunal. There was also ongoing funding and capability work taking place (particularly in relation to understanding and implementing Te Mana o te Wai in the National Policy Statement for Freshwater

Management). The National-led Government, however, repealed the Natural and Built Environment Act 2023 and the Spatial Planning Act 2023 soon after taking office and announced its own reform package. Implementation of this is underway with a blueprint for replacing the RMA due to the Minister at the time of writing this chapter.[128] A range of funding cuts were also made, including the closing of the Environmental Legal Assistance Fund, which provided funding to groups, including iwi and hapū, to take cases to the Environment Court and bring appeals.[129]

Put simply, the Waitangi Tribunal's stage two recommendations remain unimplemented. However, some of its recommendations have been engaged with and no doubt will continue to feature in officials' advice to ministers through the development of the next phases of RMA reform. It is difficult to see the Tribunal's recommendations on freshwater being substantially addressed in the current political environment.

Conclusion: Rangatiratanga and Hope for a Generation[130]

The expectations and aspirations of hapū and iwi with respect to their rights and obligations to wai, as often expressed by the Waitangi Tribunal jurisprudence, are not being met. The sphere of kāwanatanga remains unconstitutionally large. The current freshwater management system does not allow Māori to "exercise tino rangatiratanga over their resources or taonga in accordance with their own cultural and management preferences and in accordance with their own ways of life".[131] The Tribunal remains a site for Māori to air their grievances against the Crown and assert tino rangatiratanga over their wai as a taonga. The Tribunal has consistently responded to these claims by making findings and recommendations that successive governments have either ignored or failed to adequately resolve (or, when an attempt is made, it is wound back by a following government). The Tribunal has grounded a number of their findings concerning hapū and iwi rights and obligations to wai in the Article 2 guarantee of tino rangatiratanga. This has gone some way to steering the broader constitutional conversation about wai towards rangatiratanga, rather than a lesser reflection of rights and obligations, but the recognition of these rights and obligations remains unresolved.

The lack of resolution cannot continue. Māori rights and obligations to wai must be addressed. It will require strong leadership from within hapū and iwi, and likely the use of some levers within our current constitutional arrangements (such as the courts). It may be, with the Ngāi Tahu claim being heard by the High Court in 2025, that this matter will come to a political head again. It will also likely be addressed further through the Tribunal's Natural Resources and Environmental Management Kaupapa Inquiry. Whatever the result for Ngāi Tahu, or further recommendations of the Waitangi Tribunal that may come, the broader issue for Māori needs to be addressed for the interconnected well-being of the wai and ourselves.

Advocating for kaupapa Māori approaches, or rangatiratanga to be upheld, in relation to the way freshwater is managed is both a privilege and a challenge. At times, it feels like the tides coming in and out; some progress is made, and then it is washed away again with a change in priorities or, as we have seen recently, a change in political ideology. Hope is essential, as is perseverance and resilience. The Tribunal has an ongoing role in helping us as citizens of Aotearoa, of members of hapū and iwi, learn our history and retain hope that te Tiriti may help bring us together as a nation. The Tribunal has a role in keeping constitutional transformation in the realm of possibility. While its findings and recommendations may not always completely satisfy claimants or the Crown, it provides a space for a conversation that is recorded with suggested steps forward. It remains an essential part of our constitutional framework.

Me mihi, ka tika

Te Ao Hurihuri,
te ao huri ai ki tōna tauranga:
te ao rapu;
ko te huripoki e huri nei
i runga i te taumata o te kaha.
Te Ao Hurihuri
is a world revolving:
a world that moves forward
to the place it came from;
a wheel that turns
on an axle of strength.[132]

Finally, we want to formally acknowledge the work of the Waitangi Tribunal over the past fifty years. Writing this chapter has given us cause to pause on the Tribunal's extensive work and contribution in relation to wai and more generally. The Tribunal's work has also often taken place in highly politicised contexts and under adversity, whether that adversity is time (having to consider a range of matters under urgency),[133] budgetary constraints,[134] constitutionally inappropriate "call-outs" by Ministers of the Crown[135] or the very nature of the task the Tribunal is statutorily mandated to undertake – namely, to assess whether Crown acts or omissions are in breach of the principles of the Treaty of Waitangi.[136] Despite the challenges, the Tribunal's work has continued and, quite apart from producing its important work, has provided a safe space for Māori to air continuing grievances against the Crown – a place of hope. Te Tiriti is a living and breathing constitutional whāriki and blueprint for Aotearoa. The Tribunal lives on alongside te Tiriti o Waitangi, and the Crown's existence, as a part of honouring the ongoing te Tiriti relationship. We wish it strength as the axle of Aotearoa continues to turn.

"It refuted the misrepresentation that the Māori interest in the foreshore and seabed was a primarily exclusionary commercial interest. It also affirmed the relational nature of whakapapa to the natural environment."

Chapter 6

Takutai Moana

Carried by Power, Unmitigated by Fairness Wai 1071 The Report on the Crown's Foreshore and Seabed Policy 2004*

— Metiria Stanton Turei

When the Waitangi Tribunal announced in 2003 that it would hold an urgent inquiry into the Labour Government's foreshore and seabed policy, it said "We consider the level of animosity among Māori to the substance of this policy is such that no process of interaction that did not involve a major reworking of the policy would meet Māori demands."[1] The policy was the intention of the Crown to unilaterally extinguish the long-held property rights of iwi and hapū Māori in the takutai moana – the foreshore and seabed.

Māori opposition to the government's policy arose not just because of the property rights and rule of law breaches inherent in the government's proposed policy. It also reflected frustration at the duplicity of that and previous governments that insisted that Māori conform to the rule of law while the government knowingly breached that same constitutional rule.

The Tiriti-breaching, unlawful actions of the Crown over the takutai moana were neither unusual nor uncontested. When the Waitangi Tribunal released its Wai 1071 report in March 2004, the report was a new-millennium testimony in a 160-year examination of the customary rights held by iwi and hapū Māori in the takutai moana.[2] These rights were asserted against the Crown as early as 1851.[3]

The government's foreshore and seabed policy also drew one of the most significant campaigns of Māori opposition in history and set the tone for mistrustful Māori–Crown relationships into the new millennium. The compounding issues of unilateral policy making, legislative extinguishment of rights with no compensation and the removal of Māori legal rights to satisfy political ambitions triggered the largest protest hīkoi at that time to the steps of Parliament. The foreshore and seabed hīkoi of May 2004 was conservatively estimated at 15,000 people.[4]

In this chapter, I explore how the Tribunal came to its conclusions in its Wai 1071 report on the Crown's foreshore and seabed policy. The report is rich in its analysis of the gulf that exists between Māori and the Crown when Māori constitutional and property interests challenge the Crown's assumption that it alone defines Māori rights. It is also rich in the tikanga of the takutai moana across many iwi and hapū, demonstrating the extent of the pūkenga expertise that contributed to the Tribunal's report.

In the opening section, I will describe the legal history of the dispute over the takutai moana. I then move to consider the tikanga that arose in the hearing and te Tiriti o Waitangi analysis that detailed the extent of the severe breaches. I conclude with a discussion on some of the political matters that surrounded the policy itself and briefly note subsequent Tribunal reports on the issue.

I acknowledge the passing of Kahurangi Tariana Turia of Ngāti Apa, Ngā Rauru, Whanganui and Tūwharetoa iwi in January 2025.[5] Kahurangi Tariana was renowned for her unwavering commitment to the self-determination of Māori people, whānau, hapū and iwi. She entered Parliament in 1996 as a Labour MP and served for eighteen years. In 2004, she resigned her ministerial portfolios and membership of the Labour Government because of its foreshore and seabed policy. Her courage at that difficult time inspired a resurgent Māori political movement, spearheaded by the then Māori Party (now Te Pāti Māori), influencing and motivating mana motuhake and mana mokopuna across Aotearoa since that time. Her parliamentary legacy, so closely tied to the foreshore and seabed issue, will not be forgotten.

Legal History of Dispute over the Foreshore and Seabed

The 2003 intention to legislate to assert Crown dominance over Māori rights in the takutai moana was not novel. In 1872, the Crown issued a proclamation preventing the Native Land Court from issuing titles in the takutai moana to Hauraki Māori to preserve gold-mining rights for the mining industry in Thames. This proclamation was at once a statement of the legitimacy of Māori customary property of the takutai moana and the beginning of the Crown's interventionist policies in the takutai moana. The Crown has a long history of using its legal authority over Māori property rights to suit its political interests and support for non-Māori industry over iwi Māori customary rights. It was this approach that drove the foreshore and seabed issue of the new millennium.

Aquaculture applications in the Marlborough Sounds

The dispute that led to the Wai 1071 report arose first in 1997.[6] Ngāti Apa, among other iwi, had made numerous applications to Marlborough District Council to establish mussel marine farms in their traditional waters.[7] The council had repeatedly denied their applications while approving non-Māori applicants for the same activity in the same water bodies.[8] Out of sheer frustration at both the consent rejections and the Crown's intention to impose a moratorium on marine farms in the Marlborough Sounds because of a shortage of space, Ngāti Apa, Ngāti Koata, Ngāti Kuia, Ngāti Rarua, Ngāti Tama, Ngāti Toa, Rangitāne and Te Atiawa applied to the Māori Land Court for a declaration that land below the mean high-tide mark in the Marlborough Sounds was Māori customary land.[9]

Māori customary land is that land held by Māori in accordance with tikanga Māori under section 129 of the Te Ture Whenua Māori Act 1993.[10] The applicants sought an order under section 132 of the Act to have the Māori Land Court investigate the customary title of the land to determine the Māori owners of that land. The title could then be converted from Māori customary land to Māori freehold land and vested in the Māori owners.[11] This would have the effect of giving the Māori owners the right to develop on that land, such as with mussel farms. The Marlborough District Council and the Crown opposed the declaration application, arguing that Māori customary rights in the foreshore and seabed had been extinguished at common law, most particularly in the 1963 Court of Appeal decision of *In Re the Ninety-Mile Beach,* combined with section 7 of the Territorial Sea, Contiguous Zone, and Exclusive Economic Zone Act 1977 and section 9A of the Foreshore and Seabed Endowment Revesting Act 1991.[12]

Māori Land Court preliminary decision

The Māori Land Court issued its interim decision in favour of the iwi.[13] Judge Hingston rejected the council and Crown's argument that the takutai moana was vested in the Crown. He held that the legislation was not sufficiently clear to have fully extinguished customary rights.[14] He also distinguished the decision of *In Re the Ninety-Mile Beach* as applicable only in limited circumstances.[15]

In Re the Ninety-Mile Beach had formed the basis of Crown assertions of Crown ownership of the foreshore because that court had held that the Crown had acquired ownership, or dominium, over all New Zealand land at the assumption of sovereignty. That assumption of sovereignty extinguished all customary rights in the foreshore and seabed. But *In Re the Ninety Mile Beach* had been argued with some complexity and was widely considered poor law.[16] Judge Hingston therefore considered that *In Re the Ninety Mile Beach* applied only in circumstances where the adjacent land had already lost its customary status, rather than as a blanket extinguishment of all customary titles.

The Crown had intervened in the Māori Land Court hearing and, along with the Marlborough District Council (among others), appealed the decision to the Māori Appellate Court.[17] The Crown also argued that as the matter concerned significant precedent, the Māori Appellate Court should refer the case to the High Court. To expedite the process, the Māori Appellate Court did just that.[18]

The High Court

The High Court upheld the decision in *In Re the Ninety-Mile Beach* that, under common law, land below the low-water mark was owned by the Crown, and that the two statutes previously relied on confirmed this.[19] For the foreshore area between high- and low-water marks, the High Court supported the proposition that the Māori Land Court had the jurisdiction to investigate whether the foreshore was Māori customary land. However, any such rights, if they had existed, were extinguished once the adjacent land above the high-water mark lost its status as Māori customary land. The iwi appealed this decision to the Court of Appeal.

Court of Appeal decision

In a politically surprising, but legally orthodox decision, the Court of Appeal upheld the iwi appeal of the High Court decision. It agreed unanimously that the Māori Land Court does have the jurisdiction to determine the status of the foreshore and the seabed. It also held that the customary title to the foreshore and seabed was not contingent on the customary land status of the adjacent land above the high-water mark. It clarified that its decision was based on the common law doctrine of aboriginal title, which aims to protect indigenous peoples' pre-existing rights on the establishment of British sovereignty.

The Court also held that the decision in *In Re the Ninety-Mile Beach* that British sovereignty automatically extinguished Māori customary rights was not just wrongly decided but "contrary to other and higher authority".[20] Instead, the Court affirmed that the Crown's acquisition of sovereignty under te Tiriti o Waitangi granted territorial authority (imperium), not ownership (dominium), and that Māori customary rights persist unless explicitly extinguished by law.[21] Further the Court held that despite various acts of Parliament purporting to manage the foreshore and seabed, there was no legislation sufficiently clear to extinguish Māori customary property interests.

Before the *Ngāti Apa* decision, the Crown had persisted with the legal fallacy that Māori customary rights below the high-water mark had been extinguished when rights to the adjacent dry land were extinguished. Others also believed, erroneously, that the Crown owned the foreshore and seabed as part of its prerogative rights and that this was supported by subsequent legislation. However, the *Ngāti Apa* decision dispensed with these assumptions, affirming the High Court's ability to apply the doctrine of aboriginal title to the foreshore and seabed and the Māori Land Court's jurisdiction to determine the customary status of that land.

The Crown's response

Four days after the Court of Appeal decision was released, the Crown announced it would legislate away the extant customary rights of iwi and hapū Māori in the foreshore and seabed and award itself the full ownership of the land.[22] This announcement and the policy proposal to do it caused an uproar among Māori and Pākehā.[23] Māori held to the claim that to legislate for Crown ownership would be an extinguishment of customary rights.

Many Pākehā supported these Māori objections. However, many Pākehā did not after political scaremongering claimed that Māori would restrict access to beaches for swimming and/or sell the beaches to overseas interests. Rather than work through the policy options with Māori and with care, the government conceded this ground to the political opposition. In August 2003, the government released a policy proposal "The Foreshore and Seabed of New Zealand: Protecting Public Access and Customary Rights", leaving six weeks for public consultation on the proposal.

Several iwi and hapū sought an urgent inquiry by the Waitangi Tribunal into the government's proposal, and the Tribunal confirmed in September 2003 that it would hold an urgent inquiry on the matter. The Waitangi Tribunal's report, released in March 2004, found that the government's policy expropriated Māori property rights, violated the rule of law, discriminated only against Māori and was both unclear and uncertain.[24] The Tribunal ultimately recommended that the government withdraw its proposal and engage in a "longer conversation" with iwi and hapū Māori to find a more reasonable resolution.[25]

The fragility of the assertion

The *Ngāti Apa* decision took the Crown by surprise. The Crown had relied on its own assertions of ownership for so long that it had failed to appreciate the fragility of the constitutional foundation on which that claim was made. The Crown's approach to Māori rights had become quite transactional such that the constitutional nature and the Tiriti-basis of customary rights had become obscured by its own assumptions of authority. For Māori, however, the constitutional weight of te Tiriti o Waitangi was front of mind, as it was for the Waitangi Tribunal.

Tikanga of the Takutai Moana

The opening chapter of the Tribunal's report reframed the dispute away from the property rights narrative of the Crown to a narrative on the primacy of relationships inherent in tikanga Māori. This was important in two ways. It refuted the misrepresentation that the Māori interest in the foreshore and seabed was a primarily exclusionary commercial interest. It also affirmed the relational nature of whakapapa to the natural environment. The Tribunal brought the matter back to the pre-Tiriti authority that Māori exercised for te ao tūroa and the principles that drove that authority. The Tribunal considered the tikanga of such import that two of the six days of hearings were dedicated to tikanga evidence:[26]

> *Tikanga is both a consequence and a source of Māori identity. Unlike most Western law, tikanga is not a norm that is external to the person. Without his relationship through tikanga to land by whakapapa, in a fundamental sense, he does not exist. Tikanga defines him; protects him; shapes his idea of himself and his place in the world. If a regime is to be imposed on the foreshore and seabed that cuts across tikanga, that damages and undermines it, then every Māori person who maintains his or her connection with land in the foreshore and seabed of their tribal area is in some way diminished. Some will feel it more than others, of course, because their lives are lived closer to tikanga, and closer to the land and sea.*

The Tribunal took care to describe how tikanga was relevant to its Tiriti analysis and therefore the Tiriti obligations on the Crown:[27]

> *the Crown's guarantee of te tino rangatiratanga is meaningless if the tikanga that sustain and regulate the rangatira and his relationship to the people, and the land, are discounted and undermined. Indeed, we go further. We say that in order properly to fulfil the role of Treaty partner, and actively protect the cultural foundation of what it is to be Māori, the Crown must itself be schooled in the essentials of tikanga.*

The Tribunal described five tikanga themes that arose from the evidence that was delivered in the two tikanga hearing days.

Indivisibility of the natural world

The Māori conception of the natural world considers its elements as indivisible, where the land, sea, sky and freshwaters are not separated into distinct parts.[28] Rather all land, whether dry, under lakes and rivers or under the ocean, belongs to Papatūānuku. The various waters form part of a single life cycle that restores and replenishes that land. The regulatory approach that separates, for example, land above and below the high tide mark is contrary to tikanga.

Oneness of the spiritual and natural world

Inherent in tikanga is the relationship between the physical and spiritual worlds. They are not distinct from each other as the authority of tikanga concepts, such as mana, tapu and noa, are sourced from the spiritual world.[29] Karakia and other legal protective practices, such as rāhui and wāhi tapu, are means to "reflect aspects of the spiritual dimension of the coast and its resources".[30]

Mutuality of the relationship

The indivisibility and oneness of the natural world creates a mutual relationship between people and the land where people are part of the natural world rather than masters of it.[31] That can be expressed as kaitiakitanga, where the natural environment is kaitiaki over its people, ensuring the well-being of the community, and in response, the people care for the health of the environment. Tikanga creates a set of mutual obligations that ensures physical and spiritual survival of everyone and everything.[32]

Connections through whakapapa, kōrero and naming

A key means of communicating relationships between people and places is the recitation of whakapapa. Kōrero and the naming of places reconnects people to place.[33] The relationships that whānau, hapū and iwi Māori have with the natural world are essential to their identity and therefore very personal. This is evidenced in the recitation of pepeha, which directly connects a person to specific land and bodies of water.[34]

The endless cycle of reciprocity

Reciprocity or utu is the cycle of respect and mana that maintains the balance between all aspects of the natural and spiritual world.[35] Reciprocity is a regulator of nurturing relationships, or manaakitanga. The Tribunal took the opportunity to explore with the mātanga (tikanga experts) how this value would inform iwi Māori approaches to public access to the foreshore, a concern of many Pākehā.[36] The mātanga gave several examples of iwi and hapū who had retained mana over these areas while keeping them open for use by manuhiri. In these descriptions, the mātanga made a direct link between mana and manaakitanga, a relationship determined by tikanga Māori.

In its later discussion on tikanga and how far out to the ocean that mana might extend, the Tribunal confirmed:[37]

> *a worldview in which Māori extended their deep sense of spirituality to the whole of creation, acknowledging atua who bequeathed all of nature's resources to them, in their creation stories. We heard of the interrelationships of the various atua, especially of Tangaroa and Papatūānuku, and the merging of their energies with those of Ranginui where they meet on the papamoana, forming a lasting mauri.*

In this way:[38]

> *Māori have a holistic view that does not compartmentalise the beach and sea into dry land above high tide, tidal land uncovered at low tide, land permanently covered by the sea, and the waters of the sea itself. Māori law, use, authority, and rights extended seamlessly from land fronting the beach, out into the ocean.*

The tikanga chapter of the Wai 1071 report set out the tikanga expertise as the guiding principles for how the Tribunal would consider its Tiriti analysis of the government's foreshore and seabed proposal. It also gave the Tribunal the opportunity to put on record the tikanga values held by Māori that would refute much of the scaremongering about the effect of Māori acquiring customary title to the foreshore and seabed.

The Crown Proposal

Good government

The Waitangi Tribunal firmly situated the takutai moana debate in the constitutional space of the common law and tikanga Māori law. The Tribunal's letter to Minister Parekura Horomia enclosing the final report was brief but clear on the Tribunal's primary question:[39]

> *The report itself provides background and explanation for our conclusion that the policy breaches the Treaty of Waitangi in ways that we regard as fundamental and serious. Our primary and strong recommendation is that the Government accede to the claimants' request to go back to the drawing board and engage with Māori in proper negotiations about the way forward.*

It was important for the Tribunal to establish its understanding of 'good government' as a constitutional cornerstone from which complex policy discussions could be had and decisions, however difficult, could be made:[40]

> *[W]e proceed in the expectation that governments in New Zealand want to be good governments, whose actions although carried by power are mitigated by fairness. Fairness is the value that underlies the norms of conduct with which good governments conform – legal norms, international human rights norms, and, in the New Zealand context, Treaty norms. We think that even though governments are driven by the need to make decisions that (ultimately) are popular, New Zealand governments certainly want their decisions to be*

> *coloured by fairness. In fact, we think that New Zealanders generally have an instinct for fairness, and that a policy that is intrinsically fair will, when properly explained, ultimately find favour.*

In this way, the Tribunal was calling on a widely understood Kiwi value of fairness to reframe the government's approach. The Tribunal was conscious that the public debate had turned into a critique of Māori for unfairly claiming their customary rights when in fact the unfairness sat firmly with the proposal.[41] Māori objection to the proposal was sourced in shock at the deep unfairness of the government's response to extinguish rights rather than engage in dialogue and negotiation.

Crown's proposal

Before exploring the Tribunal's te Tiriti critique, it is important to understand the Crown's proposal and its justification for choosing major legislative reform over a negotiation. The submission from Crown counsel was that:[42]

> *the Government's policy seeks to establish a comprehensive, clear and integrated framework which provides enhanced recognition of customary interests of whanau, hapu and iwi in foreshore and seabed, while at the same time confirming that foreshore and seabed belongs to, and is in principle accessible by, all New Zealanders. While the development of the policy was prompted by the Court of Appeal's decision in Ngāti Apa v Attorney-General, the scope of the policy goes well beyond the narrow question addressed in that case.*

The principles behind the government's proposal

The Crown's longstanding assumption of ownership had underpinned regulatory frameworks like the Resource Management Act 1991 and other policies that had restricted (but not precluded) private titles in the coastal marine area. However, this was challenged by the *Ngāti Apa* case, which overturned these assumptions and posed complex challenges for the government.[43] The Crown focused, therefore, on achieving a fast and comprehensive solution to placing the foreshore and seabed into Crown ownership. Its proposal was guided by four principles:[44]

- Access: The foreshore and seabed should remain public domain, accessible to all New Zealanders.
- Regulation: The Crown is responsible for regulating the use of these areas for present and future generations.

- Protection: Customary interests of whānau, hapū, and iwi should be acknowledged, with specific rights identified and safeguarded.
- Certainty: Clear processes should ensure that all users and administrators of the foreshore and seabed understand their rights.

The central feature of the policy was the proposal to vest the areas, excluding existing private titled land, nominally in the "people of New Zealand" but legally into government ownership. The Crown had proposed this urgent intervention for several reasons.

First, the Crown argued that there was a widespread assumption among both Māori and Pākehā that the foreshore and seabed were communal and publicly accessible spaces.[45] This belief underpinned the legal and regulatory framework that governed the foreshore and seabed. The Crown felt that the provisions of Te Ture Whenua Maori Act 1993 were inadequate for assessing the full spectrum of Māori rights in the unique legal context of the foreshore and seabed.[46] The Crown also believed that there was insufficient guidance for the Māori Land Court in interpreting tikanga Māori in this area

Finally, the government was concerned that a grant of fee simple title to Māori could destabilise existing legal and regulatory regimes.[47] It would introduce uncertainty affecting other stakeholders, such as those involved in fishing, navigation and coastal access. The government was balancing several interests in its proposal including those who had a vested interest in access to the coast, Māori with specific customary interests, industries such as fishing, marine farming, transportation, mining and tourism and local government and public agencies with administrative roles in the coastal environment.

Māori property rights replaced with administrative engagement

The Crown's offer to Māori was to exchange the right to go to court to have their customary property rights assessed with a set of administrative and use rights the breadth of which would be determined by the government.[48] Under the proposal, the Māori Land Court would be able to grant new customary titles recognising the mana and ancestral connections of whānau, hapū or iwi to specific areas. These titles would coexist with public domain ownership and record specific customary rights or activities that the rights holders could exercise. The activities included extraction of sand, use of the area for waka launching and preservation of burial sites.[49]

The rights holders would also be able to participate in management and decision-making processes for coastal marine areas, facilitated by regional working groups comprising central and local governments and Māori representatives. Māori would also benefit from binding agreements, formalised through Orders in Council, to ensure compliance with those processes.[50] Customary right holders would be able to engage in commercial activities related to their rights, provided the rights fit within regulatory frameworks. However, new commercial activities beyond the scope of recognised customary rights would not be allowed.[51] Finally, redress would be provided in a narrow set of cases where the rights were found to exist but unable to be exercised.

A fundamental tension

The Tribunal described a fundamental tension between the Crown's justification for intervention and the claimants' concerns about fairness and adequacy.[52] While the Crown viewed its proposal as necessary to address legal uncertainty and safeguard public access, the underlying concern was the potential impact of Māori property rights on public access. The government feared that court-recognised exclusive Māori rights could limit access, challenging the belief that the foreshore and seabed belong to all New Zealanders. But this was a political matter, and the political heat of the debate, fuelled in large part by the Crown's knee-jerk reaction, led to unfounded, racist claims. One of the most pernicious claims was that Māori would sell the takutai moana to overseas buyers.

Māori criticisms of the proposal

Māori roundly rejected the Crown's justification for its expropriation of the takutai moana. They argued that the Crown's proposal was deeply flawed, unfair and inadequate. The proposal extinguished Māori property rights, violated the common law, international law and Tiriti principles. It undermined basic rights, particularly customary ownership and the ability to pursue claims through judicial processes. The proposal was incomplete and lacked clarity on critical matters, making its implementation and outcomes uncertain. Despite the assertions of the Crown counsel, the government's proposal failed to provide a robust mechanism for recognising and protecting Māori rights.

The claimants disputed the Crown's assertion that a legislative intervention was unavoidable. Allowing the courts to determine the legal tests for assessing claims would mean that each claim would be considered on its facts under the court's jurisdiction. The government's proposal imposed a one-size-fits-all approach that disregarded the diverse Māori customary interests and provided only for a limited set of Crown-determined activities. In constructing this novel process, in haste and without proper discussion with iwi and hapū Māori, the Crown was introducing greater uncertainty into the law for the foreshore and seabed.

Māori fiercely disputed the claims that the effect of a tikanga-based customary title would be to exclude people from the beaches, as the Tribunal noted:[53]

> *It was repeatedly emphasised before us that what Māori seek in relation to the coastal marine area is a recognition of their tikanga connections to it rather than the ability to keep others out. Indeed, the tikanga underlying the assertion of power comprised in the term 'mana' requires the holder(s) of the mana to exercise that power in a spirit of generosity (manaaki) towards others. The effect of this is that those with mana in land have a reciprocal duty to manaaki others. In turn, the exercise of manaaki reinforces the mana of the right-holders. There is an endless cycle of entitlement, responsibility, and generosity.*

The Crown's concern that Māori property interests in the foreshore and seabed could result in saleable titles being created and sold, potentially to overseas buyers, was also roundly rejected by the claimants:[54]

> *We have nowhere heard expressed by Māori the desire to sell any titles that may be declared in the foreshore and seabed. On the contrary, we were told that this prospect is culturally repugnant to Māori – equivalent, in tikanga terms, to selling your mother ... It appears that the undesirability of titles being created that may be sold is a matter on which Māori and the Government agree. Would it not be possible to introduce by legislation a simple limitation on any title that might be issued to effect this common objective?*

Beyond these specific critiques of the government's proposal was the constitutional objection to the Crown extinguishing extant Māori property rights without consultation, discussion or compensation. The Crown was appropriating the property to itself. It was prioritising the public's right to access the takutai moana over iwi and hapū pre-existing (if yet unrecognised) property rights to which all other access, use and legal rights must, in law, yield. Those pre-existing rights were guaranteed to Māori under te Tiriti o Waitangi and should be weighted against later and lesser interests. To do otherwise was an absolute and fundamental breach of te Tiriti o Waitangi.

Tribunal's Tiriti o Waitangi Analysis

The power to govern granted by te Tiriti to the Crown is not unfettered. Te Tiriti assured the full, exclusive and undisturbed possession of iwi and hapū natural resources and estates for as long as Māori wish to retain them. The Crown's right of pre-emption was a right asserted against other non-Māori interests, not an acquisition of ownership over the whole of the country. This was the starting position for the Tribunal's analysis of the breaches of te Tiriti o Waitangi.

Breach of Article 2

The Tribunal said that while kāwanatanga gave the Crown the right make policy and enact legislation to empower that policy, that right was to be exercised considering the guarantee of rangatiratanga in Article 2.[55] But the Crown's action, historically and in the present case of the foreshore and seabed proposal, breached that arrangement openly and knowingly:[56]

> *Instead, the Crown actively assumed ownership of the foreshore and seabed for itself, without the consent of the Māori right-holders, and without compensation. Occasional and specific extinguishment of Māori rights through purchase (such as parts of the Thames foreshore) were the exception that proves the rule. Because it was aware of Māori claims to own the foreshore and seabed and to exercise authority over it, the Crown acted in breach of the Treaty when it took those rights for itself. The Crown assumed (incorrectly) that it was acting according to the common law. It ignored or made inadequate responses to many Māori protests over its actions.*

The government repeated this with the foreshore and seabed proposal so that "[t]he right for Māori to go to court to prove the nature and extent of their property rights in the foreshore and seabed is thus being removed, notwithstanding wholesale objection from Māori".[57] The Crown needed to not revert to its historical response of attempting to expropriate that property and extinguish Māori property rights.

Breach of Article 3

Article 3 guarantees to Māori the rights of equal citizenship, equal treatment under the law and protection of the rule of law. Under the rule of law, all citizens are entitled to the protection of their property rights. No other property rights, including existing private titles in the foreshore and seabed, would be abolished or expropriated, meaning that the proposal would solely disadvantage Māori and no other New Zealand citizen. While the outcome in *Ngāti Apa* was unfavourable for the Crown, the correct legal process was followed, and the court had not exceeded its jurisdiction. The Crown's intention to strip the court of that jurisdiction to disadvantage Māori, and Māori alone, was a contravention of the rule of law, a breach of Article 3, and the principles of reciprocity, partnership, active protection, equity, options and redress.

The Tribunal acknowledged that the principles of reciprocity and partnership authorised the Crown to develop policy on the takutai moana, but that it must do so "in a way that gives meaningful effect to te tino rangatiratanga" which it did not do.[58] The government was expropriating property rights before the rights were sufficiently defined, was acting without Māori consent and lacked an emergency justification for its proposal.

The principle of active protection requires proactive measures to safeguard Māori rights and interests as far as is practicable, requiring honourable conduct, fair process and mutual recognition of authority. The Crown consulted Māori and received overwhelming rejection of the policy. Despite this, the Crown proceeded hastily and made no meaningful changes in response to Māori concerns. The Crown's rushed and inflexible approach to consultation breached the principle and showed a lack of good faith.

The principle of equity guarantees equal protection and fair treatment for both Māori and non-Māori citizens. Māori tribes should also be treated equitably relative to one another. The Crown breached equity when it expropriated Māori property rights while preserving other classes of private property and recognised similar rights for other iwi, such as lake-beds for inland iwi.[59] The principle of options protects the freedom of Māori to pursue traditional and modern governance and resource management according to their preferences. The Crown's policy to abolish Māori rights to seek legal definitions of property breached the right to choose legal avenues.

The principle of redress obliges the Crown to remedy breaches by restoring mana and tribal resources and addressing grievances.[60] Māori possess an "inchoate" property right – a right to prove their ownership in the courts. Denying this right amounts to taking property, which legally requires compensation, not just redress.[61] The Tribunal concluded that redress alone could not rectify the breach caused by the Crown's actions as it failed to honour legal rights and restore Tiriti integrity.

The Tribunal concluded that the prejudice caused by the proposal was severe by devaluing Māori citizenship, imposing powerlessness through greater legal uncertainty and causing the deliberate loss of mana and property rights.[62] Māori would suffer the loss of opportunities for affirming ancestral mana, exercising kaitiakitanga and deriving benefits as resource holders. The Crown offered no commitment to compensate for these losses. Instead, the proposal offered reduced rights in a process that would not deliver meaningful benefits.

Recommendations

The Tribunal offered the Crown six options for revising its policy:[63]

1. A longer conversation to explore the issues and options more fully with iwi and hapū Māori and allow for options to arise within a "Treaty compliant regime".[64]
2. Do nothing – Allow the court processes to continue and address any unacceptable issues as and when they arise.
3. Access and inalienability – Address public anxiety by restricting the remedies available to the courts when addressing Māori claims to the takutai moana.
4. Improve the courts' toolkit – Legislate to enable the courts to simply make declarations about the nature and scope of the customary interests.
5. Protect mana – Affirm Māori ownership of the land, Crown and Māori co-management of the land, statutory public access and inalienable title.
6. Consistency – Be consistent between its approach to the beds of freshwater bodies and the takutai moana.
7. And finally, compensate for the loss of property rights. This would be the minimum standard required for fairness, good governance and recognition of te Tiriti.

A Comment on the Politics

The government's knee-jerk reaction to the Court of Appeal's decision turned a twenty-year political practice of negotiating Tiriti matters between the government and Māori on its head. In the 1980s, Māori had succeeded in landmark Tiriti-based claims in the courts and used those wins to force an engagement with a reluctant Crown. That case law included the *Lands case*, the *Forests case*, the *Spectrum case* and the *Broadcasting case*.[65]

Those cases demonstrated a smart use of legal forums in the pursuit of Tiriti-based relationships with the Crown. The process required iwi having to work over many years and across many layers of law and governance to get their issues close enough to the Crown to have a reasonable conversation about their resolution. The governments of that period mostly responded in a reasonably mature way. They generally held to constitutional norms, accepted the legal decisions and used the principles from the case law to develop the Treaty settlement process through which they could achieve Crown-acceptable outcomes.[66] The Treaty settlements that arose were (and remain) neither generous nor complete, but by and large they opened a dialogue between iwi and the Crown.

Iwi and hapū Māori had adapted, uneasily and with significant contestation, to the settlement approach preferred by the Crown.[67] But they were, nonetheless, engaging with that process to achieve some restitution for the impact of the Crown's Tiriti breaches for land confiscations and other rohe-specific violations. By 2003, there had been several Treaty settlements, including two of the largest – Waikato-Tainui in 1995 and Ngāi Tahu in 1998 – and the highly contentious Sealord deal, legislated through the Treaty of Waitangi (Fisheries Claims) Settlement Act 1992.[68]

In the late 1990s and early 2000s, the issues that Māori were raising were more challenging for the Crown. During the term of government 2002–2005, several claims related to takutai moana were made that had significant impact on valuable natural resources in the area. Arguably, these compounding matters were feeding government anxiety over its ability to effectively regulate the valuable natural resources found in the foreshore and the seabed land. Those matters included the allocation of fisheries resources in the Maori Fisheries Bill, the settlement of Māori claims to aquaculture space and the Waitangi Tribunal's *The Petroleum Report*.

In May 2003, just a month before the *Ngāti Apa* decision was released, the Waitangi Tribunal issued *The Petroleum Report Part 1* – Wai 796.[69] That report, also the result of an urgent inquiry, addressed claims by Ngā Hapū o Ngā Ruahine of Taranaki and Ngāti Kahungunu from Heretaunga and Wairarapa about the government's management of petroleum resources, but more immediately, it addressed concerns about the government's intention to sell its interests in the Kupe natural gas field license in the Tasman sea.[70] The Tribunal found that prior to 1937, Māori had legal title to the petroleum in their land. A Tiriti breach occurred when the land was alienated prior to 1937 and then again when the Crown nationalised the petroleum resources under the Petroleum Act 1937 without paying compensation to the landowners.

When the Wai 796 report was released, the Minister for Treaty Negotiations at that time, Margaret Wilson, rejected outright any negotiations with Māori about compensation or royalties for that Tiriti breach, arguing that the national interest overrode any Tiriti breaches.[71] The oil and gas industry was lobbying the government to prevent any royalties being required, and the leader of the National Party, Don Brash, was also putting the government under pressure to reject compensation to Māori.

Also in 2003, the Maori Fisheries Bill was introduced into Parliament, which implemented the quota management allocation from the Treaty of Waitangi (Fisheries Claims) Settlement Act 1992. Section 9 of that Act had fully and finally settled all Māori commercial fishing claims. Section 10 provided that claims arising from Maori non-commercial fishing rights might still give rise to customary rights but that the government would create regulations to recognise and provide for customary non-commercial food gathering.

The Wai 1071 tribunal considered the impact of the 1992 Act on takutai moana claims. They reviewed the jurisdictional question of whether the Act would interfere with either High Court or Māori Land Court inquiries into the customary land status of areas of the takutai moana. The Tribunal, in a narrow discussion, found that while the Act might preclude the High Court from including fishing rights in a bundle of takutai moana customary rights, the Act would not impede the Māori Land Court from considering customary fishing practices on the takutai moana as evidence of the tikanga connection of the iwi or hapū to that takutai moana.[72]

Beyond this narrow jurisdictional analysis, the 1992 Act and the Maori Fisheries Bill that was proceeding through Parliament in 2003 were likely impacting the government's political attitude to the takutai moana issue. The Maori Fisheries Bill was the result of ten years of fractious negotiation and litigation between the Crown and almost every iwi and urban Māori organisation in the country over matters of difficult allocation and property rights arising from the Sealord deal.[73] The Bill was highly contentious and remained so from its introduction into Parliament in November 2003 to its third reading ten months later. In the same year, the government was also developing the Aquaculture Reform Bill, which included the provisions for the settlement of Māori commercial aquaculture claims and the allocation and management of aquaculture settlement assets, the very issue that drove the foreshore and seabed litigation in the first place.[74]

Arguably, the collective political and economic pressure arising from the Maori Fisheries Bill, the aquaculture settlement allocation and Māori oil, gas and petroleum claims drove the government into a reactive and highly defensive position in response to the Court of Appeal decision on Māori customary property in the takutai moana. Its defensive positioning was reframed as a set of legal fictions, a narrative of protecting the public's unimpeded right to go to the beach, Māori greed at wanting to sell off the beaches and the government's right to assert its legislative power.

But of greater import was the possibility that Māori property rights might extend beyond Crown-determined allocation into broader rights to valuable natural resources in the ocean and the seabed, the control by Māori of access to those resources and the financial power that would accrue to Māori from these property rights.[75] Good government, fairness and upholding constitutional norms were not driving the government's foreshore and seabed response. The Tribunal recognised that the government's overriding motivation was none of these things in its final recommendations:[76]

> *[A] government whose intention was to give full expression to Maori rights under the Treaty in 2004 would recognise that where Maori did not give up ownership of the foreshore and seabed, they should now be confirmed as its owners. Pragmatically, however, we recognise that giving effect to te tino rangatiratanga is not currently on the political agenda.*

The Legislation

The Foreshore and Seabed Act 2004 was passed into law on 18 November 2004 giving effect to the government's proposal. The impact of the legislation on the political landscape was severe. While the Labour Party was able to form a minority coalition government after the 2005 general election, the National opposition had a very significant increase in its vote, in large part off the back of a campaign against "special treatment" for Māori arising from the foreshore and seabed issue, neatly summarised by their Iwi/Kiwi billboard. The Māori Party, formed by Pita Sharples and Kahurangi Tariana Turia, after she left Labour, gained four electoral seats and became the first standalone kaupapa Māori party to hold seats in Parliament.[77] The Māori Party did not enter a coalition with Labour in the 2005–2008 term, but in 2008 it entered into a coalition with the National Party led by John Key.

As a result of the Māori Party coalition agreement with National, the Foreshore and Seabed Act 2004 was repealed and replaced with the Marine and Coastal Area (Takutai Moana) Act 2011 (MACA Act).[78] While this legislation still technically extinguished the customary rights of Māori to the foreshore and seabed, it asserted that customary rights were restored and repealed Crown 'ownership' of the takutai moana and provided for a special status that prevented the area being 'owned' by anyone.[79]

The jurisdiction of the High Court was restored such that iwi and hapū Māori could either negotiate directly with the Crown for recognition of customary marine title or protected customary rights and/or apply for such an order from the High Court before 3 April 2017. Many iwi, hapū and whānau Māori were not convinced that the MACA Act was substantially better, but nonetheless there were 201 applications under the Act by the closing date.

Epilogue

The Waitangi Tribunal has had to intervene again in the matter of government foreshore and seabed policy. In its 2024 report *Wai 3400 Takutai Moana Act 2011 Urgent Inquiry Stage 1*, the Tribunal inquired into proposed amendments to the MACA Act by the National-led coalition government.[80] The government announced that it intended to amend the MACA Act to reverse a decision of the Court of Appeal over how to interpret section 58.[81] Section 58 contains the two key tests for an applicant seeking a customary marine title: that they hold the area in accordance with tikanga and that they have either exclusively used and occupied the area from 1840 without substantial interruption or received it through a customary transfer. The majority of the Court of Appeal determined that an applicant group can be said to have exercised exclusive use and occupation if pre-1840 they had the authority to exclude others if they chose to do so, and post-1840, they had retained that right according to tikanga, even if subsequent law deprived them of the ability to exercise that right.[82]

The MACA Amendment Bill clarifies that "exclusive use and occupation" only applies if the "group or its members had both the intention and the ability to control the area to the exclusion of others" since 1840 without substantial interruption.[83] Substantial interruption is to be defined as including any activity wholly or partly in the area by a person or people who do not belong to the applicant group whether authorised or not by legislation.[84] The Bill will have retrospective effect and will override the relevant parts of six

High Court decisions under the MACA Act. Schedule 1AA, clause 6 of the new Bill confirms that no compensation will be paid to any person affected by the retrospective changes to the tests in section 58.

The Waitangi Tribunal was required, yet again, to detail the Crown's te Tiriti legal obligations to act in accordance with its principles and good governance. As it had in Wai 1071, the Tribunal repeated the extent of the breach of the principle of tino rangatiratanga, partnership and the principle of good government:[85]

> *The Crown's proposed amendments seek to radically alter the ability for Māori to have their customary rights recognised in the takutai moana. By providing no evidentiary basis for amending the Act so drastically, by ignoring the advice of officials, and by choosing to preempt the Supreme Court on the matter, we find the Crown's proposed amendments are in breach of the principle of acting in good faith, in breach of the principle of active protection and the principle of good government. We also consider that Māori will, or are likely, to suffer prejudice as a result of such radical amendments when there is no proper foundation for doing so.*

In addition to outlining its concerns that there was no policy rationale for the amendments, the Tribunal was compelled to remark on the intended retrospective application of the Bill:[86]

> *We also found the Crown breached the principles of active protection and good government by proposing amendments that are applied retrospectively (from 25 July 2024 onwards). As a result of retrospectivity, applicants will be forced to have their cases reheard, burdening them emotionally and financially through no fault of their own, and placing further strain on whanaungatanga.*

In its final recommendations, the Tribunal reflected on the Crown's wider mandate to govern well for the country as a whole:[87]

> *The enactment of the 2004 Act led to a powerful resistance from Māori, in the form of the hīkoi and the subsequent rise of the Māori Party. Recently, the tangi for the passing of the Māori King has demonstrated once again the power of kotahitanga for Māori when bound by a just cause. In the spirit of Kingi Tuheitia's call for the principle of kotahitanga to be broader and for all New Zealanders,*

> *we urge Cabinet to stand back and seriously reconsider before seeking to introduce a Bill which is the antithesis of a kotahitanga approach for the whole community of New Zealand because of its clear non-compliance with Treaty principles ... At present, the Crown's actions are such a gross breach of the Treaty that, if it proceeds, these amendments would be an illegitimate exercise of kāwanatanga.*

There is no doubt that these attacks on customary rights in the foreshore and seabed will continue to arise for iwi Māori as it is such a resource-rich space. For as long as they do, the Waitangi Tribunal will remain one of the most important legal forums through which to test iwi Māori and Crown engagements and disagreements against the founding principles of te Tiriti o Waitangi.

"... the Fisheries Settlement is more than a settlement of Treaty interests. It is recognition by the Crown that it breached iwi rangatiratanga over their fisheries."

Chapter 7

Ika

— Tai Ahu

Few Treaty settlements between Māori and the Crown could claim to be as significant as the 1992 Māori commercial fisheries settlement (the 'Fisheries Settlement'). Signed in 1992, the Fisheries Settlement remains the only truly pan-Māori Treaty settlement. It settles the commercial Treaty fishing rights of all of the major tribal groupings: Taitokerau, Ngāpuhi, Tainui, Te Arawa, Mātaatua, Porourangi, Takitimu, Ngā iwi o te Hauauru,[1] Te Moana o Raukawa[2] and Waipounamu/Rēkohu.[3] By comparison, the Central North Island Forests Settlement, while exceeding the quantum of the Fisheries Settlement, only recognises the interests of the fourteen iwi of the Central North Island.[4]

The Fisheries Settlement, like all settlements, was deeply controversial. It was achieved only after protracted proceedings in both the courts and the Waitangi Tribunal, culminating in the publication of several reports, the most substantive of which were the *Report of the Waitangi Tribunal on the Manukau Claim (Manukau Report)*, the *Report of the Waitangi Tribunal on the Muriwhenua fishing claim* (*Muriwhenua Fishing Report)* and *The Ngai Tahu Sea Fisheries Report*. The Waitangi Tribunal reports produced between 1986 and 1998 were critical in articulating the extent of Māori customary and commercial fishing interests and practices and creating the leverage required to achieve a negotiated settlement with the Crown. That period generated a flurry of government, parliamentary and judicial activity. The Law Commission at the time spoke of "a rapid and even perhaps dramatic change of perceptions of the Treaty of Waitangi's place in New Zealand law and the relationship between many aspects of the law and the Treaty".[5]

If the Fisheries Settlement was designed to put an end to Treaty claims by Māori in commercial fisheries, it certainly did not put an end to litigation. On the contrary, the nature and effect of the Fisheries Settlement continues to be the subject of deeply contested litigation and policy debate. Proceedings in relation to the preferential allocation rights under section 28N of the Fisheries Act 1983,[6] the National Government's proposal in 2015 to create an ocean sanctuary[7] and the creation of marine reserves over areas of the seabed and foreshore illustrate a divergent view about the legal effect of the Fisheries Settlement between the Crown and Māori.

Such claims are brought by Māori claimants who see those shifts in government policy as diminishing the Fisheries Settlement and failing to protect and uphold the guarantee of tino rangatiratanga under Article 2. The Crown on the other hand has generally sought to protect the right of the government of the day to make policy. The purpose of this chapter is to analyse the long-term impact of the Waitangi Tribunal's role on Māori fishing rights and interests. It will also discuss recent case law on the nature and extent of Māori fisheries interests today and assess the durability of the Fisheries Settlement.

Recognition of Māori Customary Fishing Rights

Statutory recognition

The issue of the nature and extent of Māori fishing rights had, prior to the Fisheries Settlement, vexed the government for decades. Since the late 1800s, legislation had recognised extant Māori fishing interests in one way or another. The first piece of legislation to provide for Māori fishing rights was the Fish Protection Act 1877. That Act contained a savings provision that stated nothing in the Act "shall be deemed to repeal, alter, or affect any provisions of the Treaty of Waitangi" or "take away, annul, abridge any of the rights of the aboriginal natives to any fishery secured to them thereunder".[8]

The savings provision was not included when Parliament enacted the Sea-fisheries Act in 1894. It was, however, later amended in 1903 to make it clear that nothing in the Act "shall affect any existing Māori fisheries rights" but failed to reference te Tiriti.[9] From that point onwards, fisheries legislation recognised Māori fishing rights but did not describe or substantively codify those interests. Furthermore, the form of recognition was ill-defined and fraught with assumptions. For example, the Waitangi Tribunal in the *Muriwhenua Fishing Report*, while acknowledging the Fish Protection Act 1877 provided limited protection, was critical that the Act could address Māori fishing rights "in a general way, and although nearly everything else in the Act might be contrary to the Treaty principles".[10]

Similarly, section 77(2) of the Fisheries Act 1908, which provided a general protection that "Nothing in this act shall affect any Māori fishing rights", nevertheless only applied to sea fisheries.[11]

Early court decisions

Early court decisions appeared to uphold Māori fisheries rights. In the 1910 case *Baldick v Jackson*,[12] which concerned ownership of a whale, Stout CJ found that an English statute during the time of Edward II was deemed not to apply to the circumstances of the colony on the basis that the prerogative "would have been impossible to claim without claiming it against the Maoris, for they were accustomed to engage in whaling; and the Treaty of Waitangi assumed that their fishing was not to be interfered with".[13] The broadly framed statutory protections caused the section to come before the Supreme Court in 1914 in *Waipapakura v Hempton*.[14] That case concerned an alleged infringement of regulations under the Fisheries Act 1908. The defendant, Waipapakura, who had used more than one set net with groynes to capture whitebait, argued she was exercising a Māori fishing right. John Salmond, appearing for the Crown, argued that section 77(2) did not create rights. The Court agreed, finding that a general protections clause was not sufficient, and any Māori fishing rights relied on had to be provided for in statute.[15] Other cases, such as *Keepa v Inspector of Fisheries* (*Keepa*), supported the approach that Parliament could give effect to Māori customary rights.[16] In *Keepa,* which concerned the taking of undersized toheroa, the Court found that preexisting Māori fishing rights were extinguished in the foreshore when title was granted or a freehold order made over adjoining land.[17] Hardie Boys J found that the grant of a freehold order for land adjacent to the foreshore "established the Crown as owner" and extinguished former Māori rights, including customary fishing rights over the land.[18] The Court also found that fishing rights claimed would have been exclusive, including of the Crown and others who were not of the two claimant tribes.

It was not until 1986 in *Te Weehi v Regional Fisheries Officer* (*Te Weehi*), where the High Court departed from that approach and found that "if Parliament's intention is to extinguish such customary or traditional rights, then it will no doubt do so in clear terms following its exploration of claims by Māori Tribes to specific customary rights".[19] Williamson J distinguished *Waipapakura* and *Weepu* on the basis that the customary right being sought was not exclusive and non-territorial, and had not been extinguished by statute.[20]

The Court in *Te Weehi* referred specifically to the *Waitangi Tribunal's Report on the fishing grounds in the Waitara District*, the *Manukau Fishing Report* and the *Report of the Waitangi Tribunal on the Kaituna River claim (Kaituna River Report)* in support of its position.[21] Substantial customary evidence was given in *Te Weehi* to establish the existence of Māori fishing rights, including from university lecturers and kaumātua from Ngāi Tahu. The later case *Green v Ministry of Agriculture and Fisheries* confirmed that the onus is on the applicant to prove that he or she is exercising a Māori fishing right.[22]

While the *Te Weehi* case has been distinguished in a number of cases,[23] the presumption of continuity and requirement of clear extinguishment of customary rights remains the orthodox approach and was followed in leading decisions on te Tiriti o Waitangi and customary rights, including *Ngati Apa v Attorney General*.[24] *Te Weehi* continues to be referred to in significant cases as authority for the proposition that Māori customary rights were not displaced by British sovereignty, including *Takamore v Clarke*.[25] More recently, in determining whether to grant recognition orders under the Marine and Coastal Area (Takutai Moana) Act 2011, the High Court in *Re Tipene* referred to *Te Weehi* to support the recognition of non-territorial-based customary rights.[26] The *Te Weehi* case is still described by Tā Tipene O'Regan as "the great turning point" that enabled the Fisheries Settlement.[27]

Early Waitangi Tribunal Reports

The *Te Weehi* decision obviously did not occur in a judicial or political vacuum. The early Waitangi Tribunal reports between 1975 and 1985, while often disregarded by governments, helped to bring Māori fisheries rights to the fore. The media attention surrounding the *Motunui-Waitara Report*, for example, has been argued to have played "an important role in supporting Te Āti Awa's claim and helping to disseminate information about their worldview and culture to Pākehā".[28]

In 1978, eight years prior to *Te Weehi*, the question of Māori fishing rights came before the Waitangi Tribunal in Wai 2, the *Waiau Pā Power Station Claim*.[29] Two claims were brought; one by Waikato hapū and one from the Waiau Pā community, protesting the impact on fishing resources of the proposed construction of a power station on a site close to Waiau Pā, on the south-western shores of the Manukau Harbour. The Tribunal declined to make any recommendations on the basis that the Crown decided not to proceed with the project. However, the Tribunal found the claims to be well founded and the claimants prejudicially affected by the impact on fish life from construction of cooling towers.[30]

The Tribunal also recognised Māori fishing rights in the *Kaituna River Report* in 1984. The claim was brought by Ngāti Pikiao in 1978, the same year the Tribunal released its report on the Waiau Pā Power Station Claim. The claimants opposed the construction of a pipeline discharging treated effluent from Lake Rotorua into the Kaituna River, including on the basis that contamination would impact the cultural and spiritual values and traditional fishing as a taonga. The Tribunal found, amongst other things, that the Kaituna River had been owned by many generations of Ngāti Pikiao and Te Arawa and that the traditional rights of ownership "carry with them the free and uninterrupted right to fish the river, the estuary and the sea, together with the use and enjoyment of the flora ..."[31] Notably, the Tribunal found that no matter how the effluent was treated (or "scientifically pure" the discharge became), its discharge into the Kaituna River was contrary to Māori cultural and spiritual values.[32]

The Waitangi Tribunal's 1983 *Report of the Waitangi Tribunal on the Motunui-Waitara Claim* was perhaps the boldest statement of Māori fishing rights in the earlier reports.[33] The claim was made by Te Ātiawa, who protested discharge of waste, including from Muldoon's Think Big projects from reefs in northern Taranaki. The original claim alleged that the Crown had failed to "properly control discharge of sewage and industrial waste into the sea between New Plymouth and Waitara" which had "adversely affected fishing grounds known as Tauranga, Te Puna, Titi Rangi and Orapa Reefs".[34] The Waitangi Tribunal's decision was unequivocal in several respects.

Firstly, the Waitangi Tribunal found that the Crown has a duty of active protection. In the Tribunal's words, the Treaty required the Crown "not only to recognise the Māori interests specified in the Treaty, but actively to protect them". Failure to protect Māori interest "is as much a breach of the Treaty as a positive act that removes those rights".[35] The Crown's positive duty has been instrumental in other cases, including the revitalisation of te reo Māori.[36]

Secondly, the Tribunal found that the Treaty required the Crown to distinctly recognise Māori cultural values. The Treaty "must accord with the Māori perception of those fisheries". The discharge of animal waste into the waterway "is as offensive as a physical disruption ... the guarantee of undisturbed possession or of rangatiratanga means that there must be a regard for the cultural values of the possessor".[37] The Tribunal emphasised that the Treaty was not stagnant but capable of meeting new challenges:[38]

> *The Treaty was also more than an affirmation of existing rights. It was not intended to merely fossilise a status quo, but to provide a direction for future growth and development. The broad and general nature of its words indicates that it was not intended as a finite contract but as the foundation for a developing social contract.*

Thirdly, the *Motunui-Waitara Report* was not simply a bare faced assertion of Māori Treaty rights. The Tribunal centred its analysis on the guarantees provided in the Treaty but also endeavoured to allay public concern by acknowledging and attempting to balance what it saw as a competing national interest: [39]

> *We do not therefore consider that both the Maori and the Crown should be so bound that both sides must regard all Maori fishing grounds as inviolate. In our view it is not inconsistent with the Treaty of Waitangi that the Crown and Maori people should agree upon a measure of compromise and change.*
>
> *In particular, it is not inconsistent with the Treaty that the Te Atiawa hapu should accept a degree of pollution in respect of certain of their fishing grounds, on the basis that other grounds will not be spoilt.*

While the immediate political response was dismissive,[40] Kathryn Cammell has argued that the *Motunui-Waitara Report* was a cornerstone decision and pressured Muldoon's Government to change their response to the Tribunal's recommendations.[41] In any event, the Tribunal played a direct role in shifting entrenched assumption and increasing awareness about Māori culture and landscape generally. As James and Pawson note:[42]

> *For Pakeha in the early 1980s, the exposure of a hidden history of places such as north Taranaki was radical. It questioned the assumed universality of Pakeha landscape ideals. In this sense, the newfound accessibility of Maori place alongside that of the dominant tradition was a 'reinterpretation'; in another sense it was a retrieval for Pakeha of a geography that had always been there; the reading of a narrative that they did not know how to see.*

Furthermore, the earlier reports continue to be referred to in case law today, particularly where Treaty principles bear on the matter or are incorporated into the governing statute. The 2023 decision of the Court of Appeal in *Greenpeace Aotearoa Inc v Hiringa Energy Limited* is one such case.[43] The case concerned a decision of an expert consenting panel under the COVID-19 Recovery (Fast-track Consenting) Act 2020 to grant resource consent to Hiringa Energy Limited to construct a hydrogen plant at Kapuni, Taranaki. Ngā Hapū o Ngāruahine, an interested party in the appeal, argued the relevance of Treaty principles based on section 6 of the COVID-19 Recovery (Fast-track Consenting) Act 2020, which provides that:

> *In achieving the purpose of this Act, all persons performing functions and exercising powers under it must act in a manner that is consistent with—*
> *(a) the principles of the Treaty of Waitangi; and*
> *(b) Treaty settlements.*

Although the Court ultimately dismissed the appeal, it referred extensively to the *Waiau Pa Power Station Claim* report, the *Kaituna River Report*, the *Motunui-Waitara Report* and the *Mangonui Sewerage Report*[44] and accepted that the principle of active protection could have real teeth:[45]

> *... consistency with the principle of active protection may have both procedural and substantive implications. That is, not only must the Crown adopt fair consultative processes with Māori in respect of planned projects that may engage Treaty principles, the principle of active protection may be relevant to whether the project should proceed on the site proposed or at all.*

The Muriwhenua Fishing Report and the Ngāi Tahu Fishing Reports

Much has been written about the period in which the *Muriwhenua Fishing Report* and *Ngāi Tahu* reports were released. The claim was based on the introduction of the quota management system (QMS) and the allocation of a private property right in perpetuity in the form of quota beyond the ability of the Waitangi Tribunal or the Crown to provide for Māori interests. During that period, the political landscape was quickly changing. Parliament was considering the State-Owned Enterprises Bill (SOE Bill) and the Fisheries Amendment Act 1986, which introduced the QMS. The Waitangi Tribunal found itself in a difficult position and took the remarkable step of responding by letter and issuing an interim report directly to Koro Wētere, the Minister of Māori Affairs, on the SOE Bill without having had a hearing or heard any evidence on the Bill specifically. The Tribunal noted that:[46]

> *The guarantee, in Article Two, to the undisturbed possession of lands so long as the Maori owners wish to retain the same, must be read in the context of the preamble, that the Crown is anxious to protect their just rights and property. The element of protection was, we consider, a most compelling reason for the execution of the Treaty. We must look to the surrounding circumstances and the expectations of those very Chiefs of the far North, and Panekareao in particular, that the Governor would remain their father and protector. His descendants are now before us. The honour of the Crown is at stake. We think it inconsistent with the principles of the Treaty of Waitangi that that particular relationship of the Maori and the Crown should in any way be diminished, or even threatened with compromise. We do not think in particular that the Crown should dispose of lands that are the subject of claims and risk thereby some prejudice to the Claimants' position.*

As Stephanie Milroy has argued, the Tribunal was performing "a very delicate balancing act" and "had to be careful not to overstep the mark separating its statutory functions from intrusion into the political arena".[47] The QMS was initially considered under the Muldoon Government, prior to the snap election in 1984, but its full introduction came by way of the Fisheries Amendment Act 1986. The Minister of Fisheries declined the Tribunal's request not to allocate quota under the QMS, forcing Māori (initially Muriwhenua claimants, and then subsequently Ngāi Tahu) into the position of seeking urgent interim relief from the High Court. Grieg J found, on the basis of the Interim Muriwhenua Report, that there was a strong case Māori had "a highly developed and controlled fishery over the whole coast of New Zealand, at least where they were living".[48] The Court acknowledged that hapū and tribes "had the dominion, perhaps the rangatiratanga, over those fisheries", and that they had "a commercial element and were not purely recreational or ceremonial or merely for the sustenance of local dwellers".[49]

When the Tribunal published the *Muriwhenua Fishing Report* a year later, its findings were unequivocal. The QMS was determined to be "in fundamental conflict with the Treaty's principles and terms, apportioning to non-Maori the full, exclusive and undisturbed possession of property in fishing that to Maori was guaranteed".[50] A central finding was that, traditionally, Māori fishing was not merely subsistence but was a substantial commercial undertaking. It was accepted by the Crown in *The Ngai Tahu Sea Fisheries Report* that traditional Māori fishing rights included a commercial element, and there existed a right to develop the fishery to reflect modern fishing practices.[51]

The Tribunal in both *Muriwhenua* and *Ngai Tahu* recognised Māori have the "right to develop" their fishing resources "beyond the capabilities that existed at 1840".[52] Similarly, in *The Ngai Tahu Sea Fisheries Report*, it was common ground between the claimants, the Crown and even the fishing industry that the right to development is inherent in the Treaty of Waitangi.[53]

Importantly, the Waitangi Tribunal in both *Muriwhenua* and *Ngai Tahu* reports were explicit that the reports were designed to facilitate negotiations between Māori and the Crown.[54]

There was also a concern that the allocation of quota was forcing Māori to be shut out of the opportunity to exercise and develop commercial fishing.[55] Originally, quota was to be allocated to "commercial fishermen" based on historic catch. The statutory definition did not include part-time fishermen and therefore shut many Māori out of being able to receive a property right in perpetuity.[56] Many aspects of the Fisheries Settlement were designed to address or rectify the breaches identified by the Waitangi Tribunal by the introduction of the QMS.

The impact of the Muriwhenua and Ngai Tahu Fisheries Reports

The Tribunal's later reports made an immediate impact. It was relied on by both the High Court and Court of Appeal in support of the interim injunctions preventing the allocation of quota under the QMS. The Law Commission at the time was complementary of the Waitangi Tribunal, describing the *Muriwhenua* and *Ngai Tahu* reports as "a class apart", and noted that:[57]

> *Without the Tribunal's thorough and painstaking analysis of issues, history and law, and the unique body of evidence it has received from the tangata whenua, the preparation of a document such as this would at best have required extraordinary and prolonged labours.*

More recently, the *Muriwhenua* report has been referred to in cases involving interpretation of Māori fishing rights. The defendant in *Taranaki Fish & Game Council v McRitchie*, who had been charged under section 26ZI(1)(a) of the Conservation Act 1987 for fishing for freshwater trout without a licence, relied on section 26ZH of the Act, which provides that "Nothing in this Part shall affect any Maori fishing rights". Notwithstanding that trout is a species introduced after 1840, he claimed that his people "have had the customary right to fish for all species in the river (including trout) from time immemorial".[58] The Court referred extensively to the *Muriwhenua* report in finding that the Māori fishing rights protected by section 26ZH is both an "Aboriginal right" and a "Treaty right" and should be construed expansively and generously. However, the Court found that the exercise of the Māori fishing right has to be made on the evidence, including in accordance with local kawa, for personal and whānau consumption for hui and tangi, and that it does not impact on the sustainability of the trout resource.[59]

The Court anticipated the argument that the outcome resulted in inequality and frustrated the purposes of the Act, but found that:[60]

> *... that is precisely the position that the Treaty of Waitangi, incorporated into the Conservation Act creates. As was said by Williamson J in Te Weehi "I am conscious that the same argument [as to injustice] can be made whenever any person or class of persons are exempted from particular provisions. Viewed in a more general way, such an equality between persons may indicate an overall justice rather than an injustice." If the Treaty is to be paid more than lip service it seems to me inevitable that consequences, such as this decision, will flow from it.*

The Court's judgment was overturned on appeal to the High Court. Greig and Neazor JJ emphasised the history of legislation and degree of legislative control over the management of trout historically to distinguish *Te Weehi*.[61] However, they also acknowledged that:[62]

> *The issue in this case in the end comes down to a narrow one because it is not disputed that Maori had Treaty-based rights to take freshwater fish. We can see no justification for treating the Maori fishing rights reserved by Article II of the Treaty more narrowly than has been said by the Waitangi Tribunal to be the proper approach in respect of sea-fisheries; that what is protected by Article II are the available fish, the places where fish were caught and the methods and practice of fishing, but because of the basis of our decision it is not necessary finally to decide that.*

The *Muriwhenua* report was referred to extensively by the Court of Appeal in *Takamore v Clarke* as supporting authority for the proposition that Māori have a choice about whether customary rights should or should not apply to them (a point not determined conclusively by the Supreme Court on appeal).[63] Other cases also continue to refer to *Muriwhenua* and *Ngai Tahu* reports to recognise Māori customary rights in general.[64]

The Fisheries Settlements

The 1989 Interim Fisheries Settlement

In 1989, the Crown and Māori negotiators agreed the 1989 interim fisheries settlement, which was given effect by the Maori Fisheries Act 1989. This interim settlement created the Māori Fisheries Commission, which received 10 per cent of available quota for fish species in the QMS over a four-year period and approximately $10 million to be held and managed by a new company, Aotearoa Fisheries Limited, on behalf of all Māori.

The Commission's role was also to promote Māori involvement in the business and activity of fishing. Where the Crown was unable to provide the agreed 10 per cent of fish species in the QMS, Māori were provided the equivalent value in further cash.

The 1992 Fisheries Settlement

Māori commercial fishing claims were finally settled with the signing of a deed of settlement in September 1992. The deed was given effect through the Treaty of Waitangi (Fisheries Claims) Settlement Act 1992, creating the Treaty of Waitangi Fisheries Commission, which later became Te Ohu Kai Moana Limited, a corporate trustee of a trust created by the Maori Fisheries Act 2004. The broad components of the Fisheries Settlement included:

1. agreement to make regulations to allow self-management of Māori fishing for communal subsistence and cultural purposes;

2. providing funds for Māori to assist in buying a 50 per cent stake in Sealord Products Limited (now Sealord Group Limited);
3. granting Māori 20 per cent of commercial fishing quota for all new species brought within the QMS; and
4. undertaking to ensure the appointment of Māori on statutory fisheries bodies.

The Fisheries Settlement settled all Māori commercial fishing rights and interests, required Māori to endorse the QMS and accept regulations for customary fishing, and ceased litigation relating to the QMS.

Importantly for Te Ohu Kai Moana, the Fisheries Settlement is more than a settlement of Treaty interests. It is recognition by the Crown that it breached iwi rangatiratanga over their fisheries. The preamble to the 1992 Fisheries Settlement provides recognition that:

> A. *By the Treaty of Waitangi the Crown confirmed and guaranteed to the Chiefs, tribes and individual Maori full exclusive and undisturbed possession and te tino rangatiratanga of their fisheries.*

The conceptual difference between Māori/Te Ohu Kai Moana and the Crown about the nature of the Fisheries Settlement has led to ongoing litigation.

Customary (non-commercial) fishing rights

The Fisheries Settlement was also, in some way, a precursor for recognition and resolution of non-commercial fishing rights of Māori, which were not settled under the Fisheries Settlement. Paragraph K of the Preamble provides that:

> K. *The Crown recognises that traditional fisheries are of importance to Maori and that the Crown's Treaty duty is to develop policies to help recognise use and management practices and provide protection for and scope for exercise of rangatiratanga in respect of traditional fisheries.*

The recognition of rangatiratanga was codified in section 174 of Part 9 of the Fisheries Act 1996 (relating to taiāpure-local fisheries and customary fishing) which states that:

> *174 Object*
> *The object of sections 175 to 185 is to make, in relation to areas of New Zealand fisheries waters (being estuarine or littoral coastal*

> *waters) that have customarily been of special significance to any iwi or hapu either—*
> *(a) as a source of food; or*
> *(b) for spiritual or cultural reasons,—*
> *better provision for the recognition of rangatiratanga and of the right secured in relation to fisheries by Article II of the Treaty of Waitangi.*

Today, there are different customary (non-commercial) fishing regulations for different areas. The Fisheries (Kaimoana Customary Fishing) Regulations 1998 apply to the North Island and Chatham Islands. The Fisheries (South Island Customary Fishing) Regulations 1999 apply to the South Island.

Other specific regulations arise from the Treaty settlements of particular iwi, such as the Te Arawa Lakes (Fisheries) Regulations 2006 and Waikato-Tainui (Waikato River Fisheries) Regulations 2011. Customary (non-commercial) fisheries management tools under the Fisheries Act 1996 include:

1. Mātaitai reserves, which recognise and provide for traditional fishing through local management. They allow customary and recreational fishing but do not typically allow for commercial fishing.
2. Taiāpure (local fisheries). These are estuarine or coastal areas that are significant for food, spiritual or cultural reasons. They allow all types of fishing and are managed by local communities.
3. Temporary closures and restrictions on fishing methods (sections 186A and 186B closures). These are areas that are temporarily closed to fishing or certain fishing methods.
4. Fisheries bylaws. These are changes to fisheries management rules made by tangata whenua or tangata kaitiaki/tiaki (guardians) for their Crown settlement area or mātaitai reserve.

Durability of the Fisheries Settlements

There is a strong argument to say that the Fisheries Settlement has been durable. Firstly, it was negotiated in a politically fraught environment and under commercial and legal timeframes that are seldom seen in Treaty settlements. Secondly, the institutional mechanics of the Fisheries Settlement have been largely resolved. The majority of iwi (fifty-six out of fifty-eight) recognised in the Maori Fisheries Act 2004 have met statutory requirements to become mandated iwi organisations and receive the full benefit of the Fisheries Settlement. A substantial majority have agreed coastline agreements with their iwi neighbours, have had their settlement quota transferred and are receiving dividends from Aotearoa Fisheries Limited and distributions from Te Ohu Kai Moana Trustee Limited.[65] Thirdly, in recent times independent reviews of Te Ohu Kai Moana have been positive. In the most recent four-year audit, the auditor presented a favourable review in terms of organisational performance of Te Ohu Kai Moana and its subsidiary entities. The audit notes that on balance, Te Ohu Kai Moana is performing satisfactorily in delivering its strategic pou.[66]

However, the Fisheries Settlement has given rise to strong differences in fisheries management policy between Māori and the Crown, and litigation about the nature and intended effect of the Fisheries Settlement.

In a recent settlement workshop held by Ngāi Tahu, Craig Ellison (at the time the Chief Executive of Ngāi Tahu Holdings) posed the question during an address, is the Fisheries Settlement a final settlement? His response was "My answer is that it is definitely not. It is a stage in our quest to seek rangatiratanga over our marine estate. Not the end – we still need that vigilance and action".[67] The sentiment expressed is that the Sealord deal did not simply justify the status quo of Crown kāwanatanga. It represented more than a commercial settlement of Treaty grievances but recognised and reflected rangatiratanga of Māori over the fisheries resource. There is a basis for this sentiment.

Firstly, the negotiations through the Fisheries Working Group were advanced on the basis that a fisheries settlement would only be agreed if it recognised rangatiratanga – political authority in fisheries management as a Treaty partner. When negotiations of the Working Group broke down, the Māori members released their own report seeking 50 per cent ownership of the fisheries resource and "equal say with the Crown in management and control of the fisheries of New Zealand".[68] The basis came from the wording of the Treaty of Waitangi that guaranteed Māori "the full, exclusive and undisturbed possession of the fisheries of New Zealand". It claimed there was "common ground that the settlement must be such as to give effect to the Treaty promise that <u>te tino rangatiratanga</u> in their fisheries was confirmed and guaranteed to the Māori people".[69] The Māori members were critical of the Crown members' report, noting that:[70]

> *... the Crown approach applies the term "rangatiratanga" to the fisheries in a sense unknown to Māori – as apt to describe a minority interest in a corporation controlled by the Crown in which Maori benefit is limited to receipt of a share of net resource rentals paid by holders of fishing quota.*

Secondly, the Māori members rejected the Crown's proposal on the basis that "the corporation model locks Maori into a minority position with Crown having control".[71] A settlement was not just to deliver a share of the fisheries resource but "access to the fisheries for iwi and Māori" and "equality with the Crown in control and management of the resource".[72] The Crown's members noted that "any solution must involve recognition of Māori claims to tino rangatiratanga" and that it could be given effect to by providing for "Māori participation in the management and control of the fisheries".[73] The Crown members recommended "a new fisheries control institution, with commercial objectives, owned and managed jointly by Crown and Māori".[74]

Thirdly, while the deed of settlement never delivered fully on either proposal, it explicitly recognised rangatiratanga at clause K of the preamble, and, for example, in section 174 in the Fisheries Act 1996.

More recent litigation has challenged the extent to which Crown policy infringes the Fisheries Settlement. Te Ohu Kai Moana brought proceedings seeking declaratory relief after the Kermadec Ocean Sanctuary was announced by the National government in 2016. The sanctuary was considered by Te Ohu Kai Moana to be inconsistent with the Fisheries Settlement and tantamount to a confiscation of Māori fishing rights.[75]

Where there is a Bill proposed or before the House, such proceedings may rub up against the constitutional role of Parliament and the principle of comity – that a court cannot prohibit the introduction of legislation or make adverse comments while the Bill is before the House.[76] The Court of Appeal's decision in *Ngāti Mutunga o Wharekauri Asset Holding Company Limited v Attorney General* [2019] NZCA 2 struck out an application for a declaration that the Kermadec Sanctuary was inconsistent with the Treaty and the Fisheries Settlement. Te Ohu Kai Moana's proceedings were granted an interim stay;[77] however, the National-led coalition government decided not to proceed with the Kermadec Ocean Sanctuary Bill.

More recently, the High Court has made strong statements about the underlying property rights in the Fisheries Settlement in the context of section 28N rights. Section 28N of the Fisheries Act 1983 gave preferential allocation rights in lieu of compensation to quota holders, after the QMS was introduced. When the total allowable commercial catch in a fishery is increased, section 28N rights holders are granted a preferential quota allocation that results in a proportional decrease in fisheries settlement quota.

In granting the declaratory relief sought, the High Court rejected the Crown's argument that the Fisheries Settlement was not enforceable and did not create legal relations between Māori and the Crown. The Court noted there is "ample and conclusive evidence that Māori understood the transfers of quota would provide them with a permanent or perpetual stake in New Zealand's fisheries",[78] and emphasised that the Fisheries Settlement "recorded that the Crown and Māori wished to 'seek a just and honourable solution in conformity with the principles of the Treaty of Waitangi'".[79] The Court described the resulting decrease in settlement quota as a "[u]nilateral expropriation of Māori fishing assets, without compensation" which "is the antithesis of active protection" and a "direct breach of [Article] 2".[80] The Court ultimately found the Crown to be in direct breach of the Fisheries Settlement and the Treaty of Waitangi.[81]

The decision is the latest – and arguably the strongest – judicial statement of the effect of the Fisheries Settlement. The Court was clear that the transfer of settlement quota under the Fisheries Settlement was intended to be permanent, and not re-acquired by dint of statute without compensation. Nevertheless, the arguments raised by the parties reflect the ongoing and strong divergence about the ongoing legal effect of the Fisheries Settlement.

Conclusion

More than thirty years on, the Waitangi Tribunal's earlier work continues to be instrumental for framing Māori fishing rights. The quasi-judicial nature of its role provided the flexibility required to achieve the settlement in a politically fraught environment, balancing pragmatism and political necessity in a principled way. However, the Waitangi Tribunal's work and the Fisheries Settlement in general did not, of course, comprehensively address the complex interaction between the government and Māori in fisheries generally. Tension between Māori aspirations for Treaty settlement rights and the policy and legislative functions of government will continue to be litigated. Rather than merely a settlement of prior Treaty breaches, many Māori see the Fisheries Settlement as establishing a framework to enable tino rangatiratanga in fisheries into the future.

“In our search for justice and fairer remedies, claimants often seek help from the Tribunal.”

Chapter 8

Issues Relating to Treaty Settlements

The Most Dishonourable Process of Managed Chaos

—Margaret Mutu

While the Waitangi Tribunal has upheld the vast majority of historical claims, the settlement of those claims has proven traumatic for claimants. Since 1992 and the Fisheries Settlement, many Tribunal reports have referenced problems with settlements. The Tribunal has issued no fewer than twenty-six reports that deal with settlements. The difficulties continue to arise because of the Crown's ongoing refusal to uphold te Tiriti o Waitangi. Instead, it clings to the legal fiction of indivisible parliamentary sovereignty to retain to itself all the power, wealth, prosperity and privilege it gained from dispossessing Māori.

As the Tribunal started upholding claims, the Crown dictated that Māori were to have no say in how it would address our claims. It unilaterally determined the policy and process for settling claims. The policy aimed to legally extinguish all historical claims to prevent the Tribunal using its powers to order that lands be returned. The Crown's policy and practice have no legislative framework and seek to complete the Crown's mission of forced assimilation of Māori. The English societal and cultural norms it imposes come into direct conflict with the kaupapa and tikanga of claimants. The policy relies on officials being able to inveigle claimants, along with our whānau, hapū and iwi, into a political framework that renders Māori powerless. The Crown then tells the country it is restoring the honour of the Crown and that Māori are happy with the settlements. Māori strongly disagree. Settlements, which on average return less than 1 per cent of what was stolen, have divided Māori communities throughout the country.

In our search for justice and fairer remedies, claimants often seek help from the Tribunal to address the most egregious aspects of the Crown's Treaty claims settlement process. The Crown's mandating process has resulted in eight reports. There are four reports on overlapping claims and another eight on settlements. There are also six reports on remedies.

This chapter provides an overview of the Crown's Treaty claims settlement policy and process that resulted from the *Lands* case, and its legal alternative, binding recommendations. It also considers claimants' views as recorded in submissions and interviews. It then discusses the issues identified in Tribunal reports on claims against the process, noting recurring themes and recommendations. Further actions taken by both claimants and the Crown are also considered along with the need for constitutional transformation.

The Lands Case –
Waitangi Tribunal's Power to Order Lands be Returned

The power the Tribunal has had since 1988 to order the government to return land to Māori were legal rights that Māori won in the *Lands* case, *New Zealand Maori Council v Attorney-General* 1987. The New Zealand Māori Council challenged the decision of the fourth Labour Government to corporatise "52 per cent of the land area of the country, other assets worth some $11.8 billion at that time, and 54,000 staff members"[1] into state-owned enterprises. The Court of Appeal directed the Crown to prepare safeguards to ensure that the transfer of lands was consistent with Treaty principles. The Crown reached an out-of-court settlement with the Māori Council that empowered the Waitangi Tribunal to order that state-owned enterprise and certain other lands be returned to successful claimants. Then, after the Crown was subsequently caught out trying to sell the Crown forests, Crown forest lands would also be returned to Māori at no cost, along with compensation for the forests.[2] Rental monies that had been accumulating since the Crown sold the forests were also to be paid to successful claimants. For the first time, Māori had legal rights to recover their lands and associated income. The Court of Appeal advised the parties they could reopen the litigation "in case anything unforeseen should arise".[3]

Clawing Back Māori Legal Rights – the 'Fiscal Envelope' Policy

In 1990, a newly appointed Minister in Charge of Treaty of Waitangi Negotiations, Douglas Graham, took exception to the implications of the *Lands* case and its accompanying legislation. Rather than Māori getting recommendations for the recovery of their lands that the government ignores, they could now get recommendations that were binding on the Crown and once ordered, the land had to be returned to its rightful owners.[4] In his book *Trick or Treaty?*, Graham falsely assumes that the Crown can dictate to Māori and declares "only the government can decide ... The courts cannot do this. Neither can Maori".[5] Rather than repealing the legislation, which would have reopened the *Lands* case, he set about removing the threat, demonstrating the powerlessness of courts in New Zealand to restrict Parliament's behaviour.[6] Without consultation with Māori, he developed a policy that aimed to evade Treaty claims protection systems by shutting down claimants' access to the legal remedies available in the Tribunal. Rather, he sent them into direct negotiations with the government where claims are restricted to the realm of politics. In that arena, with no statutory framework to protect Māori interests, Māori are powerless and are at the whim and mercy of Pākehā politicians and bureaucrats dedicated to preserving power, wealth and privilege in the hands of Pākehā.[7]

The Government Treaty Claims Settlement Policy and Practice

Publications from the Office of Treaty Settlements detailing the development of the policy and then explaining its implementation disingenuously obfuscate the true intent of the policy. The Crown's 'motivation and objectives' are couched in terms of moral, social, legal and political principles that seek to achieve positive, harmonious and peaceful race relations. They seek to acknowledge and resolve historical injustices. They seek to restore the honour of the Crown and to remove the sense of grievance felt by Māori. They seek to improve the social and economic status of Māori and to assure claimants and the New Zealand public that the settlements would be fair, full and final.[8]

In several of its reports on issues relating to settlements, the Tribunal has provided advice and made recommendations that urge the Crown to adhere to its published motivations and objectives.[9] Claimants have a legitimate expectation that the Crown will do so.[10] However, the published Treaty claims settlement policy is a charade. Cabinet minutes and memoranda show that the true intent of the policy bears little resemblance to the publications made available to claimants. It can be summarised as:

- to unpick the legal rights won by Māori in the *Lands* case;
- to extinguish all historical claims and remove Māori rights to make further claims; and
- to preserve Pākehā control over Māori lives, lands and resources.[11]

Understanding the true intent of the policy helps to explain the otherwise inexplicable behaviour of the Crown towards Māori in the Treaty claims settlement process. Such a punitive and racist Crown regime violates many Treaty, human and indigenous rights of Māori. To successfully implement it, the Crown had to prevent the courts intervening. Hence, there is no Treaty Settlement Process Act,[12] so the courts have repeatedly refused to step in.[13] The only avenue available is the Tribunal, whose powers are restricted to providing advice and making recommendations although that does include the binding recommendations made possible by the *Lands* case.

A close reading of Office of Treaty Settlement publications alongside the Cabinet documentation indicates how the Crown maintains complete control over the settlement process.[14] It sidesteps individual claims and only negotiates settlements with 'large natural groupings' of iwi. It extinguishes whānau, hapū and even iwi claims without negotiating or settling them, denying claimants the legal right to conduct their own claims.[15] The Crown exerts pressure on claimants to settle as quickly and as cheaply as possible. Deadlines are arbitrarily determined to suit electoral cycles. Thus far, four ministerially imposed deadlines for the settlement of all claims have passed: 2000, 2008, 2014 and 2020. Under such political pressure, the Office of Treaty Settlements often takes shortcuts and makes up policy on the hoof.[16] Lands administered by the Department of Conservation, which make up one third of the country's lands, are not generally available, and public access and recreation is guaranteed if any of these lands are included in settlements.[17] Lands that the Crown has sold and continues to sell to individuals or companies are referred to as 'private' and are not available, and the Crown will continue to sell land regardless of whether negotiations are taking place for its return.[18] Natural resources including minerals, seas, water, airways, foreshore and seabed, and flora and fauna are not available.[19] In order to receive any proceeds of a settlement, iwi must reorganise themselves as Pākehā corporate structures referred to as 'post-settlement governance entities', which are then subject to Pākehā law rather than to tikanga.[20] The proceeds are then transferred to that body rather than to the whānau and hapū from whom they were stolen.[21] And the Doctrine of Discovery and its imperative to assimilate Māori underpin and inform settlements, not te Tiriti o Waitangi.[22]

The Cabinet papers and memoranda also show that if claimants remain in the Tribunal seeking binding recommendations, they face lengthy and costly delays as the Crown fights to stop them recovering potentially large tracts of their lands along with compensation.[23] We have been fighting through the Tribunal, the courts and, more recently, the United Nations[24] for more than thirty years for binding recommendations.[25] To date, no one has succeeded although there are now several decisions from the courts that have ordered the Tribunal to make binding recommendations despite the ongoing obstruction by the Crown.[26]

Claimant Experiences of Direct Negotiations

Interviews were conducted with more than 150 claimants and negotiators between 2015 and 2020[27] about the way the Crown implements its Treaty claims settlement policy. These interviews provide more detail and explanations about the experiences of claimants and negotiators that resulted in them making applications to the Tribunal and submissions to both the Justice and Law Reform and the Māori Affairs select committees.[28] They provide unequivocal evidence that the Crown is unprincipled and appears oblivious to and uncaring of the damage it causes. One negotiator described the Treaty claims settlement process as "the most dishonourable process" and "managed chaos".[29] Overall, the process has traumatised claimants, divided their communities and delivered, on average, less than 1 per cent of what was stolen.[30] Claimants know that despite what settlement legislation may say, the settlements are not full, not fair and not final and that, like all previous settlements, they will be revisited.[31]

While every hapū and iwi has its own story to tell of its experiences, common themes are apparent. These include that:

- The Crown predetermines redress before 'negotiations' commence.[32]
- The Crown adopts divide-and-rule tactics and pursues them ruthlessly.[33]
- Claimant negotiators report that the divisions and conflict caused will take generations to repair and heal.[34]
- The Crown requires negotiations to be conducted confidentially. This puts negotiators under enormous pressure from their own people who demand openness and honesty in all matters.[35]
- Negotiators report that there is no negotiation; the Crown dictates.[36]
- Public servants and ministers frequently mislead claimants and misrepresent facts to entice claimants into negotiations and then drive settlements through,[37] which has resulted in accusations of fraud.[38]
- Deeds of settlement are lengthy, dense legal documents that obscure numerous undisclosed conditions imposed by public servants, including the removal of rights.[39]
- Public servants fully exploit the gross inequality between the Crown with its endless resources and the material poverty of claimants, often running claimants into the ground financially to impose a 'settlement'.[40]
- Negotiators frequently report being bullied by public servants and Crown agents, and many report having settled under duress. As a result, many do not accept Crown apologies as they are meaningless.[41]
- The Crown will sell the land of one hapū to neighbouring iwi corporations to punish those who refuse to submit to Crown demands, fomenting further division and bitterness.[42]
- The Crown refuses to recognise or uphold mana and tino rangatiratanga in negotiations or in settlements and refuses to discuss the settlement of colonisation.
- Many report the Crown refusing to discuss Waitangi Tribunal reports upholding their claims.[43]
- International standards New Zealand has agreed to, such as the United Nations Declaration on the Rights of Indigenous Peoples, are banned from both negotiations and settlements.[44]

The Waitangi Tribunal on Treaty Claims Settlements

In our search for justice and fairer remedies, claimants often seek help from the Tribunal.[45] The sheer number of applications for urgency in respect of pending settlements has meant that the Tribunal most often declines to hear them.[46] Dealing with those it did have capacity to inquire into became an important part of the Tribunal's caseload.[47] Reports have been issued on twenty-six applications although many other reports comment on settlement practices.

The Tribunal is reluctant to intervene in settlements.[48] Its reports on historical inquiries provide irrefutable evidence of many of the atrocities committed against Māori by the Crown and make hundreds of recommendations on the remedial actions required to recognise and affirm tino rangatiratanga in respect of our lands, resources and the well-being of our people. While Māori appreciate the truth finally being told and report learning a great deal that they did not know about themselves and about the Crown, the Crown refuses to consider almost all the recommendations, focusing instead on extinguishing the claims so that their recidivism against Māori can continue unimpeded. The Crown fully exploits the lack of protection for Māori in the current constitutional arrangements and simply refuses to uphold Māori land rights.[49] For claimants, it is counter-intuitive that the convicted criminal dictates how the crimes are to be remediated, and we look to the Tribunal for support in preventing ongoing Crown violations of te Tiriti. The Tribunal has "exclusive authority to determine the meaning and effect of the Treaty",[50] but at the outset it wrongly assumed that Māori ceded sovereignty to the Crown[51] and that, therefore, the Crown could determine whether and how it would address our Treaty grievances. This misapprehension tainted some of the Tribunal's decisions so that initially, at least, they erred on the side of the Crown.[52] The 2014 report on He Whakaputanga o te Rangatiratanga o Nu Tireni and te Tiriti o Waitangi clarified that we did not cede sovereignty.[53]

Despite its reluctance to intervene in settlements, the Tribunal has found itself repeatedly admonishing the Crown for its unfair, unreasonable and unjust behaviour, providing claimants with some relief and support that many found helpful.[54] The Tribunal constantly reminded the Crown of its obligations to adhere to Treaty principles. Over the decades, the Crown has repeatedly ignored that advice, which has led to the Tribunal's reports becoming increasingly critical of the Crown. By 2020, it was clear that the Tribunal was exasperated with the Crown's recidivist behaviour. In its *Hauraki Settlement Overlapping Claims Inquiry Report*, the Tribunal castigated the Crown at length concluding, "If the Crown is to avoid continuous litigation, adverse Tribunal findings, and delays to its settlement programme, it is high time for it to act on those previous Tribunal recommendations as well as these ones."[55]

The Tribunal identified the major issues impacting the settlement process as mandate, overlapping/cross-claims and the settlements themselves, and where the settlement process has failed, remedies. It classified the inquiries accordingly. There are eight mandate reports, four overlapping/cross-claims reports, eight settlement reports and six remedies reports although each of these often includes reference to the other issues, and many other reports reference these issues relating to the settlement process.

Settlement Process Issues

Mandate

The mandate problem arises because the Crown insists on negotiating with 'large natural groupings' and 'picking favourites'[56] while it eschews tikanga, denies the tino rangatiratanga of hapū and fails to prioritise Māori legal traditions.[57] The Crown's 'large natural groupings' policy requires all the claimants in a Crown-determined geographic area to work towards a single settlement that extinguishes all their claims. The Tribunal endorses this policy in many of its mandate reports because of the strong whakapapa ties and whanaungatanga between many of the groupings. For the Crown, the policy is a convenient tool for extinguishing as many claims as possible within a single settlement.

In 'picking favourites' the Crown recognises the mandate and enters negotiations with those most likely to deliver a settlement that suits the Crown. The individuals involved often have long-established relationships with ministers or government agencies or work for the Crown.[58] Representatives mandated by claimant groups often struggle to gain Crown recognition of their mandate when challenged by 'favourites'. Many claimants are excluded from the negotiations and lose control of their claims as the Crown lists them in the deed of settlement as extinguished when they have not been addressed, leading claimants to apply to the Tribunal for relief. The group whose mandate is recognised by the Crown must then establish a government-approved post-settlement governance entity that prioritises Pākehā governmental political, economic, social and cultural requirements over whānau and hapū realities.[59]

In the 1992 Fisheries Settlement, the Tribunal struggled to address the mandate issues and ended up siding with the negotiators and the Crown.[60] However, its approach changed over the following decades as it gave greater weight to the tino rangatiratanga of hapū and their right to determine who should represent them.[61]

The Tribunal's mandate urgency reports include:

- the three Te Arawa mandate reports of 2004, 2005 and 2007;

- *The Ngāpuhi Mandate Inquiry Report* of 2015;
- *The Ngātiwai Mandate Report* of 2017;
- *The Whakatōhea Mandate Inquiry Report* of 2018;
- *The Mana Ahuriri Mandate Report* 2020; and
- *The Maniapoto Mandate Inquiry Report* of 2020.

Several other settlement-related reports and decisions dealt with mandate issues, including *The Pakakohi and Tangahoe Settlement Claims Report* of 2000, *The East Coast Settlement Report* of 2010 and the *Decision of the Tribunal* in 2021 in the urgent claims of Wairarapa Moana ki Pouākani Incorporation, Ngāi Tūmupūhia-ā-Rangi hapū and Rangitāne Tū Mai Rā Trust.

Overlapping claims/cross-claims

Disputes arise with overlapping or shared interests because the English cultural land tenure notions of exclusive ownership that the Crown imposes are incompatible with mana whenua, kaitiakitanga and the tikanga by which hapū and iwi share common interests between our territories. Crown settlements use legislation to reduce the absolute and paramount power and authority of mana whenua to government-determined titles and to restrictive rights that mean Pākehā governmental bodies may consult with us about certain matters relating to our own ancestral lands instead of ignoring us. The legislation extinguishes mana whenua claims to our ancestral territories. In doing so, the Crown rekindles old animosities and actively fuels them, damaging kin-based relationships, creating divisions and retraumatising claimants.

The Tribunal receives numerous urgent applications to intervene in proposed settlements that threaten the delicate balance between neighbouring hapū and iwi. Most are declined. The cross-claims or overlapping claims reported on include:

- *The Ngāti Maniapoto/Ngāti Tama Settlement Cross-Claims Report* of 2001;
- *The Ngāti Awa Settlement Cross-Claims Report* of 2002;
- *The Ngāti Tūwharetoa ki Kawerau Settlement Cross-Claim Report* of 2003; and
- *The Hauraki Settlement Overlapping Claims Inquiry Report* of 2020.

Settlement Reports

The settlement reports include:

- *The Fisheries Settlement Report* 1992;
- *The Pakakohi and Tangahoe Settlement Claims Report* 2000;

- *The Tāmaki Makaurau Settlement Process Report* 2007;
- *The East Coast Settlement Report* 2010;
- *Te Aroha Maunga Settlement Process Report* 2014; and
- *The Priority Report on the Whakatōhea Settlement Process* 2021.

The Tribunal's decision concerning Treaty settlement with Ngāti Kahungunu ki Wairarapa Tāmaki nui-a-Rua and the trustees of the Ngāti Kahungunu ki Wairarapa Tāmaki nui-a-Rua Settlement Trust 2021 is covered in the remedies section.

Issues that arose repeatedly in claims against settlements included the Crown's refusal to adhere to the Treaty guarantee of tino rangatiratanga and its callous disregard for the fresh grievances it keeps creating as it imposes settlements. In the *Fisheries* report, the Tribunal considered it wrong that Treaty-based fishing rights would be extinguished. The Crown ignored the recommendation that there be a twenty-five-year moratorium on Māori fishing claims rather than extinguishing them completely.[62] Fifteen years of harrowing litigation and legal carnage followed.[63] Māori did eventually take control of some fishing quota and grew the settlement so that Māori now have a significant presence in commercial fishing[64] even though the traditional whānau and hapū fishers who derived their living from trading their catches were driven out of the industry by rapacious commercial fishing companies. The *Pakakohi and Tangahoe* report, on the other hand, did not uphold the hapū claims that they not be included in the Ngāti Ruanui's settlement. In the *Tāmaki Makaurau* report the Tribunal severely criticised and rebuked the Office of Treaty Settlements, noting that it had addressed the same questions relating to the unfairness and divisiveness of the settlement process several times in previous reports. The Tribunal asked, "If these problems keep arising, and are indeed getting worse, is there really something fundamentally wrong with the way Treaty claims are being settled?"[65] By 2010, for Te Tairāwhiti (East Coast), the Tribunal was still trying to persuade the Office of Treaty Settlements to correct the flaws in its processes, in particular, that it reveal the full list of claims it would extinguish in the settlement before voting on the mandate took place so that claimants would know that the Crown had taken control of their claims and was about to extinguish them.[66] However, it largely supported the Crown in not recommending that at least part of Te Aroha Maunga be vested in Ngāti Rāhiri Tumutumu in the *Te Aroha Maunga* report, despite the strong resistance to and the long and painful mandate issues that arose from the Crown shoehorning twelve iwi of Hauraki into a single entity.[67] In the *Whakatōhea Settlement* report, the Tribunal found that the Crown's condition – that Whakatōhea's claims could only be heard as part of the North-Eastern Bay of Plenty Inquiry if the Tribunal did not make findings or recommendations on Whakatōhea's historical claims – was not fair or reasonable and that the Crown fell short of Treaty compliance in not allowing hapū to withdraw from the settlement.[68] Once again, the Crown ignored the findings and recommendations and, instead, extinguished all Whakatōhea claims, passing legislation in 2024. It continued to deny the tino rangatiratanga of those who fought to stop their claims being extinguished, including those of the iwi Ūpokorehe and the whānau Mokomoko.[69]

Remedies/Binding Recommendations

The Crown's Treaty settlement policy requires the Office of Treaty Settlements to redirect potential and successful applicants away from seeking binding recommendations. Binding recommendations are the alternative to government settlements. They do not extinguish claims and do not allow the Crown to dictate to Māori. As such, they enhance our tino rangatiratanga in respect of both our lands and the well-being of our people.[70] For many years, governments have relied on the lack of constitutional protection for Māori to threaten to remove the Tribunal's powers to make orders or to abolish it if it ever used binding recommendations,[71] which is a serious violation of the rule of law.
The seven remedies reports considered here are:

- *Muriwhenua Land Report* 1997;
- *The Ngāti Kahu Remedies Report* 2013;
- *The Mangatū Remedies Report* 2014 ;
- *The Mangatū Remedies Report 2021;*
- *Te Whanganui-a-Orotu Report on Remedies* 1998;
- *The Turangi Township Remedies Report* 1998; and
- Wairarapa Moana ki Pouākani 2022.

Despite the threats to the Tribunal, it indicated in its 1997 *Muriwhenua Land Report* on the pre-1865 claims of Ngāti Kahu, Te Rarawa, Ngāi Takoto, Te Aupōuri and Ngāti Kurī of Te Hiku o Te Ika (the Far North) "that recommendations would be appropriate, and binding recommendations if need be"[72] should negotiations for a settlement fail. The Minister of Treaty Negotiations, Doug Graham, was furious and told the claimants he would abolish the Tribunal if we sought binding recommendations. His successor,

Margaret Wilson, did the same.[73] The Office of Treaty Settlements was adamant that claimants could not apply for binding recommendations, disingenuously declaring "they do not exist" and refusing to discuss them.[74]

Ngāti Kahu returned to the Tribunal several times after negotiations failed repeatedly.[75] Initially, like many others, we were denied a hearing. The other four iwi of Muriwhenua finally accepted Crown settlements fifteen years after the release of the *Muriwhenua* report, while Ngāti Kahu continued its application for binding recommendations. When Mangatū Incorporation of Te Tairāwhiti (East Coast) was successful in having their decision denying them a hearing judicially reviewed, Ngāti Kahu followed and secured a hearing. However, the Tribunal deferred to Crown policy instead of adhering to its legislation and refused to make binding recommendations, telling Mangatū and Ngāti Kahu claimants to negotiate settlements instead.[76] Both Mangatū and Ngāti Kahu took the Tribunal to the High Court on judicial review, and both their remedies reports were quashed. The Tribunal was ordered to reconsider the applications and "to make an adjudicatory recommendation", if the statutory prerequisites for binding recommendations have been met, that either the land is ordered to be returned to Māori, or it is not.[77]

In 2021, the Tribunal released *The Mangatū Remedies Report*, making an interim recommendation for the return of all the Mangatū Crown forest licensed land and the payment of all available compensation to the claimants.[78] At the time of writing, some thirty-three years after the claims were first filed, the decision is progressing through yet another round of judicial review before the appellate courts.[79] For Ngāti Kahu, the Muriwhenua claims had only been heard and reported on to 1865. The Tribunal decided to complete the inquiry to the present day before making the binding recommendations first indicated in 1997. At the time of writing in 2025, forty-one years after the Ngāti Kahu claims were first filed, research for the inquiry is still being completed.

In July 1998, sixteen months after the *Muriwhenua* report and two years after negotiations between Ngāti Tūrangitukua and the Crown had broken down, the Tribunal released *The Turangi Township Remedies Report* on Ngāti Tūrangitukua's application in respect of the township. This was the first application for binding recommendations where the Tribunal ordered not only the return of land but also the amount of compensation to be paid. In the event, Ngāti Tūrangitukua and the Crown negotiated a settlement within the ninety-day period allowed before the Tribunal's decision would have become binding, and a deed of settlement was signed in September 1998.[80]

However, two months before *The Turangi Township Remedies Report* was issued, seven mana whenua hapū of Te Whanganui-a-Orotu (Ahuriri Lagoon or the Napier Inner Harbour) were denied binding recommendations.[81] Instead, the Tribunal deferred to the Crown's settlement policy and told the claimants to negotiate for the return of their lands. For the very few who have succeeded in having their applications for binding recommendations heard, including Mangatū and Ngāti Kahu, the result was the same until the Court of Appeal intervened in 2016.[82] Since then, the Tribunal has indicated it will make binding recommendations for Mangatū and for Wairarapa Moana ki Pouākani Incorporation.

Wairarapa Moana ki Pouākani

In 2022, when the government exploited the lack of constitutional protection for Māori to legislate the extinguishment of Wairarapa Moana ki Pouākani's claim to their lands, the United Nations intervened.[83] The Crown knew the Wairarapa Moana ki Pouākani Incorporation had the legal right to recover its lands that the Crown had confiscated as a site for the Maraetai Power Station in 1949 using the Public Works Act. The land and station are now owned and operated by Mercury NZ Ltd, a state-owned enterprise. The land is therefore subject to binding recommendations; Wairarapa Moana had applied for them in 2017, and in 2020, the Tribunal indicated it would make the recommendations.

The Crown also knew when it signed a deed of settlement with Ngāti Kahungunu ki Wairarapa Tāmaki nui-a-Rua Settlement Trust in 2021 to extinguish the Wairarapa Moana claim to its lands at Pouākani that the trust did not have a mandate to do so. Wairarapa Moana had made it very clear when it applied for binding recommendations that its claim was not to be included in any settlement. The Tribunal's 2020 preliminary determination said it "should make binding recommendations for the return ... of all the land titles ... [and] for the payment of compensation ...".[84] In 2010, the Tribunal upheld Wairarapa Moana's claims to the Pouākani lands having fully considered the fact that the Pouākani lands are in Ngāti Raukawa's and Ngāti Tūwharetoa's territories, but Wairarapa Moana claimants are Ngāti Kahungunu from further south in Wairarapa.[85]

In October 2021, the Crown signed the deed of settlement with Ngāti Kahungunu ki Wairarapa Tāmaki nui-a-Rua and the trustees of Ngāti Kahungunu ki Wairarapa Tāmaki nui-a-Rua Settlement Trust that extinguished all the claims to the Pouākani lands without returning or compensating for them.[86]

In November 2021, the Tribunal issued findings that the trust did not have a mandate to settle the claims to those lands.[87] On 7 December 2022, the Supreme Court confirmed the Tribunal's decision to make binding recommendations.[88] On 12 December 2022, the Tribunal issued a memorandum indicating that it would finalise its binding recommendations.[89] The next day, the government passed the Ngāti Kahungunu ki Wairarapa Tāmaki nui-a-Rua Claims Settlement Act forcing a settlement on Wairarapa Moana against their wishes, extinguishing the Wairarapa Moana claim to its Pouākani lands, removing the Tribunal's power to make the binding recommendations, nullifying the Supreme Court's decision and stripping Wairarapa Moana of their legal and human rights. Despite the best efforts of the Tribunal and the Supreme Court to ensure that the rights were not violated, the Crown simply annihilated them.

The Human Rights Commission expressed its utmost concern saying, "Such action is abhorrent to the rule of law, fundamental human rights and Indigenous Peoples' rights under the UN Declaration on the Rights of Indigenous Peoples."[90] Wairarapa Moana took the matter to the United Nations. Three Special Rapporteurs intervened, issuing the government a 'please explain'.[91] The Crown responded disingenuously, effectively dismissing their well-founded concerns, justifying its behaviour by providing its Treaty claims settlement policy and its version of Wairarapa Moana's Pouākani claim.[92] Wairarapa Moana is continuing to pursue the matter through the New Zealand courts.[93]

Solutions – Constitutional Transformation

Treaty claims extinguishments through government-imposed settlements and the inevitable fallout from them are a direct result of the ongoing application of the myths that have grown out of the Doctrine of Discovery. Māori leaders have always been outspoken about their refusal to accept the resulting colonisation and its illegitimate power structures. When the government established the Waitangi Tribunal to divert attention away from Māori anger and protest, the evidence produced unravelled the carefully woven myths, including the lie that Māori had ceded sovereignty to the British Crown. Yet still the Crown refused to mend its ways and honour He Whakaputanga and te Tiriti. When they confiscated the country's foreshore and seabed from Māori in 2004 in the face of Māori and significant non-Māori outrage, the chairpersons of thirty iwi established the National Iwi Chairs Forum. The forum has since grown to eighty-four members. It picked up the call to revisit the country's constitutional arrangements that had been discussed in Māori gatherings for several decades.

Matike Mai Aotearoa – the Independent Working Group on Constitutional Transformation was established in 2010. Their 2016 report proposed six indicative constitutional models. The models follow on from the 2014 report of the Tribunal into He Whakaputanga and te Tiriti. They are based on tikanga, He Whakaputanga and te Tiriti and provide for Māori to exercise our mana and tino rangatiratanga, including our sovereignty in a 'sphere of influence' where Māori make decisions for Māori in accordance with our laws (tikanga) and for the Crown and its government to make decisions for its people in its own 'sphere of influence' in accordance with its 'rule of law'. The two spheres were called the rangatiratanga sphere and the kāwanatanga sphere. A third relational sphere appears in several of the models. It is where Māori and the Crown engage and make joint decisions. The report recommends further dialogue over the next five years to enable Māori to agree a model and instigate constitutional transformation. There has been widespread support for constitutional transformation among Māori and a significant number of non-Māori, including both Europeans and non-Europeans.

The first steps towards constitutional transformation started when the government adopted the United Nations Declaration on the Rights of Indigenous Peoples in 2010. It was slow to follow up on its undertaking. In 2014, the National Iwi Chairs Forum established the Aotearoa Independent Monitoring Mechanism, which works closely with the Human Rights Commission. The Monitoring Mechanism's overarching priority is constitutional transformation. Five years later, the government agreed to work with the Monitoring Mechanism and the Human Rights Commission to draft a National Plan of Action to implement the Declaration.[94]

In 2022, the government withdrew as it came under attack from those intent on preserving the Doctrine of Discovery.[95] The right-wing government elected in 2023 launched a legislative and policy programme to strip Māori of our legal, Treaty and human rights won over the past fifty years and to replace te Tiriti o Waitangi.[96] It included stripping the Tribunal of its powers.[97] In 2024, the Tribunal issued six strongly worded urgent inquiry reports criticising the government's serious breaches of te Tiriti.[98] Māori united to protect ourselves from the onslaught, calling on non-Māori for support. Local, regional and national hui were convened that attracted tens of thousands. Events were organised that drew significant international attention, including the largest protest march the country has ever seen.[99] Working towards constitutional transformation took on a greater urgency as Māori and Tangata Tiriti (non-

Māori who support te Tiriti) joined forces to ensure that te Tiriti o Waitangi was not annihilated and that its promise that Māori and non-Māori can live together in peace, harmony and prosperity remained the constitutional bedrock of Aotearoa New Zealand. A working group was established in 2024 to develop proposals for the rangatiratanga sphere for consideration by whānau, hapū, iwi and other Māori groups.[100] In 2022, the Tribunal had embarked on its Constitutional Kaupapa Inquiry and has since hosted a series of wānanga around the country to help design, along with the claimants and the Crown, its process for the inquiry.[101]

Conclusion

While the current Treaty claims settlements do not remove the prejudice caused by British colonisation, they have resulted in at least a small number of hapū and iwi being able to start recovering an economic base. That has enabled us to start organising to take back control of our lives. We first sought help from the United Nations about the Treaty claims settlement process in 1992 over the Fisheries Settlement.[102] We've been back many times since then, and a range of United Nations treaty bodies as well as Special Rapporteurs and the General Assembly have urged the government to take greater heed of the Waitangi Tribunal and reach agreement with us on how our claims are to be settled.[103] But the primary interest of New Zealand governments is to preserve the power, wealth and prosperity of Pākehā that many New Zealanders take for granted. They labour under the misapprehension that returning stolen lands and resources, recognising tino rangatiratanga and settling colonisation is a threat to Pākehā comfort, privilege and entitlement. The true intent of the Treaty claims settlement policy was to remove that threat, and it has remained unchanged for thirty years.

The Waitangi Tribunal has found the Crown guilty of thousands of breaches of the principles of te Tiriti and played a leading role in correcting the country's history. It strongly supports the settlement of well-founded claims but has struggled to convince governments to adhere to their Treaty obligations when settling those claims. For a very brief period in 2007 and 2008, the government demonstrated that it could model integrity and respect for the Tribunal when it temporarily abandoned its policy and accepted the recommendation that the claimants design the Central North Island forests settlement.[104] The key ingredient for the Crown was a principled and honourable Minister of Treaty Negotiations who had the integrity to bypass the Office of

Treaty Settlements bureaucrats.[105] That was lost when the government changed, and the bureaucrats regained control.

While mandating, overlapping claims and the settlements themselves have been the most common issues the Tribunal has dealt with relating to the settlement process, the most intense and long-running battle has been over binding recommendations. For several years, as governments threatened its existence, the Tribunal would not hear applications, and then when it did, it refused to make the recommendations. The courts intervened, and since 2016, the Tribunal has fought valiantly to uphold our legal rights to recover our lands only to witness the government exploit our lack of constitutional protection and legislate the last-minute extinguishment of a claim to stop the Tribunal making the orders.

As poverty, deprivation and marginalisation continue to be the reality for most Māori, many defy governments they deem illegitimate and, where they can, return to their cultural and ancestral roots to exercise their mana and tino rangatiratanga under the tikanga they inherited from their ancestors. Formal acknowledgement of this reality and the political will to restore the peace and balance that colonisation destroyed is long overdue. It will not be achieved under the current government Treaty claims settlement process. The solution is constitutional transformation that entrenches He Whakaputanga and te Tiriti and delivers on our rights articulated in the United Nations Declaration on the Rights of Indigenous Peoples.

“I had seen, as we all had, examples of claims where, by the time an inquiry got to report and then to negotiations, the group of lead claimants and lead witnesses were all dead. What sort of intergenerational truth and reconciliation was that?”

Chapter 9

The Tribunal in the Settlement Era

Hon Justice Sir Joe Williams

(Interviewed by Carwyn Jones)

CJ: Let me begin by asking, what do you consider to be the most significant developments for the Tribunal during your time as chairperson?

JW: I think a perspective I brought to my role as chairperson, as a young chairperson, was that of being counsel for Treaty claims and of belonging to the first generation of Treaty-literate Treaty lawyers. There were many of us, but I was one of them. I'd seen the Tribunal from the other side of the bar, as it were. This was a time when historical Treaty settlements were really ramping up. The next decade and a half, probably the next two decades, after I moved in, in 2000, was the period where historical Treaty claims were the bread and butter of the Tribunal.

The changes that I tried to bring in were structural and procedural, primarily, bearing in mind that during my time as chairperson the role of the Tribunal was going to be a truth and reconciliation forum for the resolution of historical Treaty claims, by and large. So, you needed a certain degree of discipline in the inquiry process. You needed pretty good coordination across the sector so that there was enough funding to do the work, and the work was focused on the right issues. We needed to move into a new role as a kind of Treaty settlements ombudsman.

Each of those things required a raft of innovations. The first one – disciplining the historical inquiry process – led to the introduction of what was called the new approach. This was a way of getting both Crown and claimant counsel focused on what the issues were and running an inquiry on the basis of adequacy of evidence in a way that was as efficient as it could be without losing its human spirit. That's always hard. The Tribunal had always had a culture of everyone comes in, write us a letter, you've got a claim. But when you're doing inquiries covering dozens, if not more, of claims across an entire district where the claimant communities numbered tens of thousands, you needed some degree of structure and shape, otherwise an inquiry like that would just go on and on and perhaps never stop.

So, we introduced the new approach, which was a process that would resolve the issues that needed to be addressed, the statement of issues and the Crown statement of response, and that would give counsel and the witnesses a sense of the approach that we would take to the report.

We would have a series of conferences that tried to organise claimant communities and structure the inquiries in a way that meant it didn't take ten years to hear an inquiry, but it could be done in maybe eighteen months. It was a big shift. The problem with the old system was that all of the incentives, particularly the funding incentives, were against that level of discipline.

Introducing the new approach meant the hearings weren't interminable. I had seen, as we all had, examples of claims where, by the time an inquiry got to report and then to negotiations, the group of lead claimants and lead witnesses were all dead. What sort of intergenerational truth and reconciliation was that? Really, it couldn't work. It was bad.

So, my aim was practical and somewhat emotional – to run claims in a way that the people who started the claim with you were still alive when you were in negotiations with the Crown, and to encourage negotiations wherever you could. You disciplined the inquiry process and the hearings process, and you encouraged coalescing of claimant groups. You discouraged conflict as much as you could in order to get to a point where you weren't dealing with the children of the claimants when you got to the production of a report.

CJ: How did you find that approach worked?

JW: The Gisborne inquiry was the first one I chaired, and it was a brilliant inquiry to test-drive this on, and it worked pretty well there. It still took us a while to produce the report, but the hearings were done relatively quickly with agreement of all the parties. At the end of the report, we gave some recommendations about how we thought the negotiations should run and how the carve-up should work, which hurt a few of the claimants. But it put a stake in the ground that gave some structure to the discussions so that the next stage didn't involve more bloodletting, because the next stage – negotiation – is always the most difficult. They settled relatively effectively and relatively quickly compared with examples from the 1990s.

Next, we set up a stakeholders' group with the Crown Forestry Rental Trust and the Office of Treaty Settlements. This raised some eyebrows, but I thought it was really important, for the sake of getting people to settlement in as painless and as time-efficient a way as possible, that the people who ran the money, the Crown (as respondent in all claims) and the inquirer reached common understandings about process and the order of priority. This enabled the structural issues involved in a once-in-a-generation process of truth and reconciliation to be talked about and planned for in an open, transparent and accountable way. It also showed up disconnections or dissonance in the approaches of the different bodies. Sometimes these could be resolved; sometimes they couldn't.

These, to me, were structural problems. They weren't problems that should be resolved claim by claim. They were big infrastructural problems that should be thought about in an infrastructural way. The Office of Treaty Settlements and the Crown Forestry Rental Trust were pleased to be involved – the Crown Forestry Rental Trust as the primary funder, and the Office of Treaty Settlements as the single defendant.

On the Tribunal, we had superb members and staff – people like Brian Corban and Margaret Bazley, the lay people, kaumātua like Tuahine Northover, Wharehuia Milroy, Keita Walker, superb judges who sat on that group with me, historians like Dr Ann Parsonson and Dr Robyn Anderson and staff like Dr Grant Phillipson, Dr Paul Hamer and Dr Richard Moorsom. I got a sense, both within the Tribunal itself and in this sector-wide discussion group that we set up, that people agreed we were in this together for a just outcome. And I was really pleased about that.

Incidentally, we also set up a governance group in the Tribunal itself, with members of the Tribunal and members of staff. We had monthly board meetings, which were great because they brought up issues that were structural in nature that could be discussed.

So, there were three large structural changes – the new approach, the governance group and the stakeholders' group. Those were useful innovations because, it has to be remembered, we were in this decade-and-a-half process – it was like a tuna swallowing a possum – of trying to get through this huge lump of historical Treaty claims that were changing claimant communities. The process itself was changing the communities; the focusing of the Crown Forestry Rental Trust, the Office of Treaty Settlements and the Tribunal, the pumping in of funds and the energy and expectations were having impacts – sometimes good, sometimes not so good – on claimant communities. I felt we should tread as lightly and as encouragingly as we could, and to do that we needed to think structurally about what we were doing. So, that's probably what I would say were the most significant developments in my time.

CJ: You've talked about the historical inquiries during this period and also needing to take on a role of monitoring the settlement process. The settlement process was still relatively young when you became chairperson, but it was picking up speed quickly.

JW: That was largely because of the work Eddie Durie and his Tribunal and staff had done in terms of Rangahaua Whānui, his series of research reports under Alan Ward's leadership, the creation of Tribunal capacity to research and write, and the experience of getting Ngāi Tahu and Tainui claims to settlement in that mid to late 1990s period.

By the time I came to take over, those basic ingredients had already been set up. I think you can see from the way that I'm describing what I did that I was very much fine-tuning and learning from experience about the need to coordinate in a more transparent, open and thoughtful way, within the organisation and between the organisation and other players and in the inquiry process with lawyers and communities. But all of it built on foundations set up by Eddie, Gordon Orr and others.

The third element, the negotiation ombudsman, if you like, was quite an important role, and it could be deployed with great effectiveness, as Carrie Wainwright's report on settlement negotiations in Tāmaki shows, but there were lots of others. Mandate and process errors, those sorts of things where the Tribunal could be deployed to hear a matter and then give an answer relatively quickly or bring the parties back together was an inevitable role; there was nowhere else. Sometimes claimants went to court, but mostly those who were unhappy with what was happening came to the Tribunal. The Tribunal being a kind of inside outsider, in the sense that there were Māori members who were pretty familiar with the claims process from a client point of view, meant that it really added value in giving an opportunity for those matters to be aired and finding ways to encourage parties to come together. This was particularly so where claimant groups and subgroups were in conflict with one another, which is how this often played out. It didn't always succeed, but it was a place to go, and you always got a thoughtful response from the Tribunal. I've always thought this third element was really important.

CJ: Would you say that the flexibility of the Tribunal process also contributed to the way the Tribunal was able to respond?

JW: Absolutely because the Tribunal is an inquisitor, the commission of inquiry rather than a court. It's just much lighter on its feet and much wiser and knowing about these issues than were the mainstream courts. You can see that in the different way the Tribunal dealt with issues compared with the way the courts tended to deal with similar issues.

CJ: Were there particular challenges for the Tribunal during that time?

JW: There were lots of challenges. There always are, of course, but the real challenge was to respond structurally and thoughtfully to the challenge of the time, which was how do we get through this? Carrying out the necessities of truth and reconciliation without killing the patient in the process was the biggest challenge. By and large, the Tribunal did okay. It wasn't perfect at all, but it was better than any other model I've seen.

CJ: Being a commission of inquiry and having some flexibility and control over your own process is really helpful in that respect. I was also thinking about the membership of the Tribunal. You talked earlier about how important it was having those good people around you in those governance spaces and settings. You've also got a body that is Māori and Pākehā, and you've got a mix of backgrounds and experience. Is that also an important factor in terms of why the Tribunal has been able to respond in the way it has?

JW: Absolutely. It's the great secret of the Tribunal that it's a mix of Māori and Pākehā and others now too. But not just any Māori and Pākehā. The Māori are people of mana, and the Pākehā are people of mana. Historians and people from the business community were often appointed. We had the president of Federated Farmers, and we had the chairperson of the National Bank, former National Speaker of Parliament, former Minister of Māori Affairs and Minister of Fisheries, and, by and large, they were brilliant. They ended up, in my experience, being more radical than the Māori. Being exposed, for many of them for the first time, to te ao Māori and the love of te ao Māori for the Tribunal, those members, including members in my time, were often really moved by that – the generosity of spirit that claimant communities brought to this, an oppressed people brought to this, because of the trust they reposed in the Tribunal. And the funny thing was, they loved the Pākehā on the Tribunal as much as they loved the Māori. They knew the Māori, and they saw themselves in the Māori, but I think they felt that their mana was enhanced by the fact that these important Pākehā cared enough to sit and listen to their stories, to their histories and to their pain. The bicultural as well as bijural nature of the Tribunal was its absolute magic, and it still is.

CJ: Were there particular inquiries you were involved with that really stood out for you as a Tribunal member or as counsel? And are there things in recommendations and reports that you think would be useful to revisit and explore and develop further?

JW: Every inquiry that I acted on as a lawyer or sat on as a judge felt really important. I know that sounds a bit of a cliché, but it's true. Certainly, I acted in many claims; a lot of them were historical, but not all of them. I acted in the wānanga claim, and in the urban Māori authorities claim, the Waipareira claim, as well as the Te Roroa Māori claim, my first one, which was very controversial, the Muriwhenua land claim, which was mind-bendingly difficult, the Tauranga raupatu claim, and the Hauraki claim. I often said that I had more claims on my books than Crown Law did.

It would be unfair to single any of those out as more powerful or more important than the others because they were all unbelievably impactful on me. And I'm not just saying that. I still remember the individuals who were involved and what I learned from them. The young people involved in the claims for their communities, the young energetic people who were doing the running around, and the witnesses, the kaumātua and historical witnesses, in particular, every single one of those people taught me life-changing lessons. Actually, it's really quite difficult to say this one was more significant than that one because these people still live on in me in quite powerful and impactful ways.

And that's true also in my time as a judge presiding over claims where you don't get as close, obviously, as you do when you're working with claimants as your clients. When working with claimants as your clients, more often than I can remember, I was moved to tears by the resilience, strength and optimism of people for whom resilience, strength and optimism were thoroughly unjustified. They're superhumans, really, in many ways – a generation above me, two generations in some cases – amazing people.

When I came to the Tribunal, that relationship with claimant communities, by necessity, had to be a little more distant. But even then, I can't really pick between the Gisborne inquiry, which was my big historical inquiry, the Wai 262 inquiry that I had to pick up after the presiding officer passed away, and the petroleum inquiry and various other things that I did as chairperson.

There were some small claims, like the one mandate claim I did. It was relatively small, maybe a week of hearings, maybe two weeks of hearings, and then a report. And still, it's incredibly important to the people involved, life changing for the people involved, however this was to turn out. I was always struck with a sense of fear and the privilege of being in that position where you see whole communities sitting there on the edge of their seats waiting for you to do something that fixes this problem, whatever it might have been. It's litigation, of course, but it's litigation like no other. It's kind of a cross between the Canterbury Earthquakes Royal Commission of inquiry and ordinary litigation. Whole communities are sitting there, their lives, their sense of well-being and healing hanging in the balance while you try to do your best to find wisdom with the mess that's been handed up to you. They were all incredibly important in their own way, and that was the great privilege of being on the Tribunal. It was the most important work I ever did, really, and will be the most important work I've ever done because of its impact not just on individual lives but on the lives of whole communities and because of the sense of hope that it could engender if it was done well.

I think my abiding memories of my time on the Tribunal are those of communities searching for a path and hoping that somehow this big, cumbersome process might provide such a path. Sometimes it did, and sometimes it didn't because it's such a complex, multifaceted, multi-community phenomenon. You weren't going to resolve everything every time, but the great gift of the Tribunal was that people felt a sense of trust in the ability of that institution to find the path. That sense of trust in the Tribunal did not happen overnight. It took years and years to build, and it's still there, of course. So, my abiding memory of the Tribunal will always be that deeper truth rather than any particular claim although every particular claim was life changing for me in some way.

CJ: What should the work of the Tribunal look like in the coming years?

JW: That's something I certainly strongly believe needs to be thought about very carefully. You can think about the Tribunal's work in phases. What really struck me about Eddie Durie's time on the Tribunal was how carefully he and others who worked with him, people like Gordon Orr, Manuhuia Bennett and a whole bunch of others, constructed a Tribunal for its time. The Tribunal became this big historical inquiry juggernaut because it had to be. That was the demand of the time.

The question is, as we watch that train disappearing round the bend, what is the demand over the next fifty years? What has changed in terms of the place of the Treaty and tikanga and te reo Māori in the life of the country, and what further contribution must the Tribunal make to that? Assuming that such a contribution is required, how should that look and how do we design it to meet the demands of that time? That, it seems to me, is going to be the great challenge for the Tribunal over the next little while, no matter who is in government.

We have to ask, what is the niche that is not being met? What is the need that is not being met? Because that's what Eddie Durie and that early Tribunal did. That's what I tried to do in the changes that I made in the early 2000s. Now that historical claims are nearly done and the whole structure of historical claims is set, what is the role for a permanent commission of inquiry into the place of the principles of the Treaty in the relationship of Crown and Māori? That's actually a very complex question that needs deep thought.

CJ: Did you have any thoughts you wanted to offer on that now?

JW: I think the Tribunal could do well to lean into its inquisitorial function a bit more now. I think the time of big juggernaut inquiries has passed. There is a great need out there for a kind of – and this is my phrase, it's not the right phrase – Treaty ombudsman for the little people who are dealing with government – the prisoners, the homeless, the people in mental health facilities, the people trying to deal with WINZ and Social Development, who need someone to go and say, this is not working, people are being treated inconsistently with Treaty principles, for whatever reason.

There are in the mainstream, I know this from my work as a judge, a lot of people for whom that would be life changing. It doesn't need a lawyer. It probably just needs an inquiry, an investigating officer producing a draft report, sending it to the relevant government department, getting a response, and then signing off a full three-member report, perhaps not even with a hearing, at least not always, to get short, sharp, Treaty-based advice from a whole-of-system perspective to government departments and institutions that need that help. No one's doing that. The Tribunal could be perfectly placed to help in that regard. For instance, where a hapū is having problems with the local authority over access, degradation of the environment, or being able to build homes in place A or place B, the Tribunal could be incredibly effective in just being an accountability spotlight on those things.

"Given that Māori are the kaitiaki of claim kaupapa, the potential effectiveness of a response may be maximised when Māori and the Crown empower Māori to lead the response."

Chapter 10

Taonga
Te Reo Māori and Mātauranga Māori

—*Jayden Houghton**

In te Tiriti o Waitangi, the Crown guaranteed that Māori would be able to exercise tino rangatiratanga (absolute sovereignty) over their taonga (tangible and intangible treasures). However, in recent decades, Māori have lodged various claims with the Waitangi Tribunal alleging that the Crown has breached those Treaty obligations. Some of those claims identified radio spectra, te reo Māori and mātauranga Māori (the body of knowledge originating from Māori ancestors, including the Māori world view and cultural practices) as taonga.

In those inquiries, the Tribunal generally found merit in the claimants' arguments and attempted to make recommendations to the Crown, which, if implemented, could help to ensure that the relevant taonga would be appropriately protected in accordance with te Tiriti. In some instances, the Crown rejected recommendations that appeared capable of improving protection for taonga and did little to respond to the Tribunal's inquiries. In other instances, the Crown has actively worked with Māori following a Tribunal inquiry to improve protection for taonga – though not necessarily in accordance with the Tribunal's recommendations.[1]

Writing on the Tribunal generally focuses on Tribunal findings, recommendations and settlements.[2] This chapter focuses on claims, inquiries and responses. It introduces the idea of a claim kaupapa, being a key thread of a Tribunal claim and inquiry. In state law, a claim kaupapa is essentially a remedy sought and the reasons for which it should be awarded. In tikanga Māori, a claim kaupapa is the utu sought to address a take (a breach of the Crown's obligations under te Tiriti) to progress towards ea.[3] A Tribunal claim usually has multiple claim kaupapa.

This chapter makes three arguments. First, it argues that a Tribunal inquiry supports a confluence of the political wills to reinforce claim kaupapa via two key functions:

1. Inquiries are bastions of claim kaupapa, which must be kept alive and beating for there to be an effective political response to the inquiry.
2. Inquiries are magnets for political will – they magnetise political will amenable to claim kaupapa around a centre and magnetise existing political will to align more closely with claim kaupapa. For example, inquiries may draw academic attention and research funding to the claim kaupapa[4] and be a vehicle for incorporating the claim kaupapa into teaching syllabi[5] and student scholarship.[6]

Secondly, the chapter argues that a Tribunal inquiry is most likely to lead to an effective response when the completion of the inquiry (the Tribunal's final report on the claim) coincides with a confluence of the political wills of Māori and the Crown to support the applicable claim kaupapa. Therefore, the Tribunal principally supports effective responses to claim kaupapa by completing robust inquiries, not in making useful recommendations (which may or may not be influential).

Coincidence may come in various forms. Sympathetic coincidence is where the political wills of Māori and the Crown were fairly aligned with the claim kaupapa during the inquiry such that the report immediately coincides with the confluence of the political wills to support the claim kaupapa.

Suspended coincidence is where one or both of Māori and the Crown have not declared their position on the claim kaupapa on the release of the report, but after some delay, there is a confluence of the political wills to support the claim kaupapa. Supervened coincidence is where one or both of Māori and the Crown opposed the claim kaupapa on the release of the report, but eventually, there is a confluence of the political wills to support the claim kaupapa. Superannuated coincidence (or settled incoincidence) is where there has been no confluence of the political wills to support the claim kaupapa, and, after some time, the report is no longer considered suitable for application in the political arena. Therefore, the horizon for suspended and supervened coincidences may not be indefinite.

Coincidence may be sustained or sporadic. Coincidence and its sustenance may be supported by stakeholders.

Thirdly, the chapter argues that the potential effectiveness of a response may be maximised when Māori and the Crown empower Māori to lead the response.

The chapter is in three substantive parts. Part 2 summarises four categories of taonga claims, and the Tribunal's recommendations with respect to each, concerning the protection, preservation and promotion of te reo Māori; the radio spectrum; flora and fauna taonga species; and taonga works, such as waiata (song), haka (ceremonial dance) and whakairo (carving), as well as works derived from these (taonga-derived works). Part 3 discusses the functions of inquiries and uses taonga case studies to demonstrate: first, that a Tribunal inquiry is most likely to lead to an effective response when the Tribunal's report coincides with a confluence of the political wills to support claim kaupapa; and, secondly, how a Tribunal inquiry supports the confluence of the political wills as bastions and magnets. Part 4 explains why the potential effectiveness of a response may be maximised when both Māori and the Crown empower Māori to lead the response.

Taonga Inquiries

Te reo Māori

In the century after 1840, the population of English-speaking settlers in Aotearoa New Zealand eclipsed the Māori population.[7] The concomitant decline of te reo Māori[8] would become the subject of three claims lodged in the Tribunal – Wai 11, Wai 262 and Wai 2336.

(a) WAI 11

The first (and perhaps most prominent) of the three claims was te reo Māori claim, which was lodged in 1984 by Ngā Kaiwhakapūmau i te Reo (Inc) (the Māori Language Board of Wellington) and its chairman, Huirangi Waikerepuru.[9] It addressed the critical state of te reo Māori. At the time, there were only around 50,000 fluent te reo Māori speakers (in a population of around 3,227,000), most of whom belonged to the older generation.[10] The number of speakers was continuing to decline despite the efforts of Māori to establish kōhanga reo (Māori language early childhood schools) across the country.[11]

The claimants asserted that te reo Māori was protected by te Tiriti, the Crown had failed to protect it and the Crown's failure to protect it was a Treaty breach.[12] The Tribunal confirmed that te reo Māori is a taonga[13] and that it is protected by te Tiriti, meaning the Crown is required to take "affirmative action" to protect, preserve and promote it.[14]

The claimants pointed to the paucity of te reo Māori in several sectors, including schools, courts, health services and media (such as radio, television and newspapers).[15] The claimants also contended that various statutes (such as the Maori Affairs Act 1953, the Broadcasting Act 1976 and the Hospitals Act 1957) and broadcasting and educational policies discriminated against te reo Māori.[16] The Tribunal agreed that laws and policies had collectively and consistently undermined the prevalence of te reo Māori. It concluded that the Crown had failed to comply with its obligations under te Tiriti (specifically Article 2 of te reo Māori text) and objected to the Crown's suggestion that government agencies were doing enough to support te reo Māori.[17]

The Tribunal made five recommendations to improve protection for te reo Māori, including that Māori be recognised as an official language and that courts and government agencies allow the use of Māori.[18] The former is what the claimants originally sought. The Tribunal emphasised that official recognition should not be a mere symbolic act but complement the active promotion of the language and Māori culture.[19]

(b) SUBSEQUENT CLAIMS

In 2011, in its Wai 262 report, the Tribunal discussed the continuing decline of te reo Māori and ongoing efforts to revive it.[20] It concluded that while the government's Māori language agenda had improved after te reo Māori claim, that agenda still fell well short of the standard required by te Tiriti.[21] The

Tribunal's recommendations included that the Māori Language Commission be revamped and expanded.[22]

In 2012, the Tribunal again concerned itself with te reo Māori in the Wai 2336 inquiry. The claimants asserted that the Crown's integration of kōhanga reo into national early childhood education had hindered the "organic development" of kōhanga reo kaupapa and otherwise failed to meet the Crown's obligations under te Tiriti to protect, preserve and promote te reo Māori.[23] The Tribunal agreed, echoing its comments in the Wai 262 report, and recommended that the Crown work with Māori to establish procedures to improve the funding, quality and, ultimately, participation statistics of kōhanga reo across the motu.[24]

Radio spectrum

The electromagnetic spectrum covers waves from 30 hertz to 3000 gigahertz.[25] It can be utilised through technology, and, for the purposes of systematic and effective management, it is divided into specific radio frequency bands. Among these are those used for wireless transmissions, such as radio stations and television channels.

Owing to their social and economic significance, spectrum resources have generally been regulated by national agencies.[26] Indeed, the International Telecommunication Union (an agency of which Aotearoa New Zealand is a member) recognises the regulation of spectrum resources as a state sovereign right (with associated responsibilities).[27] In Aotearoa New Zealand, the number of private radio broadcasters increased sharply in the 1970s and 1980s, and successive governments attempted to maintain control of the radio spectrum.[28] The Fourth Labour Government, driven by a free-market ethos, spearheaded the Radiocommunications Act 1989, which deregulated broadcasting and allowed the radio spectrum to be converted into commercialised assets. Subsequently, the Crown began to sell spectrum rights on the free market.[29] Sales were originally facilitated through tender processes. Eventually, the Crown conducted spectrum auctions,[30] which drive competitive bidding for spectrum rights and usually generate enormous revenue.[31]

(a) WAI 26/150

In 1986, in its report on te reo Māori claim, the Tribunal found that the predominance of the English language across broadcasting media in Aotearoa New Zealand had seriously undermined te reo Māori.[32] Within the next few years, two claims (Wai 26 and Wai 150) were brought before the Tribunal, each concerning the use and management of the radio spectrum and frequencies and their potential role in revitalising te reo Māori via broadcasting.[33]

In Wai 150, for example, the claimant (New Zealand Māori Council and Ngā Kaiwhakapūmau i te Reo (Inc)) asserted that, when te Tiriti was signed, the Māori chiefs and nations exercised rangatiratanga over "[t]he whole of New Zealand ... all that was below, upon and above the surface".[34] It sought an "interim ruling and recommendation that nothing be done to pursue the spectrum management policy embodied in the Radiocommunications Act 1989" to halt the Crown's imminent tender of radio frequencies.[35] In addition, it sought the lodging of caveats on the titles of radio spectrum products to protect Māori interests.[36]

Wai 26 and Wai 150 were eventually amalgamated as Wai 26/150.[37] The claimants asserted that "the radio spectrum was a taonga" on the basis that radio spectra are natural resources,[38] a view supported by the literature.[39] If so, the claimants contended that te Tiriti (specifically Article 2 of te reo Māori text) would guarantee rangatiratanga over the radio spectrum, and the Crown would be required to "bargain for any use of the spectrum in the broader public interest".[40] Further, the claimants contended that the principles of the Treaty "imposed an obligation on the Crown to ensure that Maori had sufficient access to the spectrum to maintain cultural integrity and security".[41]

The Tribunal concluded that the claim was "well-founded".[42] While the Tribunal regarded the radio spectrum as a natural resource and taonga, it was "a taonga to be shared by the tribes and by all mankind".[43]

The Tribunal recommended that the Crown suspend its tender for six months to allow for consultation with "iwi suitably qualified and experienced".[44] It noted that Māori access to radio frequencies could help to change broadcasting norms and facilitate the revitalisation of te reo Māori, and it recommended that FM frequencies be made available to Māori in Auckland and Wellington.[45] It emphasised that partnership should be central to the Crown's relationship with Māori, and, as radio frequencies were taonga, they were not to be monopolised.[46] Further, it warned the Crown against making light of te Tiriti, and Crown obligations under it, highlighting the importance of consultation to the "spirit" of te Tiriti.[47]

(b) WAI 776

Ten years later, another claim concerning the radio spectrum was lodged with the Tribunal. Wai 776 concerned the Crown's plan to auction off twenty-year management rights for the 2 gigahertz range of the radio spectrum – a range vital for mobile telecommunications.[48] Rangiaho Everton, who brought the claim on behalf of all Māori, sought an interim recommendation that the auction be suspended so that the Crown and Māori could negotiate management rights to the spectrum.

The claim was similar to Wai 26/150. The claimant asserted that the radio spectrum is a natural resource and taonga subject to the exercise of rangatiratanga, meaning that Māori have a right to control a fair and equitable share of it. They asserted that the Crown's failure to consult Māori on the tender in question breached its obligations under te Tiriti. They contended that the Radiocommunications Act breached te Tiriti because it did not contain a provision recognising rangatiratanga over the radio spectrum.[49] They also accused the Crown of attempting to protect te reo Māori only and no other aspects of Māori culture.[50]

In 1999, the Tribunal released its report on the claim. Its decision was split. The majority considered the claim "prima facie ... well founded", reaffirmed the findings from Wai 26/150 (including that the radio spectrum was a taonga) and recommended suspending the auction to allow for negotiations.[51] It especially objected to the notion that the radio spectrum could not be afforded protection under te Tiriti because it was not contemplated at the time of its signing, referencing Cooke P's judgment in *Te Runanga o Muriwhenua Inc v Attorney General*, which described te Tiriti as "a living instrument that has to be applied in developing circumstances".[52]

Judge Savage, in the minority, was not so sure. A Māori expert witness had contended that taonga in te Tiriti comprised things with "a spiritual or cultural dimension for Maori", although went on to suggest that everything had "a spiritual or cultural dimension for Maori".[53] Judge Savage cautioned that this was "perilously close" to saying that taonga in te Tiriti means "anything you like" and suggested that such a meaning would render te Tiriti "so indefinite as to be meaningless" and "cast doubt as to whether the parties to the compact were ever ad idem".[54] Te Tiriti did not reserve to Māori taonga katoa (all treasures) but rātou taonga katoa (all their treasures).[55] His Honour did not believe this included the spectrum resource,[56] even if he recognised that the failure of the claim would pose a threat to te reo Māori.[57] His Honour also contemplated that if the claim were accepted, the principle of partnership would apply to an unreasonably expansive list of resources and activities.[58]

Taonga species

(a) WAI 262

In 1991, six claimants brought the Wai 262 claim.[59] The claimants contended that the Crown had, through various actions, undermined rangatiratanga over "indigenous flora and fauna me o ratou taonga katoa".[60] Broadly, the actions included dismantling "Iwi political power structures" and generally pursuing "social and economic policies" that undermined the ability of Māori to exercise rangatiratanga, such as creating protected species, and selling, disposing of and exporting flora and fauna and the genetic resources of these.[61] These actions undermined kaitiakitanga and led to a loss of mātauranga Māori.[62] The claim identified how the Crown's actions and inactions had harmed the ability of Māori to protect, preserve and promote specific flora and fauna species, such as kūmara and tuatara.[63]

The Tribunal released its report in 2011.[64] The report was in eight chapters. Chapter 2 concerned the protection of taonga species. The Tribunal recommended that kaitiaki relationships with taonga species and mātauranga Māori regarding those species receive "a reasonable degree of protection", assessed on a case-by-case basis.[65] It also recommended that those who commercially use mātauranga Māori regarding taonga species be required to, depending on the context, obtain the consent of, consult with or disclose their activities to the relevant kaitiaki, even where that knowledge is already publicly available.[66] More specific recommendations included the creation of a bioprospecting regime compliant with the principles of the Treaty, reform of the existing genetic modification regime to better uphold Māori interests, and the establishment of a Māori committee to advise the Commissioner of Patents on tikanga Māori and kaitiaki interests relating to intellectual property.[67]

Taonga works

(a) WAI 262

The Wai 262 claim focused initially on flora and fauna but eventually expanded to other matters, such as the protection of taonga works, rongoā Māori (traditional medicine) and taonga under Crown control (such as in museums and archives). Chapter 1 concerned the protection of taonga works.

The Tribunal distinguished between taonga works and taonga-derived works, which derive to varying degrees from mātauranga Māori. It defined mātauranga Māori as "the unique Māori way of viewing the world, incorporating both Māori culture and Māori traditional knowledge".[68] It defined taonga works as fixed or unfixed works that are wholly expressions of mātauranga Māori that invoke whakapapa connections and traditional narratives,[69] and, in accordance with tikanga Māori, possess mauri and have living kaitiaki. In contrast, it defined taonga-derived works as works that, while drawing inspiration from mātauranga Māori or taonga works, do not directly reflect whakapapa connections or traditional narratives.[70] While taonga-derived works are undoubtedly Māori works, they do not have mauri nor a living kaitiaki.

The claimants contended that the Crown's policies and actions had undermined rangatiratanga over taonga works by allowing the use and development of these works "in isolation of the original creator's cultural and spiritual concepts", leading to the loss or damage of the taonga and their associated knowledge.[71]

The Tribunal also recommended two new mechanisms for the legal protection of taonga: a general objection mechanism prohibiting the derogatory or offensive public use of mātauranga Māori, taonga works and taonga-derived works; and a mechanism that kaitiaki could use to prevent the commercial exploitation of mātauranga Māori and taonga works.[72]

The Tribunal also recommended the creation of an expert commission overseeing the legal protection of taonga works, taonga-derived works and mātauranga Māori.[73] The commission would have three functions: a facilitative function to create best practice guidelines for dealing with taonga works and taonga-derived works; an administrative function to establish and maintain a register of kaitiaki relationships with publicly available taonga works; and an adjudicative function to determine kaitiaki, categorise taonga works and taonga-derived works, and resolve disputes over uses of taonga works and taonga-derived works.[74]

Functions of Tribunal Inquiries

This part uses the Treaty partners' responses to the taonga claims to reflect on Tribunal inquiries. It contends that Tribunal inquiries have two key functions – as bastions and magnets. First, an inquiry is a bastion of claim kaupapa, which must be kept alive and beating if there is to be a meaningful response to the inquiry. Secondly, an inquiry is a magnet, which magnetises political will amenable to claim kaupapa around a centre and magnetises existing political will to align more closely with claim kaupapa.

Bastions

Claimants lodge their statements of claim, which may be developed in a statement of issues; the claimants, their legal representatives and their expert witnesses provide written and oral submissions; the Tribunal commissions experts to investigate aspects of the claim; and the Tribunal produces a report that summarises the claims, issues, submissions and evidence. These are not the only aspects of Tribunal inquiries, which also include, for example, recommendations. But in these ways, Tribunal inquiries are bastions of claim kaupapa.

The bastion function is crucial because it keeps claim kaupapa alive, which enables a confluence of the political wills of Māori and the Crown to support the claim kaupapa and increases the likelihood of an effective response to the relevant inquiry.

This section explores three case studies that demonstrate the bastion function. First, it examines te reo Māori claim kaupapa, where there is a sympathetic coincidence of a Tribunal report with a confluence of the political wills to support claim kaupapa, resulting in an effective response. Secondly, it considers taonga works claim kaupapa, where there is a suspended coincidence of a Tribunal report with a confluence of the political wills to support claim kaupapa, resulting in an effective response. Thirdly, it looks at radio spectrum claim kaupapa, where there is no coincidence of a Tribunal report with a confluence of the political wills to support claim kaupapa, resulting in no effective response.

(a) TE REO MĀORI CLAIM KAUPAPA

Te reo Māori claim kaupapa include the recognition of te reo Māori as an official language of Aotearoa New Zealand and the increased use of te reo Māori in several sectors, including the school system and broadcasting. On the release of the Tribunal's Wai 11 report, there was a confluence of the political wills of Māori and the Crown to support the recognition of te reo Māori as an official language of Aotearoa New Zealand.[75] The government pre-empted the Tribunal's recommendations with the Māori Language Act 1987. While the Act recognised te reo Māori as an official language, it did not confer any additional rights by this declaration.[76] Further, while it allowed te reo Māori to be spoken in the courts, this fell short of the Tribunal's recommendation that te reo Māori be made an official language that could be used in spoken or written form in all dealings with public bodies.[77] The Act also established the recommended Māori Language Commission,[78] an independent Crown entity designed to promote and support te reo Māori, as recommended by the Tribunal.[79]

The government also spearheaded the Education Act 1989, which recognised and promoted kura kaupapa and whare wānanga (institutions of learning).[80] The Act responded to the Tribunal's criticism of the paucity of te reo Māori in the school system.[81] However, the government ignored the Tribunal's recommendations to promote te reo Māori in broadcasting and bilingualism in the public service.[82]

In each case, there was a sympathetic coincidence of the Tribunal report and confluence of the political wills to support these claim kaupapa. In the case of te reo Māori claim, the Tribunal's recommendations were aligned with the claim kaupapa. Still, its recommendations were not adopted as the government's political will was only for a watered-down response.

(b) TAONGA WORKS CLAIM KAUPAPA

The Wai 262 claimants sought a sui generis system that would enable the exercise of rangatiratanga in the protection, preservation and promotion of taonga works. The Tribunal's recommended expert commission would provide Māori with no or only limited opportunities to exercise rangatiratanga in protecting, preserving and promoting taonga works.[83] Kaitiaki would primarily be consulted and provide advice.[84] The Tribunal's recommendations "largely fell short" of the claimants' aspirations.[85]

The government has demonstrated a genuine commitment to a meaningful response to Wai 262. Te Pae Tawhiti, the work programme for the Wai 262 response, has been through two iterations.[86] The first iteration, the Overlapping Spheres Model, would enable Māori to exercise rangatiratanga in co-designing the substantive response with the government. The government supported that model for about four years until it was scaled back due to pressures on the government during the COVID-19 pandemic. Further, the Treasury has allocated significant funding to Te Taumata Whakapūmau to coordinate a Māori-led response to Wai 262.[87] Some of that funding has been allocated to Kahu Aronui, an advisory group of Māori technical experts, to develop responses to Wai 262 claim kaupapa, including a sui generis regime to protect, preserve and promote taonga Māori for which protection was sought in Wai 262.[88]

It took the government six years to formally respond to the Tribunal's report and propose Te Pae Tawhiti.[89] So, there was a suspended coincidence of the Tribunal's report and the confluence of the political wills.

Te Pae Tawhiti explicitly responds to Wai 262 rather than the Tribunal's report, and the emphasis is often on the statements of claim.[90] Te Pae Tawhiti has also diverged from the Tribunal's recommendations,[91] which Māori and the Crown have generally dismissed as "useful guidance".[92] For example, Māori and the Crown have decided not to adopt the Tribunal's recommended expert commission but instead invest in the design of a sui generis regime to protect, preserve and promote taonga works (and other taonga). Accordingly, this case study supports the contention that it is the completion of the inquiry that spurs further action, not the recommendations, which may or may not be influential.

(c) RADIO SPECTRUM CLAIM KAUPAPA

In Wai 26/150, the claimants sought a suspension of the imminent tender of the radio spectrum on the basis that the radio spectrum was a taonga. The Tribunal's report endorsed the substance of the claim and recommended the suspension.[93] However, there was no confluence of the political wills to support the claim kaupapa. The Crown rejected the Tribunal's findings and refused to delay the tender. It strongly disagreed that the radio spectrum was a taonga under te Tiriti, stating that Māori did not possess exclusive rights to it.[94] It also contended that while delaying the tender process might help to promote Māori language and culture, it would inconvenience other potential bidders for the spectrum.[95] In summary, the Crown prioritised its dealings in the market over the claim kaupapa.

Wai 776 was prompted by years of Crown inaction on broadcasting issues following Wai 26/150 nearly a decade earlier.[96] In the Tribunal inquiry, the Crown insisted that the radio spectrum could not be a taonga because radio spectra were merely "artificially generated radio waves".[97] It contended that Māori did not need to own management rights to use radio technologies and that the government could support te reo Māori through alternative means.[98] When the Tribunal released its interim report, the Crown delayed its planned auction of the spectrum in question by three months to pursue negotiations with iwi.[99] However, the Crown ultimately rejected the Tribunal's final report recommendations and proceeded with the delayed auction,[100] doing little else to respond directly to the claim kaupapa.

There has been no confluence of the political wills of Māori and the Crown to support the radio spectrum claim kaupapa. Accordingly, there has been no coincidence. There may yet be supervened coincidence before the Tribunal reports are superannuated.

Magnets

Assertions that the Crown has breached its obligations under te Tiriti are often dismissed in the political arena for lacking formalisation and legitimation. For example, protests on Treaty issues are often dismissed as mere political activism.[101] Tribunal claims formalise assertions that the Crown has breached its obligations under te Tiriti; Tribunal inquiries legitimise formalised claim kaupapa (through submissions, evidence and hearings); and Tribunal reports transition claim kaupapa into the political arena in a way that formalises and legitimates them. In many instances, this will improve the political perception of assertions that the Crown has breached obligations under te Tiriti and increase the likelihood that they will motivate a response in the political arena.

In formalising, legitimating and transitioning claim kaupapa, Tribunal inquiries magnetise political will amenable to claim kaupapa around a centre and magnetise existing political will to align more closely with claim kaupapa.

This section provides case studies, each from a different category of taonga claim (te reo Māori kaupapa, the taonga species kaupapa and the radio spectrum kaupapa, respectively) and demonstrating a different category of coincidence (sympathetic coincidence, suspended coincidence and supervened coincidence, respectively).

(a) TE REO MĀORI CLAIM KAUPAPA

The Wai 11 inquiry magnetised existing political will to align more closely with claim kaupapa. A sympathetic coincidence of the Wai 11 report with the confluence of the political wills to support the claim kaupapa led to an immediate effective response, including recognising te reo Māori as an official language. The coincidence has been sustained since.

In the Wai 262 inquiry, the Tribunal canvassed many of the issues previously raised in te reo Māori claim (and the findings reached by the Tribunal in that inquiry), noted that they had not been appropriately addressed, and made multiple recommendations for Crown action to properly ensure the language's revitalisation.[102] The Crown and Māori responded favourably to this, leading to developments like the enactment of the Māori Language Act 2016 – legislation that (among other things) established Te Mātāwai, a new entity to help revitalise te reo Māori in a manner that loosely reflected the vision of the Tribunal in Wai 262.[103] Further, in the Wai 2336 inquiry, the Tribunal explored the importance of kōhanga reo to ensure the ongoing survival of te reo Māori, investigated how the Crown had breached its obligations under te Tiriti by integrating kōhanga reo into national early childhood education, and recommended the Crown work with Māori to improve the state of kōhanga reo.[104] In response, the Crown allocated funding in the 2021 and 2022 budgets to support increased pay for kōhanga staff in addition to increased funding for all teachers, and the Crown and Te Kōhanga Reo National Trust have worked together to decide how to apply the funding.[105]

In these ways, the Tribunal's inquiries concerning te reo Māori magnetised political will amenable to claim kaupapa around multiple centres (being the Wai 11 report and relevant chapters of the Wai 262 and 2336 reports). The cumulative inquiries served as ascending foundations for subsequent Tribunals' inquiries to build on and refreshed claim kaupapa so they stayed relevant and did not become superannuated.

(b) TAONGA SPECIES CLAIM KAUPAPA

The Wai 262 inquiry also magnetised political will to support a Māori Plant Varieties Committee (MPVC). While the inquiry was in its infancy, the legislature enacted the Trade Marks Act 2002. Section 17(1)(c) requires the Commissioner of Trade Marks to reject any matter that "the use or registration of which would, in the opinion of the Commissioner, be likely to offend a significant section of the community, including Māori". The Act created the Māori Trade Marks Advisory Committee (MTMAC) to advise the commissioner on whether an application for a trade mark or the prospective mark would be likely to offend Māori. The MTMAC is only advisory. The commissioner ultimately decides.[106]

In 2011, the Tribunal released its report. During the claim, while rejecting the need for any fundamental reform to the law relating to plant variety rights, the Crown accepted that mātauranga Māori and relationships with taonga species justified a higher degree of protection.[107] In response, the Crown proposed introducing a Māori advisory committee for plant variety rights.[108] The Tribunal noted this proposal and recommended adapting it so that any plant variety rights legislation included a power to refuse a plant variety right because of the effect on kaitiaki relationships with the relevant species. It also recommended that the committee be adequately informed of the relevant Māori interest, such as by providing for joint decision-making when a kaitiaki relationship is at risk.[109]

In 2017, some years following the completion of the Tribunal's inquiry, Cabinet agreed to a review of existing plant variety rights legislation, including how to account for the Tribunal's recommendations in the Wai 262 report.[110] In 2021, Cabinet approved the introduction of the resulting Plant Variety Rights Bill 2021, which included a proposal for a Māori committee for plant variety rights.[111]

The Plant Variety Rights Act 2022 created the MPVC.[112] The Committee's powers were far more extensive than those of the MTMAC. For example, the Act requires the Commissioner of Plant Variety Rights to reject an application if it is adverse to kaitiaki interests. The MPVC has the power to investigate and can require the commissioner to reject the application, giving Māori decision-making authority, which is far closer to rangatiratanga than the MTMAC's advisory powers.

A robust Tribunal inquiry allows the claim kaupapa to be elaborated in detail. In the Wai 262 inquiry, the claimants were able to amend the statements of claim multiple times, allowing them to develop their submissions over several years and draw on extensive expert evidence.[113] The process helped the claimants to refine what exactly they were seeking for each claim kaupapa and this was recorded in the submissions and evidence, as well as the Tribunal's report. This enabled and made it easier for Māori and the Crown to deviate from the Tribunal's recommendations and revert to the claim kaupapa when there was a coincidence of the Tribunal report with a confluence of the political wills to support claim kaupapa.[114]

The Tribunal inquiry magnetised political will to support an MPVC. First, the submissions and evidence endorsed a Māori committee for plant variety rights similar to the MTMAC for trade marks. Secondly, the legislative process in designing the Act explicitly referenced the Tribunal inquiry and was guided by the taonga species claim kaupapa.

The Tribunal's recommendations were aligned with the claim kaupapa, so the recommendations were adopted.

(c) RADIO SPECTRUM CLAIM KAUPAPA

The radio spectrum claim kaupapa in the Wai 11 and Wai 26/150 inquiries received no response. The radio spectrum claim kaupapa in the subsequent Wai 776 claim again received no response. Nonetheless, the claims magnetised political will, which exerted pressure on the Crown to respond, and the Crown would take some steps to enhance Māori rights in the spectrum.

In 2000, after the completion of the Wai 26/150 inquiry, Te Huarahi Tika Trust was incorporated as a charitable trust to enable Māori a right of purchase over a block of 3G spectrum being auctioned by the Crown that year. The Crown provided the trust with a $5 million cash contribution and a 5 per cent discount on the block of spectrum.[115] While not what the claimants sought specifically, it was not without value, with the trust leveraging the cash contribution and discount into a 20 per cent stake in the 2degrees telecommunications provider.[116]

Māori were more successful in the broadcasting and radio spectrum arena, although it remained unrecognised as taonga.[117] In 2003, the Crown passed legislation establishing the first Māori Television Service the following year.[118] In 2023, following negotiations with the Māori-led Māori Spectrum Working Group, the Crown transferred the long-term management rights of 100 megahertz of the 3.5 gigahertz spectrum and $17.8 million to the Interim Māori Spectrum Commission.[119]

The Tribunal received recurrent claims on similar issues (regarding closely related taonga). Without the Tribunal's inquiries into the radio spectrum and broadcasting issues, it is doubtful whether Māori would have secured these rights and interests. The inquiries magnetised political will around multiple centres, exerting continuous and growing pressure on the Crown.[120] It becomes increasingly politically difficult for the Crown to hold out on all claim kaupapa relating to a given taonga.[121] The confluence of the political wills of Māori and the Crown to support these minor claim kaupapa have allowed the Crown to alleviate some of that pressure.[122]

Maximising the Effectiveness of a Response

An effective response is most likely when the Tribunal's report coincides with a confluence of the political wills of Māori and the Crown to support claim kaupapa. The more that Māori and the Crown support claim kaupapa, the more effective the response could be. Given that Māori are the kaitiaki of claim kaupapa, the potential effectiveness of a response may be maximised when Māori and the Crown empower Māori to lead the response.[123]

The taonga works claim kaupapa provides a good example. As mentioned, the Crown has allocated funding to Te Taumata Whakapūmau, which directs some of that funding to Kahu Aronui to lead the design of a sui generis regime to protect, preserve and promote taonga works (and other taonga). Kahu Aronui involves descendants of the original Wai 262 claimants[124] and is influenced by the voices of those most directly affected by the Wai 262 claim kaupapa.[125] Accordingly, Kahu Aronui is empowered by Māori and the Crown to take a leadership role in responding to Wai 262.

The Kahu Aronui-led "Voices of 100 Māori Creatives" project surveyed Māori creative practitioners on the "policy and legal gaps in the protection of taonga Māori". It asked creative practitioners about their experiences with the misuse and misappropriation of Māori creative works and their awareness of and the efficacy of existing protections for these works.[126] Kahu Aronui intends to use the information collected to pursue its mahi, drawing on the results to develop Māori-led solutions for protecting taonga Māori in response to the Wai 262 claim.[127] It is unlikely that Māori knowledge and experiences would as effectively inform the response if it were not being led by Māori.

The confluence of political wills to support the te reo Māori claim kaupapa has arguably been sustained. However, the government has not pushed hard to significantly increase language fluency rates, and rangatiratanga is compromised, which hinders the ability of Māori to respond independently. Coincidence is at risk as the current government backslides on its commitments.[128]

A political landscape less insistent on Māori leadership in the response can risk jeopardising the effectiveness of that response. The Overlapping Spheres Model was designed to enable Māori to exercise rangatiratanga in co-designing the substantive response with the government.[129] In 2022, it was replaced with a Levers Model to "more clearly give effect to the aspirations of the Wai 262 claims".[130] However, that model prioritises partnership over rangatiratanga such that the Māori sphere has been subsumed into the Māori–Crown relationship.[131] While Māori are presently empowered to take a leadership role in the response, the Crown determines the extent of Māori authority in Te Pae Tawhiti.[132] There is now a risk that Māori and the Crown will regress to a competitive relationship[133] like that from the six years between the release of the Tribunal's report and the Crown's long-awaited formal response.[134]

Conclusion

This chapter made three arguments. First, a Tribunal inquiry is a bastion of claim kaupapa and magnetises political will to support claim kaupapa, with each function supporting a confluence of the political wills of Māori and the Crown to support claim kaupapa.

Secondly, a Tribunal inquiry is most likely to lead to an effective response when the completion of the inquiry (the Tribunal's final report on the claim) coincides with a confluence of the political wills of Māori and the Crown to support the applicable claim kaupapa. The Tribunal's recommendations may or may not be influential. In other words, the effective response to a Tribunal inquiry may or may not involve adopting the Tribunal's recommendations. On the one hand, there was a confluence of political wills to support te reo Māori claim kaupapa, and Māori and the Crown adopted the key Tribunal recommendations on that claim. For example, the government officially recognised te reo Māori as an official language and established the Māori Language Commission, each recommended by the Tribunal.[135] On the other hand, there was a confluence of political wills to support the taonga works claim kaupapa, and Māori and the Crown largely disregarded the key Tribunal recommendations on the claim. Māori and the Crown may each support claim kaupapa and adopt all, some or none of the Tribunal's recommendations on the claim. If recommendations are adopted and lead to an effective response, it is likely because they align with the claim kaupapa.

Thirdly, the potential effectiveness of a response may be maximised when Māori and the Crown empower Māori to lead the response. A response can be effective yet fail to fulfil its potential. There are also different degrees of empowerment, and Māori leadership at the Crown's discretion is no substitute for rangatiratanga.

The Sixth National Government does not seem likely to meaningfully advance Māori aspirations. The previous National-led government did not have a robust track record of endorsing the kaupapa of Tribunal claims (or accepting the importance of Māori authority in the responses to those claims), and, in the 2023 general election, both the ACT New Zealand and New Zealand First parties campaigned on anti-co-governance policies.[136] Unlike Budget 2022, which increased the funding for Te Pae Tawhiti to $22 million over 2022–2026,[137] Budget 2024 allocate no funding to Te Pae Tawhiti.[138] The risks to the protection, preservation and promotion of taonga are real on the fiftieth anniversary of the Tribunal.

“I have always reflected on the importance of the Māori–Crown relationship going forward and that what we are attempting to do is ensure that that’s sound and stable, in the interests of New Zealand society.”

Chapter 11

From Historical Claims to Kaupapa Inquiries

Judge Wilson Isaac

(Interviewed by Carwyn Jones)

CJ: What do you see as some of the most significant developments for the Waitangi Tribunal that took place during your time as chairperson?

WI: When I became chairperson at the end of 2009, the Tribunal, in terms of its inquiry programme, was well into the district inquiries and the historical inquiries. At the same time, we were starting to receive a number of kaupapa inquiries, which we didn't really know what to do with. And at a similar time, the government was pushing settlements. Within that mix, we had a huge number of urgent inquiries that were concerned with the government settlement process. I guess you could call it hectic; there was a lot going on. I was fairly new to the game, and I had never been in a leadership role within the Tribunal. What I tried to do initially was bring around me a good team of people to sit down and work out what we were going to do with what I thought was a fairly limited resource, both in terms of finance and staff, and to develop a system where we could deal as fairly as possible with what we had in front of us.

On our team, I had the likes of Richard Moorsom, who was fantastic; Grant Phillipson had just been taken off as the chief historian and had become a Tribunal member; Pat Savage was the deputy chairperson; and Julie Tangaere was the director of the Waitangi Tribunal unit at the time I was appointed as chairperson, and then Grace Smit was brought into the role of director. We worked very well as a team.

We set up priorities for the Tribunal and how to utilise our resource. Our first priority was to deal with the urgencies. They had to be dealt with straight away. Pat Savage, as the deputy chairperson, was pretty ruthless in dealing with those, but he dealt with them in a very fair and concise manner so that everyone knew exactly where they were. Our next priority was to deal with the historical claims because, at that time, we thought we had most of them covered. I think there were only about six running at the time, and Te Paparahi o Te Raki was one that carried on. We had some stragglers, like the Eastern Bay of Plenty claim, but we had most going. At that time, I think we had about 90 per cent of the country covered in terms of the historical claims, but we wanted to have those out of the way by 2020 and transition into the kaupapa inquiries. They were the priorities: urgencies, historical claims and kaupapa inquiries. Within that mix, we had to ensure that the resource was spread evenly, or as evenly as possible, across those claims. Every claim that's filed has got to be heard in some shape or form, and we ensured there was some order around that. That's what we achieved.

From 2010 through to 2020, we completed most of the historical inquiries, or if they weren't finished, they were in the report-writing phase. Then, we set up a transition to move into the kaupapa inquiries. In 2015, I issued a direction that set out how we were going to transition into the kaupapa inquiries. Really, it was a movement of resource and mindset away from the historical inquiries towards dealing with matters of national significance for Māori that were right in front of us. I started with the Military Veterans Kaupapa Inquiry, which is still going on. By the time I left, I wanted to get most of the significant ones underway, like justice, education and the constitutional inquiry, and that essentially happened.

It was a challenging time in terms of ensuring that we had a full membership. When I started as chairperson, I had a good relationship with the Minister of Māori Affairs – Parekura Horomia, he was first, and Pita Sharples was next and Te Ururoa Flavell as Minister for Māori Development – we had a good, trusting relationship. I would make a recommendation to them as to whom I wanted as members, and they would turn it around. It became more difficult to get members who had integrity in both the Pākehā world and the Māori world. Back in that time, we had great historians, like Keith Sorrenson, Ann Parsonson, Evelyn Stokes and Grant Phillipson. We had amazing kaumātua – John Turei, John Tahuparae, John Clarke, Manu Bennett, and in more recent times, Pou Temara, Hirini Mead, and Te Wharehuia Milroy. All those members had the faith and the trust of both sides. In my work as chairperson, I have always reflected on the importance of the Māori–Crown relationship going forward and that what we are attempting to do is ensure that that's sound and stable, in the interests of New Zealand society.

CJ: The Tribunal does play that important role in mediating the Crown–Māori relationship, ensuring that remains stable, but it's also often right in the political crosshairs. As chairperson, how did you manage that?

WI: I didn't see that as an issue, and it was probably because of the relationship I had with the ministers, which was a good, amicable relationship. We both did our work. I think we could both see that the Tribunal was there to ensure that the Māori–Crown relationship was protected and enhanced. At that time, they didn't see the Tribunal as being a threat. They saw it as being an enhancement to that relationship, and so it wasn't an issue for me in the early times. Later, when the ministers thought we should perhaps stick to our knitting and stay out of government policy, I had to navigate the role a bit more carefully to assure them that we were following the jurisdiction that is afforded to us in the Act. I didn't come across any major issues.

We were able to manage things within the Tribunal – in the Tribunal, with the judges, the Tribunal membership and the administration – to see what was the best fit for the Tribunal and the best fit for Māori–Crown relations. I think, looking back, that had the support of all sides. What we did in our transition to the kaupapa inquiries was tweak the membership slightly so that we had members within the Tribunal who were more government savvy, more knowledgeable about parliamentary process and the bureaucracy. We brought in people like Sir Doug Kidd and Kim Ngarimu. They knew the process, and they assisted us in moving forward. We always ensured we had a skills matrix, which we shared with the Minister and said, this is why we want these people. And normally, the Minister signed off on them.

CJ: The deadline for historical claims to be lodged was almost immediately before you took on the role of chairperson. So that feeds into the focus on the completion of the historical claims.

WI: It does. There was that deadline in place, and that led to a whole raft of claims. There were also some claims that we were told, essentially, not to start because they were in direct negotiations. Ngāti Porou went to direct negotiations, but we had some urgencies from it, which had us go back into some of the historical issues faced by Ngāti Porou, the Eastern Bay of Plenty. That started quite late, but there were those underlying claims that were always there. That led to the transition out of these claims. We got to hear them, report on them, make recommendations and then move more into the kaupapa inquiries. I think by 2015, we had identified eleven kaupapa inquiries that hadn't been inquired into. Now, I think every single one of them has got a panel appointed.

CJ: You mentioned the number of urgent inquiries related to the settlement process itself. Margaret Mutu, who has written on engagements in the settlement process, has noted that these are often issues that are drawing in the courts in other ways. Were there any particular challenges around managing people coming to the Tribunal and also going to the courts?

WI: I guess the most litigious claim that I was involved in was the northern South Island inquiry, where we had the Ngāi Tahu boundary before us very clearly, and we simply had to wait on the court. I issued a decision about the boundary that went on review to the High Court. Ngāi Tahu were fairly keen to ensure that the boundary that they said had been set by the Māori Land Court was the boundary. We had cross claims from Ngāti Rārua and Ngāti Apa. It was a very litigious time, which, basically, put our inquiry on hold until we were given the green light by the courts, while they issued their decisions. They said we could inquire into cross-claims. We could set our own processes for dealing with them, which we did, and at the end of all of that, I think there was a lot of healing done between Ngāi Tahu and the northern South Island iwi. In some cases, that healing wasn't as effective as in other cases. But what it did for the northern South Island was identify where the eight iwi of the northern South Island sat in terms of their rohe, which is still significant today. I say that in light of the fact that we're getting claims in the Māori Land Court as to the ownership of taonga that are found in the northern South Island. They have come together as a joint group and said to the court how they want it dealt with, which wouldn't have happened before our inquiry. There are still differences of opinion, but, essentially, they're working together. So, that's a classic example of the court becoming involved and essentially supporting what the Tribunal was trying to do so that we could get to the truth of the matter.

CJ: In terms of moving into the kaupapa inquiry process, were there things about the process itself or procedure that needed to be adjusted?

WI: What we found with the veterans inquiry was we had to ensure that we heard from as many veterans as possible before they died. So, the first part of that inquiry was setting up a process for that to happen, and rather than go through all the filing of the claims and the responses, we said we wanted to hear from veterans. We went to where most of the veterans live – we went up north, we went to Rotorua, we went to Gisborne, and we went down south – and we heard them talk about their experiences. That was a change, and that is happening more and more in the kaupapa inquiries. I think the Mana Wāhine Kaupapa Inquiry had a similar sort of process where the inquiry heard from the people involved without the constraints of the claims in front of them. People just speak to their experiences, and some of it is not claims related at all. Now, with the veterans, we're hearing the more technical evidence and the evidence associated with the claims. It has been a very enlightening process.

CJ: Were there any other kinds of challenges through your time as chairperson?

WI: The ongoing challenge was that of dealing with the resource, in terms of the staffing resource, the member resource and the financial resource. It seemed to me that we were going cap in hand to the government all the time to ensure that we had the resource we needed to do the job. That became burdensome. We did a lot of juggling to ensure that we had the ability to hear as many claims as we could in a period of time that gave the claimants, the Crown and the members all time to give their best to those inquiries. So, that was always a challenge, but we did work around it.

CJ: I think, looking at where the Tribunal is now, it seems to have become quite a nimble organisation in terms of doing that juggling and needing to change quickly. I observed recently, partly through the work of Tribunal members and staff but also with claimant counsel, that there's more of an experienced cohort there who are able to shift, and there has been a shift in mindset from the Crown.

WI: I think, if I take it back to the Mike Doogan days, he brought a different mindset of Crown counsel. He was very conciliatory, and he was able to bring the Crown in almost as a friend of the claimants, which hadn't happened a lot before. That's now playing out in some inquiries I've been involved in where, previously, the Crown had been the respondent and they were there to question everything. In some inquiries I've been involved in, they've been very conciliatory and have attempted to assist the process. The veterans inquiry and the geothermal inquiry are ones we're getting quite a bit of buy-in from the Crown. In some of the others, the Crown has been quite a staunch litigant in ensuring that they question everything. I think Mike Doogan was responsible for that change in mindset, which was great.

CJ: You've touched on some of the inquiries you've been involved with, but are there any other inquiries that stand out?

WI: All the inquiries that I've been involved in are important, particularly to those persons who bring the claims. The first one I had was the Mōhaka ki Ahuriri inquiry with Eddie Durie. I had just been a judge for two years. He gave it to me in 1996 and said it was a very small claim that would take six months. Ten years later, we're still involved. That was a real learning curve for me. As a presiding officer, I had a very new bunch of Tribunal members. I think, apart from Keith Sorrenson, none of them had sat on a Tribunal – Evelyn Stokes, John Clarke and John Turei.

Within that inquiry, we had the Napier Hospital inquiry, and that did stand out as we were starting to get more into the contemporary sphere of things. We looked long and hard at that inquiry, and we were very careful with the way we articulated the Treaty principles within that inquiry. We articulated a couple of new ones, but they were more about the duties that we associated with the principles, like the duty to consult, which I don't think had been looked at before. I think that inquiry essentially set out guidelines as to how Māori work with Crown organisations. That was an important report in relation to that, and I hear, it's still being used.

And then you have the National Park District Inquiry, which centered on the national park in the central North Island, on the mountains – Ruapehu, Tongariro and Ngāuruhoe. That, again, was important, I think, for the Crown, which had only previously dealt with Tūwharetoa. The Crown learnt that there are other iwi who have ownership, mana and significance in that mountain that it needed to start thinking about. Ngāti Rangi and Tūwharetoa were very gracious in saying that perhaps one side of the mountain is Tūwharetoa and the other side is Ngāti Rangi. With Turoa ski field, I know we made a recommendation that part of that ski field, up at the top of it, was owned by Ngāti Rangi and was taken in a manner akin to confiscation. All of those recommendations are still being worked on, and they're still in discussion, but now Ngāti Rangi are fully involved in the discussions. So, within that Crown–Māori conversation, the recommendations made in those inquiries are assisting things going forward.

CJ: Is there anything else that you wanted to mention?

WI: I haven't said anything much about the current inquiries I'm on. We've done our first report in the water claim as to who owns the water. We're now dealing with the geothermal inquiry, which is fascinating, about who owns the geothermal resource. Once we get into it, that is going to be different in that there is a lot of competition for that geothermal resource within Māori, and the Crown is sitting back. That's going to be quite a different inquiry in that we have to navigate the waters within Māori before we actually get to the Crown. We had a recent hearing at Whakarewarewa, and there were all the factions, which brings a different dynamic to the game. It is a dynamic that, apart from the northern South Island, you don't get very often, but there's a lot of money at stake in this one.

So, again, that will change not so much the role of the Tribunal but the manner in which we deal with things and whether we involve mediation. It's going to need some agility and flexibility in our processes. But, in terms of the way the Tribunal operates, it can set its own processes, and it can be nimble to ensure that we get where we want to in terms of the claims before us tomorrow.

"Māori ways of understanding, experiencing and accessing health have not been recognised in the way in which the health system was set up, the resources that were available, the monitoring that was undertaken and the ways in which Māori could participate in the system."

Chapter 12

Toiora

Social Policy and Well-being

— *Carwyn Jones, Jacqueline Paul and Rhiannon Jones*

The Waitangi Tribunal has engaged with significant matters of social policy and well-being over the course of its existence. People often tend to think of the Tribunal's work as being primarily to address historical claims and issues relating to land and natural resources. Although historical claims and the large-scale district inquiry programme was a key focus of the Tribunal's work for many years, it is the Tribunal's jurisdiction to inquire into contemporary Crown policy and practice that has been a constant feature of the Tribunal's role.

When the Tribunal was first established in 1975, it could only consider contemporary Crown action, being Crown acts or omissions from 1975 onwards that were alleged to be in breach of Treaty principles. In 1985, the Tribunal's jurisdiction was extended to allow it to inquire into matters going back to the signing of te Tiriti in 1840. Historical claims quickly became the key focus of the Tribunal's work as it was through past Treaty breaches that most of the loss of land and natural resources had occurred. However, the Tribunal has always had the ability to consider contemporary policy issues.

This chapter examines some of the Tribunal's inquiries that have addressed pressing social policy and well-being issues. In particular, this chapter looks at the Tribunal inquiries relating to social service delivery and the Waipareira Trust, health services and outcomes, housing and homelessness, and child welfare and protection. These are far from the only social policy issues with which the Tribunal has engaged. The Tribunal has scrutinised education policy and funding in relation to kōhanga reo,[1] kura kaupapa[2] and wānanga.[3] Issues relating to Māori rates of incarceration,[4] prisoner voting rights[5] and policy tools for assessing offenders have also been the subject of Tribunal inquiries.[6] The Tribunal's kaupapa inquiry programme includes inquiries into the justice system, eduction services and outcomes, social services and outcomes, identity and culture, and economic development alongside the ongoing inquiries into health services and housing policy, which are addressed in this chapter.

The reports on Te Whānau o Waipareira, health, housing, and child welfare and protection provide illustrative examples of the Waitangi Tribunal's contribution to issues of social policy and well-being. They show how Treaty principles are relevant to contemporary social policy. The recommendations made in those reports demonstrate how Treaty principles such as rangatiratanga, active protection, partnership, options and equity can be given practical application to improve social policy.

Te Whānau o Waipareira Report

One of the first Waitangi Tribunal inquiries to address the equitable resourcing and delivery of social services for Māori was the Te Whānau o Waipareira inquiry.[7]

Te Whānau o Waipareira Trust was established in 1981 in response to Māori urbanisation in the decades following the Second World War. West Auckland was one urban settlement that saw a rapid increase in the Māori population over that period. Māori committees under the Maori Welfare Act 1962 were established by Māori in West Auckland to address some of the new challenges presented by urbanisation. The desire to find ways of expressing Māori culture and traditions in the new urban environment led to the development of Hoani Waititi Marae. The marae was a pan-tribal intiative and was intended to become a focal point for cultural revival and support whānau ties across the Māori community in West Auckland. Hoani Waititi Marae was opened in 1980 and was an important step in the evolution towards Te Whānau o Waipareira Trust.

Another important step came through the Tu Tangata and Kokiri programmes that were rolled out by the then Department of Māori Affairs in the late 1970s and early 1980s. These programmes were grounded in the philosophy of devolution and intended to give local providers the resources and decision-making authority in relation to education programmes, youth programmes and similar matters. The Waipareira Community Management Group became one such local provider. In 1982, this group changed its name to Te Whānau o Waipareira, and, in 1984, Te Whānau o Waipareira Trust was established as a charitable trust.

Te Whānau o Waipareira Trust, at the time of the Tribunal inquiry, described itself as:[8]

> *a democratically run, charitable organisation, providing many forms of assistance to the people of West Auckland. It offers a caring service with dignity to all who request support. By doing so, the Trust aims to foster a greater understanding of matters Maori.*

In the mid-1990s, Te Whānau o Waipareira Trust had a multi-million-dollar budget and was involved in a large number of programmes relating to education, housing, employment, vocational training, health and community services.

The Trust's claim to the Waitangi Tribunal alleged:[9]

> *... that the Crown, through the Community Funding Agency (CFA) of the Department of Social Welfare (DSW), had failed to recognise the special status of Te Whanau o Waipareira as a Maori organisation and had failed to properly consult and deal with it in accordance with the Crown's obligations under article 2 of the Treaty of Waitangi. This alleged denigration of Te Whanau o Waipareira, in breach of article 2, was said to have led to further breaches, namely that the Crown developed and implemented a piecemeal approach to welfare funding that was inappropriate for Maori clients, compromised the unity and effectiveness of Te Whanau o Waipareira, and trapped its beneficiaries in a state of dependence on the Government. In the end, it was contended, funding levels and standards of welfare services declined to the point where the trust's Maori clients did not get their article 3 entitlement to the same welfare services as other citizens.*

This claim also raised an important question about the nature of the Crown's Treaty obligations in a social policy context, specifically, to whom are those obligations owed? The Crown had argued that Te Whānau o Waipareira, as a pan-Māori organisation, was distinct, in Treaty terms, from kin-based groups, such as hapū, which are referred to in te Tiriti. The Crown, therefore, contended that Article 2 of te Tiriti does not apply to Te Whānau o Waipareira. The Crown said that the Trust did not meet the criteria to be recognised as an iwi under the then recently repealed Runanga Iwi Act 1990. Furthermore, even if the Trust was recognised as an iwi, its community development activities were fundamentally different in nature from the issues of rights to land, natural resources and taonga protected in Article 2.

The Tribunal addressed this issue through the application of the principles of rangatiratanga, protection and partnership.

In articulating the rangatiratanga principle, the Tribunal noted the reciprocal relationship of trust between leaders and members of a Māori community that is essential to defining rights, obligations and accountabilities within the community and to expressing the identity and authority of the community to the rest of the world.[10] The Tribunal also noted that while kinship connections provide a vast array of ready-made social networks to draw on "it is rangatiratanga that determines which of those relationships have current significance".[11] This flexibility explains the dynamism of forms of Māori social organisation evident in the way that hapū amalgamated or split apart over time in response to a range of social and environmental circumstances. The Tribunal found that the Crown has an obligation to protect rangatiratanga "wherever it is manifest" and to protect the right of Māori communities to choose their own forms of social, political and economic organisation.[12]

The key question that the Tribunal identified as relevant to the protection principle in this claim was whether the policies and practices of the Crown "enhance the solidarity and integrity of Māori communities and empower the people, or whether they divide and rule them".[13] In this case, the Tribunal found that the way in which the Department of Social Welfare and the Community Funding Agency had engaged with Māori providers in West Auckland was in breach of the protection principle. The Crown had failed to recognise the Trust as a community expression of rangatiratanga and had undermined the rangatiratanga rights of Māori in West Auckland to organise themselves as they preferred.[14]

The Tribunal, therefore, found that the principle of partnership did not apply only between the Crown and kinship-based Māori entities, such as hapū or iwi. Partnership could certainly be expressed through devolution, though the Tribunal could see no justification for restricting that devolution in the way that the Crown was implementing its policies. The Tribunal did not dismiss the importance of maintaining kinship ties and cultural values and practices. However, the Tribunal referred to the way in which tikanga Māori, including the tikanga around social organisation, can adapt to changing circumstances. Moreover, the Tribunal found that Te Whānau o Waipareira is best placed to support many Māori living in West Auckland to restrengthen kinship connections:[15]

> *It is they who operate in the urban areas where Maori most estranged from kinship ties are found. It is they who are best located to bring in 'te pani me te rawakore' and re-establish their connections to their kin.*

The Tribunal made a range of recommendations, many of them building on the general approach outlined in *Puao-te-Ata-tu*. Amongst other things, the Tribunal recommended that the Crown should:[16]

> (a) *develop and publish evaluations of its current social service policies and programmes, based on their outcomes for Maori;*
> (b) *better coordinate its many agencies, each with its own policies and practices, in their relationships with Maori groups in order to represent its views as a whole on social service issues more effectively than it does at present;*
> (c) *ensure that any consultation with Maori about how the allocation of resources for social services might best promote community development in any given region includes both tangata whenua and non-tangata whenua in the region, irrespective of relative need and population size*

Health Services and Outcomes

The deliberate focus on partnerships with Māori and equitable outcomes for Māori has also been a feature of the Tribunal's Health Services and Outcomes Kaupapa Inquiry. In November 2016, the Tribunal's chairperson prioritised an inquiry into nationally significant health issues as part of the Tribunal's kaupapa inquiry programme. The Health Services and Outcomes Kaupapa

Inquiry brought together 100 claims that raise health issues. Among a range of other issues, these claims related to:

- the primary healthcare framework;
- the delivery of services to the deaf, blind and mentally ill;
- reducing ill-health amongst Māori caused by smoking and HIV/AIDS;
- an alleged disparity in the quality of health services provided to Māori and non-Māori;
- the accommodation of mātauranga Māori and rongoā Māori in health policy and the delivery of mainstream health services; and
- disparities in health outcomes for Māori and non-Māori.

To enable an initial targeted inquiry that addressed system issues within the primary healthcare framework, the Waitangi Tribunal decided to hear the Māori Primary Health Organisations and Providers (Wai 1315) and National Hauora Coalition (Wai 2687) claimants as a first stage of the inquiry. The Tribunal signalled that stage two was to focus on other nationally significant themes, including mental health, alcohol and substance abuse including tobacco use, and the experiences of Māori with disabilities. A third stage is also envisaged. The scope of stage three of the inquiry is to be further defined following the outcomes of stages one and two, but it is planned to address other themes of national significance and include eligible historical claims.

The inquiry is ongoing at the time of writing. However, the inquiry has already produced three reports:

- *Hauora: Report on Stage One of the Health Services and Outcomes Inquiry* (pre-publication version, 2019; and final published report, 2023);[17]
- *Haumaru: The COVID-19 Priority Report* (2023);[18] and
- *Hautupua: Te Aka Whai Ora (Māori Health Authority) Priority Report, Part 1* (pre-publication version, 2024).[19]

This chapter focuses on *Hauora*, its overarching recommendations for the primary healthcare system, and the recommendation to explore the establishment of an independent Māori health authority. As a response to the establishment and disestablishment of the Māori Health Authority, *Hautupua* is also relevant to these issues. Although *Haumaru* forms part of the broader Health Services and Outcomes inquiry and contributes an important Tiriti-based analysis of aspects of the government's response to the COVID-19 pandemic, for reasons of space, this report is not examined.

The first stage of the Health Services and Outcomes inquiry focused on primary healthcare. The claimants argued that the Primary Health Care Strategy and the broader primary healthcare framework did not sufficiently focus the primary healthcare system to achieve Māori health equity. Both claimant groups submitted that primary healthcare legislation and policy required urgent reframing in order to be Treaty compliant. In response, the Crown submitted that the existence of Māori health inequities did not, in and of itself, constitute a Treaty breach, and Crown counsel stated that the Crown wished to improve its "efforts to address" Māori health inequities "consistent with Treaty principles".

The Tribunal found that the primary healthcare system was not consistent with the principles of the Treaty of Waitangi and recommended significant changes to the legislative, policy and institutional framework of the healthcare system.[20] The primary healthcare system has not effectively let Māori govern and practise being well and is not underpinned by tino rangatiratanga and mana motuhake.

Māori ways of understanding, experiencing and accessing health have not been recognised in the way in which the health system was set up, the resources that were available, the monitoring that was undertaken and the ways in which Māori could participate in the system. Furthermore, Māori options for healthcare often did not exist and, if they did, did not always involve care in a way that understood and respected holistic and cultural needs of the communities. This has an effect on access to healthcare, including fewer Māori initially engaging with healthcare services, returning to healthcare services and prioritising healthcare services in their communities. These impacts are felt across complex individual, whānau and intergenerational levels and ultimately mean that Māori are not provided the services they need to be well.

The Tribunal identified that structural reform was necessary to ensure the principles and te Tiriti were foundational to the way in which primary healthcare is delivered. The Tribunal also found that the New Zealand Public Health and Disability Act 2000 did not go far enough to ensure that the whole primary healthcare system was te Tiriti compliant. The principles of "partnership, protection and participation" in He Korowai Oranga, the Māori Health Strategy, did not reflect te Tiriti or its principles. Though the Act did lay out terms for Māori participation in district health boards, those terms were ineffective at giving "Treaty-consistent control" over decision-making in the design and delivery of healthcare.[21] There was a lack of specific references to te Tiriti within lower-level documents, and these omissions were of concern when considering the whole-of-sector te Tiriti obligations.[22]

A notable feature of this report is the Tribunal's focus on achieving substantive equitable outcomes. While the Tribunal is careful to note that the determinants of health are complex and that "no single Crown entity or social sector agency can be strictly held to account in isolation for achieving equity", the Tribunal is also clear that the persistence of inequitable health outcomes for Māori is evidence that the law and policy settings are not Treaty compliant.[23]

The Tribunal also found that there was consistent underfunding for Māori primary health organisations from the outset. The primary healthcare funding model continually disadvantaged providers and organisations that had high populations of Māori enrolled, in particular, those serving high-needs populations and Māori primary health providers and organisations. As recognised by the Waitangi Tribunal, tino rangatiratanga is central to the ways in which Māori health providers and organisations support hauora Māori. A major Treaty breach was the failure to adequately resource these organisations alongside the failure to support governance that was effective for Māori design and delivery of systems of healthcare that protect and promote hauora Māori. Iwi/Māori partnership boards were also underfunded and often functioned in an advisory-only capacity, and their input was inconsistently sought. When considering the Act in conjunction with the funding arrangements, the Tribunal found that the primary healthcare framework "does not recognise and properly provide for tino rangatiratanga and mana Motuhake of hauora Māori".[24] Furthermore, accountability measures were insufficient to provide clear evidence as to how the primary healthcare system, as a whole, was performing for hauora Māori.

The Waitangi Tribunal made two overarching recommendations in *Hauora*. First, the Tribunal recommended that the Treaty principles provision in the New Zealand Public Health and Disability Act be strengthened to ensure there is a clear commitment to the principles of the Treaty, which underpins the primary health system.[25] The Tribunal also recommended a set of specific Treaty principles for the primary healthcare system:[26]

> *(a) The guarantee of tino rangatiratanga, which provides for Māori self-determination and mana motuhake in the design, delivery, and monitoring of primary health care.*

(b) *The principle of equity, which requires the Crown to commit to achieving equitable health outcomes for Māori.*
(c) *The principle of active protection, which requires the Crown to act, to the fullest extent practicable, to achieve equitable health outcomes for Māori. This includes ensuring that it, its agents, and its Treaty partner are well-informed on the extent, and nature, of both Māori health outcomes and efforts to achieve Māori health equity.*
(d) *The principle of options, which requires the Crown to provide for and properly resource kaupapa Māori primary health services. Furthermore, the Crown is obliged to ensure that all primary health care services are provided in a culturally appropriate way that recognises and supports the expression of hauora Māori models of care.*
(e) *The principle of partnership, which requires the Crown and Māori to work in partnership in the governance, design, delivery, and monitoring of primary health services. Māori must be co-designers, with the Crown, of the primary health system for Māori.*

The second overarching recommendation made in this report was that the Crown commit itself and the health sector to achieving equitable health outcomes.[27] The Tribunal recommended that this commitment be included in key legislation governing the health sector as well as all documents, strategies and plans that make up the policy framework of the primary health system. The Tribunal identified that an expressly stated, stand-alone commitment would be essential to move away from the language of "reducing disparities" in order to deliver equity in health outcomes for Māori.[28]

A Māori health authority

The Tribunal also made a significant recommendation for structural reform: exploring the establishment of an independent Māori health authority.[29] The Tribunal indicated that this was an interim recommendation, in part because the particular focus of this stage of the inquiry had not enabled the Tribunal to hear from all stakeholders or consider the full range of issues that might have a bearing on the establishment of an independent Māori health authority. Consequently, the Tribunal made interim recommendations that the Crown and claimant representatives design and draft terms of reference to explore the possibility and update the Tribunal on their progress within set timeframes.

The Tribunal's recommendations contributed to broader health sector reform that was already underway. The Health and Disability System Review final report was released in 2020 and highlighted "the need for legislative, governance and structural changes to create a cohesive and equitable health system for the future".[30] Reforms to the health sector were significant, and the Pae Ora (Healthy Futures) Act came into effect on 1 July 2022 as part of the response to the recommendations from *Hauora* and aligned with the timing of the Health and Disability System Review.[31] As well as giving effect to the Treaty principles (tino rangatiratanga, equity, active protection, options and partnership) recommended by the Waitangi Tribunal, the Act saw the establishment of four new entities, one of which was Te Aka Whai Ora (the Māori Health Authority).

The structural issues were addressed again by the Waitangi Tribunal in *Hautupua: Te Aka Whai Ora (Māori Health Authority) Priority Report, Part 1*. This report contained findings and recommendations from a priority inquiry into the disestablishment of Te Aka Whai Ora. Te Aka Whai Ora was a casualty of the change of government in 2023. Initially, the Waitangi Tribunal had granted an urgent hearing into the disestablishment of Te Aka Whai Ora, intending to report on the matter before legislation was introduced. When the government chose to bring forward the introduction of the Pae Ora (Disestablishment of Māori Health Authority) Amendment Bill, the Tribunal was forced to delay its inquiry until after the legislation was enacted. However, the Tribunal determined that there remained sufficient justification to hear the issue as a matter of priority within the ongoing Health Services and Outcomes inquiry. The Tribunal found that the Crown had failed to meet its Tiriti obligations in a number of ways, including failing to:[32]

- discharge its duty to consult and be sufficiently informed;
- follow its own processes for the development and implementation of legislative reform;
- recognise and respect tino rangatiratanga and the right of Māori to self-determine what is best for them for hauora Māori; and
- recognise and respect tino rangatiratanga by deciding to disestablish Te Aka Whai Ora without consulting Māori, and in the face of significant objection from Māori.

These issues mirror many of the problems identified by the Tribunal across a range of reforms undertaken by the National–ACT–New Zealand First Coalition Government, including the removal of section 7AA of the Oranga Tamariki Act discussed below.

Kāinga Kore

The Wai 2750 inquiry into housing policy and services and its report, *Kāinga Kore,* represented a pivotal moment in Aotearoa New Zealand's understanding of Treaty obligations within the context of housing policy and services.[33] Released in pre-publication form in May 2023, this stage one report provides a critical examination of Crown policies and strategies addressing Māori homelessness from 2009 to 2021. While the Tribunal originally considered a broader scope, it strategically narrowed its focus to contemporary homelessness (as part of the first phase), acknowledging this issue's connection to wider housing crisis and its challenges.

Conducted during the Labour Government's tenure, the inquiry established housing for Māori as a fundamental Treaty issue through its comprehensive examination of multiple breaches, including inadequate consultation in developing homelessness definitions, prolonged failure to collect adequate data, insufficient response to Māori experiencing homelessness and breaches of partnership principles in policy development. The report identified significant systemic issues, from housing system fragmentation (unsurprising to many working in this area) to inadequate protection of rangatahi experiencing homelessness, all constituting breaches of Treaty principles, including good government, active protection and partnership.

The inquiry and its process, including detailed Treaty analysis, has created momentum for addressing long-standing housing disparities affecting Māori communities, particularly through the report's comprehensive recommendations for reform and improved Crown coordination. The Crown's willingness to implement these reforms remains to be seen.

Treaty breaches: establishing homelessness as a Treaty issue

The report provides evidence based on Aotearoa New Zealand's housing system that the Crown has systematically breached Treaty obligations. While Māori scholars had previously argued that the Māori housing crisis (including homelessness) represented a breach of te Tiriti o Waitangi, the Tribunal's comprehensive analysis has now established this connection, creating a substantial body of evidence demonstrating systematic Treaty breaches across the housing system between 2009 and 2021.

A key example of Treaty breach examined in the inquiry was Statistics New Zealand's failure to adequately consult with Māori in developing its 2009 homelessness definition.[34] This initial breach of the Treaty duty of consultation proved far-reaching as years of subsequent inaction demonstrated a persistent disregard for Treaty partnership obligations. The breach was not merely procedural but reflected a deeper failure to recognise Māori perspectives in defining and understanding homelessness. From a te ao Māori context, homelessness encompasses spiritual and cultural dimensions that the standard definition failed to capture. This was evident in early discussions where claimants emphasised that "Māori are houseless rather than homeless" – a crucial distinction that reflected deeper cultural understandings of home and belonging. The Crown's sustained failure to collect adequate homelessness data represented a breach of both good government and active protection principles. This data deficit transcended mere technical oversight, instead constituting a fundamental failure to understand and monitor Māori housing needs. While initiatives like MAIHI Ka Ora and its associated Ka Mārama – Māori Housing Dashboard emerged as attempts to address these data gaps through a Māori-centred lens, these responses came only after years of inadequate data collection had already impeded effective policy development and implementation. The dashboard, while representing a step towards more culturally appropriate data collection and monitoring, highlighted the absence of such Māori-centered approaches in housing data systems.

The period from 2009 to 2016 was particularly significant as the Crown conceded multiple Treaty breaches. These acknowledgments encompassed failures in active protection through inadequate housing provision, in equity through escalating disparities in unmet housing need, and in good government through deficient implementation and monitoring of He Whare Āhuru He Oranga Tāngata (the Māori housing strategy before Maihi Ka Ora).[35] These breaches resulted in systematic failures to address both immediate housing needs and longer-term strategic requirements for Māori communities.

The development and implementation of contemporary housing policies further exposed significant Treaty breaches. The constrained scope of consultation during the development of both the Aotearoa New Zealand Homelessness Action Plan (HAP)[36] and MAIHI Framework for Action[37] breached partnership principles, exemplifying persistent deficiencies in Crown–

Māori engagement. Claimants like Hurimoana Dennis argued that there had been "insufficient consultation" on the MAIHI Framework.[38] While subsequent initiatives attempted to incorporate stronger partnership approaches, these consultation processes had already failed to meaningfully incorporate Māori perspectives and expertise at crucial early stages, resulting in policies that inadequately addressed Māori community needs and aspirations. This was particularly evident in the youth homelessness sector where, despite active advocacy and engagement from rangatahi providers and youth homelessness experts in the HAP process, the final policies failed to adequately capture or address the distinct challenges faced by young people experiencing homelessness – representing yet another critical gap in the Crown's response.

Defining and measuring homelessness

As previously noted, the inquiry revealed inadequacies in how homelessness was defined and measured in Aotearoa New Zealand. The 2009 Statistics New Zealand definition, developed with minimal consultation with Māori, demonstrated a broader systemic failure to incorporate Māori voices, cultural perspectives and understandings into housing policy. One of the authors of this chapter, Jacqueline Paul, in support of the Te Matapihi claim, emphasised that the Crown should partner with Māori to develop a more culturally appropriate definition, particularly concerning rangatahi homelessness.[39]

The measurement challenges extended beyond mere definition. Government agencies employed inconsistent data collection methods, particularly in recording ethnicity and service access. Critical data gaps, such as the number of people turned away from services, created blind spots in understanding the full scope of the housing crisis. These inconsistencies and gaps were not simply technical problems but represented a deeper failure to understand and address the cultural and spiritual dimensions of housing and homelessness for Māori communities.

The inquiry's examination of rangatahi homelessness revealed particularly serious breaches of Treaty obligations.[40] The Tribunal found both a breach of active protection through the Crown's failure to take vigorous action to protect this vulnerable group and a breach of good government through the failure to obtain adequate data on rangatahi homelessness. These failures were exacerbated by age inconsistencies across different government agencies and policies, creating confusion for rangatahi engaging with services and hindering effective responses.

The impact on rangatahi was particularly concerning given their vulnerability and the potential long-term consequences of housing instability. The lack of coordinated response across agencies combined with insufficient culturally appropriate support services created significant barriers for rangatahi Māori seeking housing assistance. Regional variations in service delivery further complicated access to support, while poor coordination between youth services and housing providers created additional challenges for this rōpū.

Looking forward: implications and recommendations

While the inquiry identified significant failures, it also provided a framework for future action. The Tribunal acknowledged that many Crown initiatives introduced since 2018 were too recent to assess effectively, indicating the need for ongoing evaluation. The findings suggest that addressing Māori homelessness requires not just policy changes but fundamental shifts in how housing issues are understood, measured and addressed within a Treaty framework.

While the inquiry extensively discussed culturally appropriate housing solutions and related governance structures, it notably did not include specific recommendations regarding the establishment of a Māori housing authority,[41] despite this being a frequent point raised by claimants throughout the tribunal hearings and its potential parallel to the recently established Māori Health Authority.

The inquiry established clear requirements for policy reform, emphasising the need for better coordination between agencies and the implementation of culturally appropriate service delivery models. The development of comprehensive data collection systems became a priority, alongside the essential integration of Māori perspectives in policy development and recognition of cultural dimensions in housing needs assessment.

The kāinga kore inquiry represents a pivotal moment in understanding how Treaty obligations should shape housing policy and practice in Aotearoa New Zealand. Its findings establish housing as a core Treaty issue and provide a framework for addressing both immediate needs and systemic changes required for equitable outcomes. The inquiry sets clear benchmarks for Treaty compliance in housing policy and establishes guidelines for meaningful consultation and partnership with Māori.

As Aotearoa New Zealand continues to grapple with the housing crisis, the inquiry's findings provide both a critique of past failures and a roadmap for future improvements. The challenge now lies in translating these findings into effective action to address Māori housing needs within a Treaty compliant framework. This will require sustained commitment to immediate interventions and long-term structural changes in the way housing policy is developed and implemented.

Oranga Tamariki

Child welfare and protection is another area of social policy that has been of longstanding concern to Māori. The Waitangi Tribunal has undertaken two significant urgent inquiries relating to Oranga Tamariki (the Ministry for Children), resulting in two reports: *He Pāharakeke, He Rito Whakakīkīnga Whāruarua – Oranga Tamariki Urgent Inquiry*[42] and *The Oranga Tamariki (Section 7AA) Urgent Inquiry Report.*[43] Taken together, the Oranga Tamariki urgent inquiries reinforce the importance of equity as a Treaty principle in the context of social policy and also illustrate the Tribunal's role within New Zealand's constitutional arrangements.

The first of the Oranga Tamariki urgent inquiries focused on the impact of the disproprotionate numbers of tamariki Māori being brought into state care. In July 2020, 4179 tamariki Māori were in state care – 69 per cent of the total number of children in care. The Tribunal held hearings for this inquiry over the second half of 2020 and into early 2021, and it published its findings and recommendations in *He Pāharakeke, He Rito Whakakīkīnga Whāruarua* in April 2021. Between 2017 and 2019, the Tribunal had received nine applications seeking urgent inquiries relating to the actions of Oranga Tamariki and its predecessors. Seven of those applications for urgent inquiries were grounded in historical grievances relating to Māori children placed in care. The chairperson of the Waitangi Tribunal declined those applications on the basis that the government had initiated a Royal Commission of Inquiry into historical abuse in state care and it would not be a sensible use of the Tribunal's limited resources to simultaneously conduct an urgent inquiry into those matters. However, the other two applications were granted because they dealt specifically with contemporary actions of Oranga Tamariki.[44] The two specific issues that were identified for the Waitangi Tribunal's consideration in this urgent inquiry were:[45]

> *(a) Having regard to the rising and disproportionately high number of tamariki Māori being taken into state care under the auspices of Oranga Tamariki, is Crown legislation, policy, and practice*

inconsistent with the principles of the Treaty and the Crown's Treaty duties to Māori? If so,

(b) What changes to Crown legislation, policy, and practice are required to ensure Treaty compliance?

The Crown made some important concessions at the outset of this inquiry. In particular, the Crown acknowledged "the significant disparity between the number of tamariki Māori and non-Māori being taken into the State care system" and accepted that such disparity was "unacceptable and the principles of te Tiriti/the Treaty require that active and positive steps be taken in order to address this".[46] Furthermore, the Crown conceded that:[47]

> *structural racism is a feature of Oranga Tamariki and its predecessors, and has resulted from various legislative, policy, and systems settings over time. The Crown acknowledges that this has had adverse effects on tamariki Māori, whānau, hapū, and iwi, and has detrimentally affected the relationship between Māori and the Crown.*

Significantly, the Tribunal framed its Treaty principles analysis by considering the Article 2 guarantee of tino rangatiratanga *in relation to kāinga*.[48] The Tribunal noted that 'kāinga' is specifically referred to in Article 2 of te Tiriti, which states:

> *Ko te Kuini o Ingaranui ka wakarite ka wakaae ki nga Rangatira, ki nga Hapu, ki nga tangata katoa o Nu Tirani, te tino Rangatiratanga o o ratou wenua o ratou kainga me o ratou taonga katoa. [emphasis added]*

In considering the implications of this guarantee, the Tribunal identified that 'kāinga' covers a range of meaning, including 'village' and 'home'. It is "the place where cultural identity is formed, nurtured, and sustained".[49] Its use in te Tiriti indicates that the tino rangatiratanga (chiefly authority) that is to be guaranteed there, relates not only to lands and resources, but to people as well. This leads the Tribunal to conclude:[50]

> *This is nothing less than a guarantee of the right to continue to organise and live as Māori. Fundamental to that is the right to care for and raise the next generation.*

Against that backdrop, the Tribunal identified principles of partnership, active protection, equity, options and redress as relevant to the inquiry and found significant breaches of those principles. The Tribunal acknowledged that the causes of the disparity within the child welfare and protection system have their roots in the many issues associated with colonisation. Yet, the report also notes that the disparity is continuing to be perpetuated and "cannot be considered simply the result of conditions 'external' to Oranga Tamariki and its predecessors".[51] Structural racism within the system is continuing to cause harm to tamariki and whānau Māori. The Crown breached the principle of partnership by failing to recognise the rangatiratanga of Māori and failing to engage with Māori in the design of legislation and policy in this area.[52] Oranga Tamariki and its predecessors were found to be "fundamentally Pākehā in their philosophies, values, and constructs" and, consequently, in breach of the principle of options, there was no space within that framework for the welfare of tamariki Māori to be recognised and protected in accordance with the world view of whānau, hapū and iwi.[53]

The Tribunal made a number of recommendations aimed at removing the prejudice to Māori within the child welfare and protection system. However, the Tribunal emphasised that the key change that is necessary is a fundamental structural change. Its primary recommendation, therefore, was formation of a Māori Transition Authority. The Tribunal identified that the root cause of the prejudice suffered by Māori, including the disparities across a range of social measures, has been the Crown's resistance to recognise the right Māori have to cultural continuity and to give effect to the Tiriti guarantee of tino rangatiratanga over kāinga.[54] To address that root cause, the transformation of the system must be led by Māori. The Tribunal recommended that a Māori governance group, with a role for claimant representation, be set up to engage with the Crown on the establishment of a Māori Transition Authority. The Māori Transition Authority would then "decide the framework within which future care and protection services for tamariki Māori will be placed".[55] This suggests a similar 'by Māori, for Māori' approach as recommended in the *Hauora* report in order to create a Tiriti-consistent system to address significant and longstanding inequities in social policy.[56]

Section 7AA

The Crown did not adopt the Tribunal's recommendation of establishing a Māori Transition Authority. In fact, following a change of government in 2023, the Crown undertook legislative reform to remove specific obligations in relation to tamariki Māori and partnerships with Māori communities.

Section 7AA of the Oranga Tamariki Act imposed specific duties on the chief executive of Oranga Tamariki to provide a practical commitment to the principles of the Treaty of Waitangi. These duties include ensuring that policies and practices have the objective of reducing disparities and have regard to the whakapapa of tamariki Māori and the whanaungatanga responsibilities of whānau, hapū and iwi. Section 7AA also provided for the chief executive to enter into strategic partnerships with Māori organisations. After examining section 7AA in its earlier report, the Waitangi Tribunal found that this section is "for all intents and purposes, Oranga Tamariki's Treaty clause".[57] As part of the coalition agreement between the National Party and the ACT Party, it was agreed that the Oranga Tamariki Act would be amended to remove section 7AA. The Waitangi Tribunal granted an urgent inquiry to claimants who sought to challenge the removal of this section.

Following the Tribunal's previous urgent inquiry into more general issues relating to Oranga Tamariki, the urgent inquiry into the removal of section 7AA reiterates similar themes and issues regarding the application of Treaty principles to the substantive child welfare and protection matters. The inquiry into section 7AA did, however, raise some new and significant issues in relation to policy development, Waitangi Tribunal procedure and the constitutional relationship between the Tribunal and Ministers of the Crown. These issues arose as the Tribunal sought to understand the policy rationale for the removal of section 7AA.

The background to the policy was that the coalition agreement between National and ACT included a commitment to progress the ACT Party's policy to remove section 7AA from the Oranga Tamariki Act 1989. Karen Chhour, an ACT Party Member of Parliament, was subsequently sworn in as Minister of Children. Minister Chhour made it clear to officials and at a meeting with strategic partners and iwi representatives that her intent was to repeal section 7AA. The Minister maintained this position despite the fact that the Regulatory Impact Statement prepared by officials concluded that neither a full nor partial repeal of section 7AA would address the policy concerns identified, and it recommended that the government retain section 7AA and strengthen practice and operational guidelines. The Regulatory Impact Statement noted that "[t] here is no empirical evidence to support the notion that section 7AA has driven practice decisions that have led to changing care arrangements" and, furthermore, section 7AA has been a success:[58]

> *Changes introduced in Oranga Tamariki that resulted from the introduction of 7AA have been effective at reducing some of the disparities and inequities experienced by tamariki, rangatahi, and whānau Māori. There has also been considerable progress as a Department towards honouring the principles of the Treaty of Waitangi through the current practice approach and operating model.*

The particular issues of the constitutional relationship between the Tribunal and Ministers of the Crown arose when the Tribunal sought further explanation from Minister Chhour. The evidence from Crown officials was that the policy to remove section 7AA came from a political commitment in the coalition agreement, rather than through the usual policy development process. Therefore, the Tribunal reasoned, it needed to receive evidence from Minister Chhour herself in order to understand the rationale behind the policy. It is not unusual for the Tribunal to seek evidence from a responsible minister and in most cases, the relevant minister will provide a written response. Minister Chhour initially refused to provide evidence, either written or in person, which led to the Tribunal taking the rare step of issuing a summons for Minister Chhour. This created a small political controversy, with some other government ministers alleging that the Tribunal had acted outside its authority in requiring Minister Chhour to give evidence. The Crown successfully challenged the Tribunal's summons in the High Court, though the High Court's decision was subsequently overturned by the Court of Appeal.

Although the Minister had provided the Waitangi Tribunal with a response to its questions by the time of the Court of Appeal decision, and the Bill to repeal section 7AA had also been introduced, the Court of Appeal's judgment was still significant in terms of laying out some important points about the constitutional role of the Tribunal. In particular, the Court of Appeal confirmed that the Waitangi Tribunal has a role of constitutional importance and a statutory duty to inquire into claims that a Crown policy to enact legislation is inconsistent with the principles of the Treaty of Waitangi. As a commission of inquiry, the Tribunal has significant powers to enable it to fulfil its statutory function, including the power to summons a Minister of the Crown to provide evidence. Although the Tribunal has a quasi-judicial function, the Court of Appeal noted that the context in which it operates means the relationship between the Tribunal and government ministers is slightly different to the relationship that exists between the courts and ministers. Consequently, the

Tribunal was acting within its powers when it issued a summons for Minister Chhour on the reasonable determination that she had information relevant to the Tribunal's inquiry. Although the Court of Appeal decision was not able to be issued in time to have an impact on the inquiry in relation to the removal of section 7AA, the judgment is significant for confirming the constitutional role and position of the Waitangi Tribunal with respect to Ministers of the Crown.

Conclusion

The inquiries examined in this chapter are examples of the way in which the Tribunal has engaged with issues of social policy and well-being. They each illustrate important aspects of the Tribunal's work in this space. Throughout these inquiries, there has been a focus on equity, and the reports demonstarte the importance of a Tiriti analysis in addressing social policy and well-being issues and supporting equitable outcomes for Māori. These inquiries also raise distinctive issues around the Crown's Tiriti obligations and to whom they are owed and around the constitutional role of the Tribunal itself. Rangatiratanga, partnership and equity are shown to be important Treaty principles in shaping processes for problem definition, policy design, implementation and delivery of social services. We can expect to see the foundational work of the *Te Whānau o Waipareira*, *Hauora*, *Kāinga Kore* and *Oranga Tamariki* reports develop further in the coming years as the Tribunal progresses its kaupapa inquiry programme and continues to respond to urgent social policy and well-being issues.

“Injustice is not passive. It does not sit politely, waiting to be attended to; it compounds over time.”

Chapter 13

Mana Wāhine

— *Ani Mikaere*

[E]very part of tikanga and mātauranga Māori was based on the equality and interdependence of Māori women and men ... In Māori terms, any notion of a gendered hierarchy implying the lesser status of Māori women would have been, and still is, intellectually incomprehensible and culturally impossible.
Moana Jackson[1]

Background to the Original Mana Wāhine Claim (Wai 381)

The claims that are currently being heard by the Tribunal in the Mana Wāhine Kaupapa Inquiry were born from a deep sense of frustration that the "intellectually incomprehensible and culturally impossible" had come to pass – that Māori women were indeed being relegated to a lesser status. The lodging of the claims also signalled a steely determination, on the part of the claimants, that this state of affairs must not be allowed to continue.

The original Mana Wāhine claim (Wai 381) was lodged in 1993, prompted by the removal of Dame Mira Szaszy from the shortlist of appointees for the inaugural Treaty of Waitangi Fisheries Commission, and her replacement with a young Māori male. As the claimants' lawyer, Denese Henare, explained:[2]

> *In many chapters of examples that example was yet another in the way Maori women were seen—that we have less value than young Maori males and less value than Pakeha males. Maori women saw that injustice and said to each other ... 'There's something wrong with the way the Crown continues to perpetuate this attitude of no value in Maori women'.*

It was not as though Dame Mira lacked experience for the role, having served as the only Māori woman member of the Māori Fisheries Commission (the predecessor to the Treaty of Waitangi Fisheries Commission) since its inception in 1989. But it is clear that she did not want the claim to be about her as an individual: Ripeka Evans explains that she was "reluctant to consider formal action until the higher principles at stake could be defined and articulated", insisting that the claim should be "grounded in our own beliefs and assert our own mana as women that would ultimately benefit all people".[3]

The erosion of Māori women's status had been troubling Dame Mira for some time. Her recollections of the early days of the Māori Women's Welfare League were of strong support from Māori men throughout the country, who "came in droves to the meetings and sat there with us" and of the inaugural president, Whina Cooper, being free to speak wherever they went on League business.[4] But by the early 1960s, she had noted a change in the demeanour of Māori men and an apparent willingness on the part of the Crown to align itself with them at the expense of Māori women:[5]

> *After 10 years of Māori women running the Māori world there was a reaction amongst the men, that they were being left out of things ... So the men moved to get the government to approve the establishing of a National Māori Council ... For me that was the beginning of the dichotomy of power and development within the Māori world.*

She felt that the League lost impetus in subsequent years, becoming "almost conditioned" to New Zealand Māori Council thinking. There was even a proposal, during the 1970s, for the League to come under the umbrella of the Māori Council, a move that she had opposed strongly. The independence of the League, in her view, was of the utmost importance:[6]

The organisation must retain its independence—independence from the Crown and independence from any other body, any other influences ... That was very much troubling me after my time, that undermining, in a sense, of the power of the organisation.

Her removal from the shortlist of appointees to the Treaty of Waitangi Fisheries Commission in 1993 was cited by the Wai 381 statement of claim as an example of the Crown's longstanding failure to meet its Treaty obligation to protect and ensure the rangatiratanga of Māori women as individuals, members and leaders of tribes and families. By failing to accord Māori women status and power within the structures it created, the claimants argued, the Crown was undermining their status as rangatira.

The claimants sought a review of all current and pending Crown appointments to political, social, cultural and economic organisations, urging that no further appointments be made until the claim had been reported on and a process for implementing any recommendations had been put in place. They further sought a requirement for consultation with the League as part of Cabinet appointment processes and the establishment of a commission to protect the integrity of Crown and iwi-mandated processes of selection, recommendation and appointment to organisations that were to be representative of Māori.

The response of the Minister of Māori Affairs, Doug Kidd, was revealing. He flatly refused to take responsibility for his central role in the debacle (as Minister, he had removed Dame Mira from the shortlist), citing Māori culture as the problem and claiming that Māori women had "more a friend than a foe in the Minister". He placed the blame squarely on Māori men – and, indeed, on Māori women themselves:[7]

They (Maori women) need to stand on their hind legs ... The days of the Government being the great white father to the Maori are over.

That Kidd would regard the boorish inanity of this retort as an appropriate ministerial response is a powerful commentary, not only on the arrogance of the Crown but also on the climate in which the Mana Wāhine claim was launched. At that time, the premise of the claim was widely regarded as novel.[8] Many colonisers refused to acknowledge any connection between te Tiriti o Waitangi and the challenges confronting Māori women, preferring to deny their own responsibility in the matter by characterising Māori men as irredeemable misogynists and Māori women as spineless. Tragically, some Māori had also been conditioned into believing this to be true.[9]

The Long Wait to be Heard

The original Mana Wāhine claimants sought an urgent hearing in 1993. They also pointed out the significance of the year – not only was the centenary of women gaining the vote in Aotearoa being celebrated, but it was also the United Nations International Year of the World's Indigenous Peoples – adding that these two events "in and of themselves require that the Tribunal give priority to hearing this claim". However, a further twenty-five years were to pass before the chairperson of the Tribunal formally initiated the Mana Wāhine Kaupapa Inquiry (Wai 2700) on 20 December 2018.

By this time, the argument that the status of Māori women was a te Tiriti issue had been taken up by many others. In July 2020, it was noted that over 160 claims had been lodged, raising a vast array of issues in relation to alleged Crown acts and omissions, policy, practices and legislation and their prejudicial impacts on wāhine Maori.[10] Given that the Wai 381 claimants had sought urgency, and given the subsequent proliferation of claims raising related issues, many have questioned why it took so long for the Mana Wāhine Kaupapa Inquiry to make its way to the front of the queue.[11]

According to Ripeka Evans the Wai 381 claimants, when presenting the claim in person to the Tribunal chairperson in 1993, had mentioned their concern at the direction the claims process was taking. Speaking just weeks after the claim was lodged, she noted:[12]

> *We reminded the Tribunal ... that there was a perception amongst our women that the claims and settlement process, and the Treaty debate, had been captured by resource issues. I am not saying that resource issues are not important, but the Tribunal needs to be mindful not to let the sexy issues eclipse issues of status.*

History was to prove their concerns well founded as the historic claims, centring primarily on resources, became all-consuming during the decades that followed. Not that anyone could deny the horrific impact of the wholesale land removals, theft of fisheries and environmental devastation unleashed on hapū and iwi by the Crown since 1840, or the urgent need to have those grievances resolved. But, given the chronic underfunding of the Tribunal, focusing on the iwi-centred and largely resource-based claims inevitably exhausted the limited pool of Tribunal reserves. As these claims went through the laborious process of being lodged, heard, reported on, negotiated and settled, fundamentally important issues affecting Māori throughout Aotearoa such as housing, health, justice, adoption, education, constitutional arrangements and the status of Māori women languished.[13]

The price of focusing so heavily on the resource-based claims is not limited to the ill-effects of unresolved injustice for those who have been forced to wait their turn. Injustice is not passive. It does not sit politely, waiting to be attended to; it compounds over time.[14] Moreover, prioritising the historic claims may have had the effect of setting in place additional structural barriers for Māori women. Appearing before the Tribunal in 2021, Donna Awatere observed that the delays in hearing Wai 381 had enabled the burgeoning of a Treaty settlement process that had intensified the issues prompting the claim in the first place:[15]

> *[T]he Mana Wāhine claim, made in 1993, ought to have preceded all other claims from that date. One of the first steps in the process of undermining the Rangatiratanga of the whānau and Hapū was to convince Māori men that Pākehā ideas of the worthlessness of women was superior to that of the Māori idea that women are the foundation of life itself ...*
>
> *[U]ntil the Mana Wāhine claim re-establishes the ancestral rules of the Mana and power, the centrality of the female, the balance the female elements as Atua, as ancestors, as leaders provide, then the settlements will be what they are—another way to make invisible and co-op (sic) the work and achievements of Māori women.*

Awatere is not the only person to notice the predominance of Māori men in the Treaty settlements arena. In 2012 Moana Jackson encouraged men to rise above the privilege accorded them by colonisers; and to recalibrate their priorities:[16]

> *I am aware that often tikanga was redefined by the colonisers to privilege men over our women and that some of our men now take that privilege to subordinate or silence our women. I am aware too that if I go to work for example with a group that is dealing with domestic violence, or the welfare of our mokopuna, or go to talk at a hauora hui, 90 percent of the people there are our women. However if I go to a hui about the latest possible deal with the Crown, 90 percent of people there will be our men.*

The focus on Treaty settlements – haggling over their monetary value and conforming to Crown rules of engagement in order to secure them – had clearly become a distraction. As Mason Durie pondered in 1999, we ran the risk of being remembered as the generations who became "captivated by the smallness of once vast tribal estates, blinded by the promise of a few fish, or so intoxicated with the trappings of sovereignty that we failed to make a place for our children in the new world".[17]

The longstanding emphasis on the large resource-based claims also had the unfortunate effect of allowing te Tiriti grievances to be reduced, primarily, to a squabble about property rights. This played into the hands of those who insist on privileging the document in English – a document that takes Crown sovereignty as a given, thereby enabling the Crown to curtail any Article 2 guarantees (such as protection of property or rights of citizenship) and forcing claimants to couch their arguments primarily in terms of how the Crown should most honourably exercise its unquestioned power.

This position flies in the face of what Māori signatories actually agreed to, and what Hobson himself signed up to, in te Tiriti (the document in te reo Māori). Te Tiriti o Waitangi is not simply about a guarantee of property rights, cynically curtailed by the Crown so as to cause it minimum inconvenience. Its reach is all-encompassing. Te Tiriti o Waitangi compels the acknowledgement of tino rangatiratanga, the expression of political authority by whānau, hapū and iwi to maintain a way of life based on the maintenance of whakapapa relationships between people, and between people and our non-human whanaunga. Allowing the Crown (or our own) to characterise te Tiriti as being about anything less than that encourages a dangerous diminution of what our tūpuna agreed to in 1840.

There have been some exceptions to the focus on resources. Most notable of these has been the *Te Paparahi o Te Raki Inquiry* (Wai 1040), which brought the fundamental issue of the constitutional arrangements envisaged by te Tiriti to the fore. That said, hearings for the claim did not begin until 2010 and the Stage 1 report was not published until 2014.

Meanwhile, claims concerning issues affecting Māori throughout Aotearoa were left unattended. It was not until the Tribunal was approaching the last of the large iwi-based claims that it turned its attention to issues that were not tethered, primarily, to the settlement of historical grievances. Perhaps, as its kaupapa inquiry programme gathers pace, some of the philosophical ground lost during the past twenty-five years will be regained as attention is focused on issues that cannot be minimised by the Crown as mere property rights.[18]

Not all changes that have taken place while the Wai 381 claimants have been waiting their turn have been for the worse. There has certainly been a shift in the way the Crown has seen fit to respond. In July 2019, Minister for Women Julie Anne Genter announced a budget allocation of $6.2 million to "progress the Crown's engagement" with the claim,[19] explaining that a specialist team would be assembled to work alongside Te Puni Kōkiri in order to coordinate a government response and participation in the inquiry.[20] While clearly a change in direction from the patronising stance adopted by Doug Kidd back in 1993, Wai 381 claimant Ripeka Evans (one of the handful of original claimants still living) remains unimpressed:[21]

> *I have to call it out, the Crown funding for this claim is for the Crown to bring it - not for me - not for the claimants to come and tell their stories ... It beggars belief that the lesson of the last 28 years is that the Crown has not woken up yet about mana wāhine and about the opportunities that that presents ... And we are still looking to the tribunal as our ray of hope - we don't have deep pockets.*

The Tribunal's Approach

The kaupapa inquiries have instigated a more innovative approach to proceedings, and the Mana Wāhine inquiry is no exception. The inquiry began with a number of tūāpapa hearings, held during 2021–2022 in Kerikeri, Ngāruawāhia, Whangārei, Whakatāne, Lower Hutt and Christchurch. Intended to establish a foundation for the balance of the inquiry, the tūāpapa hearings focused on the tikanga of mana wāhine and pre-colonial understandings of wāhine in te ao Māori. In accordance with guidelines produced by the claimant lawyers with the support of the Tribunal, witnesses were encouraged to explore four themes:

- Atua whāea and tipuna whāea and the blueprint for mana wāhine.
- Te ira wāhine and te ira tangata – the relationality and balance of wāhine and tāne.
- Te mana o te wāhine in Te Ao Māori, Māori society, and rangatira wāhine.
- Wāhine rangatiratanga over whenua, whakapapa/whānau, whai rawa, and mātauranga.

Over 126 witnesses participated in the tūāpapa hearings, drawing on a diverse range of sources – pūrākau, iwi kōrero, waiata, karakia, poetry, life experiences and academic research – to produce a wealth of information about pre-colonial understandings of mana wāhine.

The Tribunal has taken the unprecedented step of making this material available on its website. Te Kete Pūputu: The Online Guide to the Mana Wāhine Tūāpapa Evidence has collated the knowledge shared by witnesses and made it accessible to everyone. Users are able to read key quotes from a range of witnesses on the four main themes listed above. They are also able to access information about the tūāpapa hearings and to read all briefs of evidence. Launched online in May 2024, Te Kete Pūputu is a first for the Tribunal. It allows ready access to valuable material gathered during this early stage of the inquiry – material on which the Tribunal does not intend to make any direct findings[22] and which may otherwise have been shared only with those directly involved in the hearings.

The Tribunal also commissioned a number of reports exploring a range of issues, both historical and contemporary.[23] These too will be made available on the Tribunal website. In addition, a number of reports have been commissioned by the Mana Wāhine Joint Research Committee,[24] which was established to manage funds made available by the Crown for claimant research. The committee is comprised of representatives from the Mana Wāhine claimant community, claimant counsel, Crown counsel, Manatū Wāhine and Tribunal research staff. Its purpose is to "ensure that cogent submissions are made to the Tribunal in relation to the Inquiry's research programme or casebook".[25]

Eyebrows might well be raised at the paucity of the sum made available by the Crown to support claimant research.[26] That said, the body of knowledge produced by both sets of research reports, combined with the material made available on Te Kete Pūputu, highlights one of the most significant aspects of the Tribunal's work: its ability to generate research that has the potential to create transformation by changing the way that people think about an issue. While its reports have always played an important role in this regard, the Tribunal's commitment to making this background material readily accessible, expressed through initiatives such as Te Kete Pūputu, will serve to significantly enhance the educative aspect of its activity.

The Significance of the Mana Wāhine Kaupapa Inquiry

To fully appreciate the importance of the Mana Wāhine Kaupapa Inquiry, it is necessary to understand the pivotal role of patriarchy in the process of colonisation. Patriarchy is no mere byproduct of colonial oppression. A key driver of the British imperialist machine, patriarchy has been essential to the achievement of the coloniser's goals.

For the British colonists, hierarchy served as a powerful form of social cement. Their conception of a well-ordered society was one where every person understood and accepted their place in the pecking order, willingly submitting to some while demanding submission from others. The concept of hierarchy was also considered crucial to the success of the imperial project, with the view that "the empire was built on the principle that imperialists could dominate others because they allowed themselves to be dominated" representing popular wisdom during the heyday of the British Empire.[27] As Ashis Nandy explains, the colonial "drive for mastery over men" is rooted in a world view that:[28]

> *believes in the absolute superiority of the human over the nonhuman and the subhuman, the masculine over the feminine, the adult over the child, the historical over the ahistorical, and the modern or progressive over the traditional or the savage.*

This way of understanding the world could not have been any further removed from that of the people whom the British empire-builders came to colonise. Our tūpuna had developed their own quite distinctive philosophical framework to provide answers to life's universal questions – an accumulation of theory and understanding that explains where we came from and guides our behaviour. This body of knowledge, often referred to as mātauranga, is rooted in the relationship between the people and the world around – land, water, sky and all life that exists within and between them. In turn, the language of the people, te reo Māori, evolved over time to articulate, expand on and transmit the mātauranga.

Central to mātauranga is the concept of whakapapa, which is primarily concerned with relationships: between people; between people and their non-human relatives; and between past, present and future generations. Whakapapa reminds us that relationships must be carefully managed because everything in our world is connected. Failing to nurture key relationships will result in imbalance, which will ultimately be to the detriment of all.

The real tragedy of the historic, iwi-based claims that have been prioritised over the past several decades is not simply what they revealed about the theft of "resources" or the stifling of economic opportunity. Rather, it is what they demonstrated about the impact of Crown actions on the relationships between iwi and their non-human tūpuna. The brutal severing of whakapapa relationships with whenua, maunga, awa, ngahere and so on – those entities with whom an intimate whakapapa relationship had produced a body of mātauranga and reo that was unique to each hapū and iwi and therefore critical to their survival – did a kind of damage that defies quantification. It played a key role in the collapse of language and tikanga that brought many iwi to the brink of cultural extinction.[29]

Reliance on a whakapapa framework to make sense of our existence also informs our approach to relationships between people, requiring us to value every person as part of an endlessly expanding whole. This is not to be confused with some feel-good notion of equality or sameness; rather, it recognises that the particular qualities of every person contribute to the vitality of the whakapapa network in its entirely. Whether female or male, young or old, teina or tuakana, each person plays their part in establishing the precedents that are bequeathed to later generations. Without the unique characteristics of each and every individual, the strength of the collective is diminished.

Whakapapa is inherently, inescapably non-hierarchical. All elements in creation, human and non-human, possess mana by virtue of their whakapapa. For the coloniser, this way of understanding the world was deeply problematic. For colonisation to succeed, it was essential that the colonised come to recognise the notion of hierarchy as normal. Only then would they accept the inevitability of domination and its corollary, subordination.

But how to colonise peoples whose societies were not hierarchical? The introduction of patriarchy was a crucial first step,[30] providing a powerful incentive to half of the target population (men) to accept the logic of hierarchy because of the benefits that accrue to them. The missionaries played a crucial role in introducing patriarchy to Māori, "civilising the natives" by grooming the men to assume control of nuclear families and re-educating the women to accept their role as good Christian wives, submissive and confined to the domestic sphere.

This reordering of male–female relationships is entirely consistent with the core of Church teachings. Given the gender and colour of God (who sits at the top of the hierarchy), Christianity is inherently misogynist and racist, premised on the belief that maleness and whiteness are innately superior to femaleness and colour. Through the introduction of patriarchy, Māori were programmed to accept their "God-given" place on the lower rungs of creation, Māori men accorded an automatic advantage over their female relatives by virtue of their genitalia.

Colonisation has constituted an unrelenting attack on the whakapapa foundations of Māori philosophy. It has sought to disrupt and to sever relationships, creating a separation between human and non-human, and between different "categories" of people. It has replaced healthy relationships with exploitative ones – an inevitable result of hierarchy, which is sustained by the exercise of power over others.

Giving evidence during the first of the tūāpapa hearings, Donna Awatere was scathing about the results of the colonial endeavour and clear that patriarchy acted as the advance guard for the adoption of hierarchical thinking:[31]

> *[T]here is nothing superior in these stupid Pākehā ideas. The patriarchy's legacy is violence towards women. Capitalism's legacy is the gap between rich and poor both between nations and between citizens. Dualism's legacy is the degradation of the environment and the climate emergency ... In accepting the worthlessness of women idea, Māori men took a big step towards accepting the Pākehā superiority story.*

Patriarchy has been instrumental in the process of colonisation, underpinning the coloniser's sense of entitlement and ushering in new ways of thinking about the world that guaranteed its perpetuation by the very people who stood to lose everything by maintaining it:[32]

> *This colonialism colonizes minds in addition to bodies and it releases forces within the colonized societies to alter their cultural priorities once and for all ... The West is now everywhere, within the West and outside; in structures and in minds.*

In driving a wedge between the two key elements in whakapapa, female and male, patriarchy is designed to destroy the very fabric of whānau, hapū and iwi. It has been key to dismantling Māori resistance, turning us against one another and disrupting our attempts to mount effective resistance against colonialism.

What Might Be Achieved as a Result of the Mana Wāhine Kaupapa Inquiry?

Mana Wāhine claimants have sought a range of remedies, including a Crown acknowledgement of and apology for its breaches of te Tiriti, the implementation of appropriately funded processes to address the harms done to generations of wāhine Māori and the creation of mechanisms to monitor the Crown's progress in improving its performance.

When asked what they hoped to see come out of the claim, participants in the *Takapou Whāriki* report[33] discussed a number of possible reparations, which the report loosely organised into three groupings: acknowledgement of harm, the return of land to help rebuild mana motuhake and whānau and cultural connectedness, and the need for systems-change.[34]

Speaking to the acknowledgement of harm, Tina Ngata sought:[35]

> *A recognition of the fact that the forces of colonisation and the practices and processes of the Crown in particular have had a specific, distinct, and disproportionate impact upon the mana of wāhine. And recognition that there's been a physical impact on our lifespans; that there's been a spiritual impact upon us in terms of access to our atua wāhine ...; that there's been an impact on our economic strength; on our ability to lead in relation to rangatiratanga and mobilise our communities and whānau.*

Some wanted the Crown to acknowledge and reflect on its role in this process, while others were more focused on the importance of others – Māori and Pākehā – understanding who was responsible for the multiple challenges confronting Māori women in the present day.

On the subject of land, Awhina Cameron noted:[36]

> *I think we know that money doesn't heal. A lot of Treaty settlements ... have been about resourcing ... but they've been in a monetary form. What has been severed is the unique connections and the unique status of women on land, and women to land.*

For Ngaropi Raumati, the desire to see the return of land is tied directly to the removal of whenua from mothers following the birth of their babies:[37]

> *We should claim land because it was whenua to whenua; we did not get to return our whenua to the whenua therefore we should be compensated with land from our tribal areas. One hectare for every whenua not returned.*

Naomi Simmonds explained the return of land in terms of rangatiratanga:[38]

> *The solutions are clear to us in terms of land back, environmental restoration and protection and a clean way, having our own services*

for our own whānau, our own things like maternity care. Land back, and having our own rangatiratanga to serve our own whānau using our own knowledge and practices ...

On the matter of systems-change, participants spoke about the need to change current systems or to develop kaupapa Māori systems, or both. All noted the importance of wāhine Māori being positioned to determine policies, funding and the development of resources. They spoke about health, education and the need for wānanga to rebuild and expand our own knowledge base.

When asked about their hopes for the future, most simply wanted a world where misogyny and racism were no more:[39]

I would like to see less pressure on our wāhine Māori ... not to feel like they have to constantly fight, fight, and fight just to get the basic rights. I would love for us to not have to do that anymore, to have the space to just breathe. I would love for everybody to understand our role as wāhine Māori and our tikanga, and our reo; and that it's not something that we have to constantly make a big statement about.

Some spoke about the world they imagined for their children: one where their daughters could choose to be whatever they wanted[40] and where they would "not be questioned because they're female".[41] Kassie Hartendorp explained:[42]

I feel this really strong sense that one of the things of colonisation was always about making women's lives and dreams and souls and experiences smaller and lesser than ... I just think of my daughter, and I hope that what it means is that she never has to make herself smaller.

Many were explicit about the fact that the struggle for mana wāhine was part of the wider struggle to decolonise. Aroha Mead, for instance, said that being truly free as a wahine meant being truly free as a Māori:[43]

It means that where we need to move to as a country and as a people is a collective thing, and that the expression of mana wāhine sits within a broader connection of being Māori ... We're dependent on te reo being normalised in the country, we're dependent on the Treaty having a stable, durable, constitutional status. We're dependent on a greater awareness of racism and sexism in New Zealand society as a whole so that the behavioural changes that need to happen and the corresponding policy and legal changes that need to happen can indeed happen. We depend on the whole of society to allow that.

So, what might be achieved as a result of the inquiry? The Crown's record, when it comes to implementing Tribunal recommendations, is underwhelming to say the least. Governments are essentially reactionary, moving only when the weight of public opinion makes it politically expedient, or at least safe, to do so. The immediate outcome of the Mana Wāhine Kaupapa Inquiry, insofar as it is measured in terms of the Crown response to the remedies that claimants have sought, is bound to be disappointing.

However, few would expect the true value of bringing the claim to lie in the implementation of Tribunal recommendations. It is much more likely to be found in the extent to which it can influence societal opinion: in the contribution it can make to changing the colonial narrative about the contemporary challenges confronting wāhine Māori. A straightforward explanation of the role played by patriarchy in colonisation would go a long way towards undermining that narrative. An unequivocal statement that misogyny is the travelling companion, not of tikanga but of colonialism, would clear up a great deal of muddled thinking about the role of women according to tikanga. A finding that incentivising Māori men to buy into the notion of gender hierarchy was part of a colonial strategy to unravel the whakapapa bonds that wove us together would do much to repair what Kathie Irwin once referred to as "the first partnership lost" when the Treaty was signed: the partnership between Māori men and women.[44] The Tribunal can and should address these matters when it reports on the Mana Wāhine inquiry.

It is also important to note that the contribution of the Tribunal is not limited to the production of a report. The very act of lodging a claim can trigger a shift in our understanding of an issue. The filing of over 160 additional claims relating to mana wāhine since 1993, the evidence of over 120 key witnesses presented during the tūāpapa hearings and the careful reaction of the Crown to the instigation of the kaupapa inquiry in 2018 are all indicative of the impact that the lodging of the original Mana Wāhine claim has already had on our thinking. The Tribunal process has generated, and will continue to generate, the production of a significant body of material that will doubtless prove invaluable for future work.

The Tribunal will not begin hearing the substantive Mana Wāhine claims until 2025, so the issuing of a report is still some way off. But, with or without Tribunal engagement, the ground has shifted. The crass incredulity of the Minister in 1993, at the suggestion that mana wāhine was a te Tiriti issue, would likely be greeted with disapproval now in many circles.

Concluding Thoughts

While there has been some progress in the way that issues of mana wāhine are perceived, particularly by Māori women,[45] there is still an urgent need for these matters to be reported on and addressed. As Tina Ngata observed:[46]

> *The hearings are taking place against a backdrop of social extremes for wāhine Māori, who are at once recognised globally for their leadership in Indigenous academia, business, justice, environmental advocacy and education, but who are also significantly underpaid for their work, experience numerous barriers to adequate healthcare and social assistance, and suffer one of the highest incarceration rates for women in the world.*

The report commissioned by the Waitangi Tribunal to examine the socio-economic status and well-being of Māori women from 1990–2020 makes for grim reading, finding a persistent pattern of socio-economic disparities faced by wāhine Māori during this period. Compared to Pākehā women, wāhine Māori consistently experience lower income levels and higher rates of unemployment, are concentrated in low-paid and precarious jobs, experience poor health and well-being outcomes and are overrepresented in the social welfare system.[47]

It is also clear that colonised thinking about the role and status of wāhine Māori remains stubbornly entrenched in some quarters. In 2020 Prue Kapua, in her capacity as president of the Māori Women's Welfare League, was moved to issue a scathing response to a "misogynist and ignorant attack" by a Minister of the Crown against the young Māori woman who had been leading the defence of Ihumātao.[48] Minister Shane Jones had publicly referred to Pania Newton as a "little putiputi", accusing her of "pleasing" Pākehā and questioning her mana.

Kapua did not hold back, pointing out that the Minister had displayed the very behaviour that underpins many of the mana wāhine claims currently before the Tribunal. In her view, Newton had shown leadership and demonstrated mana "regardless of attempts by Māori men to undermine her and perpetuate the damage suffered by wāhine Māori from colonisation". Kapua also noted the irony in the fact that the young man who had replaced Dame Mira Szaszy on the shortlist of appointees to the Treaty of Waitangi Fisheries Commission in 1993, prompting the lodging of the original Mana Wāhine claim, was none other than Shane Jones – older now, but apparently no wiser. As Linda Smith once sagely observed, breaking through the psyche of the colonised man is a monumental task.[49]

The incident serves as a sobering reminder that the erosion of mana wāhine remains as pressing an issue now as it was thirty years ago. Kapua advised Jones that he "would do well to recall the words of his kuia", repeating Dame Mira's statement before the United Nations Working Group on Indigenous Peoples on behalf of the Mana Wāhine claimants in 1994 – words that provide a fitting end to this chapter:

Me aro koe ki te hā o Hineahuone
Pay heed to the dignity of women.

"... the scope and content of tino rangatiratanga can be elaborated on via the rights set out in the Indigenous Declaration and how tino rangatiratanga might be understood in contemporary times in ways that reflect and are consistent with international law."

Chapter 14

Rangatiratanga
Constitutional Issues

— *Tracey Whare*[1]

The purpose of this chapter is to analyse how the Waitangi Tribunal has interpreted and applied Article 2 of te Tiriti o Waitangi and its specific and absolute guarantee of tino rangatiratanga.[2] Tino rangatiratanga is foundational to an understanding of power within Māori society as well as how that power is to be exercised. Tino rangatiratanga speaks to the pre-existing and continual political and legal authority of Māori to determine both their collective and individual destinies within and regulated by te ao Māori values and principles, particularly those expressed as legal norms of tikanga Māori. As such, the realisation of tino rangatiratanga, both historically and in contemporary times, underpins all claims considered by the Waitangi Tribunal.

In this chapter, three kaupapa inquiries will be considered. Two inquiries have been completed, and one is ongoing. The reports of the completed inquiries are *Whaia te Mana Motuhake In Pursuit of Mana Motuhake: Report on the Māori Community Development Act Claim*[3] (the Whaia te Mana Motuhake report) and the *Report on the Trans-Pacific Partnership*[4] (the TPPA report). The interim reports on the ongoing inquiry on constitutional matters are *Ngā Mātāpono The Principles: The Interim Report of the Tomokia Ngā Tatau o Matangireia – the Constitutional Kaupapa Inquiry Panel* and *Ngā Mātāpono The Principles: Part II of the Interim Report of the Tomokia Ngā Tatau o Matangireia – the Constitutional Kaupapa Inquiry Panel*[5] (collectively referred to as the Ngā Mātāpono reports). These inquiries have been chosen because they directly address tino rangatiratanga in relation to Māori decision-making. In addition, these inquiries address issues that impact all Māori and are not geographically bound to a particular place.

As noted by Margaret Mutu, tino rangatiratanga is the exercise of paramount and spiritually sanctioned power and authority.[6] It provides for relational regulation between people, both collectively and individually, as well as between people and the environment and is exercised in accordance with tikanga Māori. It is tikanga Māori that regulates the use of tino rangatiratanga.

The relationship between tino rangatiratanga and kāwanatanga lies at the heart of the three inquiries that are the focus of this chapter. As such, the Tribunal has had to consider the scope and content of tino rangatiratanga within diverse contexts. For example, the Whaia te Mana Motuhake report requires consideration of kāwanatanga and tino rangatiratanga in relation to a statutory framework establishing Māori autonomous bodies, the TPPA report requires the Tribunal to consider the exercise of kāwanatanga in international fora that negotiate binding trade agreements and the relationship of tino rangatiratanga to both the process and outcomes of international law making. And the Constitutional Kaupapa Inquiry has, to date, considered government policy and draft legislation to radically change the legal status of te Tiriti o Waitangi, which, in turn, will have a profound impact on the ability of Māori to legally claim and exercise tino rangatiratanga.

Outline of the chapter

Each inquiry and its subsequent report will be considered in chronological order. While comparisons can be drawn between each, it is important to note that each Tribunal inquiry comprises different Tribunal members and is independent of all other inquiries. Tribunals, in many ways, start afresh, meaning they are not bound to follow findings of former inquiries and can interpret and apply the Treaty, te Tiriti and Treaty principles to the particular claim and context they are considering.

For each report, I will summarise the background for bringing the claim, how the claim was framed by the Tribunal and how the Tribunal interpreted and applied tino rangatiratanga. I will then analyse the different approaches each claim took to tino rangatiratanga as well as the consistent themes across all three inquiries that focus on the minimum standards required of the Crown in its engagement and consultation with Māori, the constitutional relationship as between the Crown and Māori, the constraint that relationship has on the exercise of kāwanantanga as well as the minimum standards required for the Crown to recognise and provide for this constitutional relationship. Finally, I will reflect on the impact on society of the Tribunal's engagement with tino rangatiratanga.

Whaia te Mana Motuhake In Pursuit of Mana Motuhake: Report on the Māori Community Development Act Claim

Background

In 2009, the government began a review of the Maori Community Development Act 1962. The Act established the New Zealand Māori Council (NZMC), a national body charged with responsibility to improve the physical, economic, industrial, educational, social, moral and spiritual well-being of Māori.[7] The Act also provided for the establishment of local Māori Committees, regional Māori Executive Committees and District Māori Councils.[8] A specific focus of the government review was the administration of Māori Wardens, which the Act vested in District Māori Councils.[9]

In response to the 2009 review, the NZMC and some District Māori Councils submitted a claim to the Waitangi Tribunal challenging the Crown's decision to conduct a review as well as the interim arrangement whereby Te Puni Kōkiri (the Ministry of Māori Development) would administer Māori Wardens. It was claimed that this approach was undermining the authority of the Māori institutions established by the Act. The claimants also argued that any review of the Act should be conducted by themselves, and anything less would amount to a breach of the Act, Treaty principles and the United Nations Declaration on the Rights of Indigenous Peoples (the Indigenous Declaration).[10] The claimants argued that the Act had constitutional status and indicated a rangatiratanga agreement between Māori and the Crown as a result of the consensus amongst Māori at the time of its enactment.[11] The claimants also claimed that the Act granted official recognition to the ongoing search for tino rangatiratanga.[12]

Framing of the claim by the Waitangi Tribunal

In considering the claim, the Tribunal focused on three issues, two of which I will canvass here. These are, first, the Crown's consultation process and, second, the claims based on constitutional status and tino rangatiratanga. In relation to the former, the Tribunal considered whether the Crown's consultation process for reviewing the Act breached Treaty principles, whether the timing of consultations breached good faith and whether the administration of the Māori Wardens programme by the government diminished the authority of the NZMC.[13] In relation to the latter, the Tribunal considered whether the government had failed to recognise the special status of the Act as self-governance legislation.[14]

I focus on two of the findings. First, the Tribunal found that as a Treaty partner, the Crown was required to reach a collaborative agreement with Māori and that a standard consultation process where the Crown informs itself and makes a final decision was not appropriate because self-governance arrangements are critically important to Māori. The Tribunal found this was a breach of Treaty principles.[15]

Second, the Tribunal found that the replacement of the NZMC by Te Puni Kōkiri in the administration of the Māori Wardens programme was a breach of the Treaty principles of partnership, active protection and good faith because it interfered with the statutory role of District Māori Councils and the NZMC under the Act. The Crown's exclusion left the authorities with no role in determining funding policies.[16] In particular, the exercise of self-determination could not occur. The Crown's actions also amounted to a breach of article 18 of the Indigenous Declaration.[17]

Analysis

The Tribunal noted that the statutory creation of the NZMC, local Māori Committees, regional Māori Executive Committees and District Māori Councils provided Māori with the ability to exercise self-governance. As such, any change or review of the Act establishing these bodies required more than the minimal level of consultation. The Crown had an obligation not only to consult with Māori but to engage in a collaborative approach given any review was likely to impact the exercise of self-governance.[18] The Tribunal also noted that the Act is the only legislative recognition of Māori self-government.[19]

In addition, the Tribunal noted that the administration of the Māori Wardens programme was a statutory obligation that the District Māori Councils were required to discharge. The takeover by Te Puni Kōkiri interfered with and undermined this statutory obligation and the ability of Māori to engage in self-governance.[20]

As this inquiry considered the exercise of self-governance within a statutory framework, it provided the Tribunal with an opportunity to consider tino rangatiratanga in a contemporary setting as opposed to traditional sites of authority where tino rangatiratanga was and continues to be exercised, such as whānau, hapū and iwi. The Tribunal looked beyond the statutory framework and focused on whether Māori used and supported such entities. As such, the Tribunal took a pragmatic approach, making it clear that legal structures such as the NZMC and the District Māori Councils are simply vehicles to support self-management and that the legitimacy of any Māori institution is founded on the support and consent of the communities themselves.[21]

In addition, the Tribunal considered the application of international law in this inquiry, particularly the Indigenous Declaration. It noted that the Indigenous Declaration carries significant weight, affirming basic human rights and creating an expectation that states will comply. The Tribunal noted that New Zealand had endorsed the Indigenous Declaration in 2010 after initially rejecting its adoption in the General Assembly.[22]

The Tribunal noted that the Indigenous Declaration, as an instrument of international law, is not directly enforceable and that it did not have jurisdiction to determine whether the Crown had acted inconsistently with it. Despite this, the Tribunal noted that the Indigenous Declaration was relevant to the interpretation of the roles of the Crown and Māori vis-à-vis the review of the Act and the application of Treaty principles.[23] The Tribunal adopted the view that the Indigenous Declaration should be used as an aid in its interpretation of the Act and the scope and content of Treaty principles.

The Tribunal's engagement with the Indigenous Declaration focused on how it complements and is consistent with te Tiriti. The Tribunal married specific articles of the Indigenous Declaration with articles of te Tiriti. When considering rangatiratanga, the Tribunal noted that articles 3, 4, 5, 33, 34 and 35 of the Indigenous Declaration were complementary. Article 3 affirms indigenous peoples' right to self-determination, while article 4 affirms the right to autonomy and self-government. Article 5 affirms maintaining and strengthening indigenous political, legal, economic, social and cultural institutions. Article 33 affirms membership of an indigenous people, article 34 complements article 5 by affirming the laws and processes of indigenous institutions, and article 35 focuses on the rights of indigenous peoples to maintain and develop relations amongst themselves, particularly those who are divided by state borders. This marrying exercise demonstrates how the scope and content of tino rangatiratanga can be elaborated on via the rights set out in the Indigenous Declaration and how tino rangatiratanga might be understood in contemporary times in ways that reflect and are consistent with international law. The Tribunal noted that this set of rights recognises that indigenous peoples should not have outcomes imposed on them by governments.[24]

The Tribunal also considered which articles of the Indigenous Declaration mirrored the exercise of kāwanatanga. The Tribunal referenced articles 19, 38, 39 and 46, which recognise the right of indigenous peoples to determine their own representatives, the requirement for the state to obtain consent prior to taking decisions that may affect indigenous peoples, including legislative changes, the requirement for the state to provide resources to realise the Indigenous Declaration and the understanding that the only justifiable limitation on rights within the Indigenous Declaration are human rights obligations. The Tribunal noted that this set of rights provides for the Crown to govern the state of New Zealand.[25] The Tribunal also noted that kāwanatanga is the exercise of state power over the state and that Māori have their own sphere of authority.

The pairing of the Indigenous Declaration articles with kāwanatanga underlined the important checks placed on the exercise of kāwanatanga, particularly the need for consent when legislative changes were being considered. It also highlighted a key component of self-determination being the right of indigenous peoples to determine their own representatives in their engagement with the state.

The Report on the Trans-Pacific Partnership Agreement

Background

This inquiry focused on the role and processes of government in negotiating and drafting international trade agreements and whether those processes as well as the content of those agreements prejudicially impact on Māori rights and interests.

Within the constitutional framework of the New Zealand state, it is the executive branch of government that is tasked with negotiating international trade agreements. This inquiry focused on one such agreement, the Trans-Pacific Partnership Agreement (the TPPA) and its replacement, the Comprehensive and Progressive Agreement for Trans-Pacific Partnership (CPTPP). Claims were lodged in June 2015 as negotiations on the TPPA were ending. The claimants sought a hearing under urgency, recommending that work on the TPPA stop immediately until Māori had been consulted to ensure that Māori rights were protected and the Crown could meet its Tiriti obligations. Claimants also recommended that the draft TPPA text be released, and they raised concerns as to whether the Treaty exception clause, which the government had included in all trade agreements since 2001, was adequate.

The Tribunal declined to grant a hearing under urgency, but it did agree that once the final draft text was available, a hearing would be held.[26] The draft text was made public in October 2015, and the hearing was held in March 2016. The hearing focused on two issues: first, whether the Treaty of Waitangi exception clause provided effective protection of Māori rights and second, what Māori engagement was required to ratify the agreement. The Tribunal also held hearings on two other matters that impact on the TPPA – the review of the Plant Variety Rights Act and the e-commerce provision of the TPPA. My focus will be solely on the Treaty exception clause and Māori engagement prior to ratification.

Framing of the claim by the Waitangi Tribunal

The Tribunal noted the decision to enter into international trade agreements rested with the government of the day; however, the Tribunal also noted it had jurisdiction to consider whether the Crown in its acts or omissions had acted inconsistently with Treaty principles.[27]The inquiry raised issues that directly impacted on tino rangatiratanga in that the Crown was representing Māori interests in international fora from which Māori were excluded. For this reason, a focus on the process itself and the lack of Māori engagement in that process was a critical issue raised by the claimants.

Claimants also argued that the inquiry should be guided by the findings of the Te Paparahi o te Raki Inquiry and its subsequent stage one report, *He Whakaputanga me Te Tiriti – The Declaration and the Treaty*.[28] The finding that sovereignty had not been ceded challenged the Crown's view that its authority included the ability to represent Māori interests in international fora.

The Tribunal took the position that each Tribunal inquiry is independent, and while it may take guidance from previous inquiries and court decisions, its mandate was to inquire into whether the Crown's actions in relation to the TPPA were consistent or otherwise with Treaty principles.[29]

The Tribunal noted that the primary issue was whether the Treaty of Waitangi exception clause was an effective protection of Māori interests. The Tribunal found that the Treaty exception clause was likely to offer a reasonable degree of protection to Māori interests.[30] However, it also noted that it is the Crown that determines what measures are necessary to accord more favourable treatment to Māori.

As a result of its finding, the Tribunal found that there was no breach of the principles of the Treaty of Waitangi arising from the inclusion of the Treaty exception clause in the TPPA. However, the Tribunal did note that the scope of the TPPA was greater than previous trade agreements because the protections and rights of foreign investors were extensive. If foreign investors were to bring claims against the New Zealand government, the Tribunal noted this, in turn, might have a negative or chilling effect on the Crown's desire to meet its Treaty obligations. While the Tribunal raised this concern, it also noted that it was unable to assess the actual or potential prejudice that may arise.[31] To address this, the Tribunal recommended further dialogue between Māori and the Crown.

In relation to process and engagement, the Tribunal noted that negotiations on the draft text were confidential and that while states involved in the negotiations had agreed that they could share draft text via domestic non-governmental consultation processes, it was the practice of the New Zealand Government not to share draft text and negotiating positions beyond government.[32]

Analysis

(a) Substance

The Tribunal chose to focus on the Treaty exception clause because of the constitutional significance of the Treaty.[33] While the Crown argued that Māori were to be treated as any other stakeholder, this perspective failed to account for the constitutional relationship between the Crown and Māori.

The Tribunal noted that while the TPPA included a Treaty exception clause, it was the same wording that had been used in trade agreements since 2001. The Tribunal noted that between the original drafted language and the time of the inquiry there had been new developments in international law and Treaty jurisprudence that should have prompted the government to review its approach and consider whether the Treaty exception clause was still fit for purpose.[34] Despite these findings, the Tribunal considered the wording sufficient to protect Māori interests, albeit with some concerns as outlined in the previous section.

(b) Process

The process by which the government engaged in the drafting of trade agreements was found to be wanting. The Tribunal noted that Māori were not treated as Treaty partners but rather as general stakeholders, that there was a lack of transparency by the Crown in its decision-making and the process by which the Crown informed itself of Māori interests was poor.[35]

This was not the first time that this issue had been raised. The Tribunal noted that the government had been made aware of this issue in a previous inquiry, noting that contrary to the findings of that Tribunal inquiry, which focused on cultural and intellectual property rights, the Crown did not seek or provide a realistic opportunity for Māori to identify their interests in the TPPA as a Treaty partner and that there had been no changes to government policy on consultation since the previous inquiry addressed the very same issue.[36] In my view, this speaks to the ability of government, particularly the executive, to ignore the findings and recommendations of the Tribunal and carry on with business as usual despite being made aware that their approach is in breach of Treaty principles.

The standards set out in *Ko Aotearoa Tēnei* envisage a proactive approach by government, informing Māori about developments in the international arena and how such developments might affect their interests.[37] Māori, in turn, can then advise the Crown as to whether their interests will be affected and how they might be protected. *Ko Aotearoa Tēnei* adopted a scale approach; if the issue is important to Māori and the consequences of it impact Māori differently, then the Crown is to prioritise Māori engagement.[38]

The Tribunal adopted the findings of *Ko Aotearoa Tēnei* that Māori interests are entitled to a reasonable degree of protection vis-à-vis international law making.[39] In taking this approach, the Tribunal affirms the view that kāwanatanga encompasses the right of the Crown to represent New Zealand and make foreign policy. It is an issue that is revisited in the third report of this inquiry, where the Tribunal draws from *He Whakaputanga me te Tiriti*

The Declaration and the Treaty, noting that the Crown had obligations to protect Māori from foreign threats and represent them in international affairs, where necessary.

This does not align with the claimants' position that tino rangatiratanga is not limited to domestic self-governance. While recognising the claimants' arguments, the Tribunal is careful to limit its scope, noting that the broader question of the Crown–Māori relationship regarding international instruments is not a matter that the inquiry would consider. The Tribunal acknowledged that a constitutional inquiry was pending that could consider the scope and parameters of both tino rangatiratanga and kāwanatanga in relation to international law making.[40] This is likely to have been frustrating for claimants; the Tribunal had an opportunity to consider the issue the claimants had raised, but it did not.

This approach is also at odds with the one taken in the Whaia te Mana Motuhake report, particularly the Tribunal's reference to and recognition of participatory rights and processes as set out in the Indigenous Declaration. In that report, the Tribunal highlighted the importance of indigenous peoples determining their own representation in contexts where decisions are being taken and of consent being obtained regarding legislative or administrative measures that may affect them.

While the Tribunal did not find in favour of the claimants, a separate development may lead to better and strategic Māori input in relation to future trade policy and negotiation. A mediation process between the Crown and claimants resulted in the establishment of a new Māori entity, Ngā Toki Whakarururanga, with the expectation that this body will advance and protect Māori interests in trade.[41] The establishment of this entity provides the Crown with a willing and able Māori collective through which it can strengthen its engagement with Māori.

Tomokia Ngā Tatau o Matangireia: Constitutional Kaupapa Inquiry

Background

The final inquiry I will consider is Tomokia ngā Tatau o Matangireia: Constitutional Kaupapa Inquiry. The claim began in 2022 with the Tribunal drawing together 187 varied claims and distilling them into nine thematic areas being:

1. *Tino Rangatiratanga, Autonomy and Self-governance*
2. *Kāwanatanga*

3. *Constitutional Legitimacy and Sovereignty*
4. *Parliamentary Sovereignty and Systems*
5. *Ngā Tikanga Māori me Ngā Ture Pākehā*
6. *Electoral Rights and Systems*
7. *Local Government and Te Tiriti*
8. *National Models of Māori Self-Government*
9. *NZ Bill of Rights Act 1990 (NZBORA), United Nations Declaration on the Rights of Indigenous Peoples (UNDRIP) and Te Tiriti*[42]

As such, this inquiry has a clear constitutional scope of national significance and will directly address the relationship between the Crown's exercise of kāwanatanga and tino rangatiratanga and the scope of each.

While this inquiry is still within its initial stages, it has already released two interim reports, which are the focus of this section.

Framing of the claim by the Waitangi Tribunal

The Tribunal has the authority to determine how each inquiry will proceed. Tribunal proceedings have often adopted formal, legal approaches based on Western judicial values with the parties represented by lawyers who engage in adversarial practices much like those used in the courts. In this inquiry, the Tribunal chose to adopt processes that more closely aligned with and reflected tikanga Māori. From the outset, the presiding officer, Dr CL Fox CJ, has sought to design the inquiry approach consistently with tikanga Māori and te Tiriti and has elevated the participation and decision-making opportunities of the claimants themselves, at times directing lawyers to participate in proceedings as observers only.[43]

One of the key areas of innovation that this inquiry has adopted is the regional wānanga approach. Regional wānanga will determine the scope of the inquiry, the issues and how those issues can be addressed. The Tribunal elaborated on this approach by directing that wānanga would allow claimants to provide evidence of their constitutionalism.[44] In addition, the wānanga will be future focused, seeking to build consensus among the parties as well as māramatanga, a clarity and collective understanding of what needs to be addressed. This approach contrasts with how previous inquiries have been conducted where individualised statements of claim have been prioritised and have determined the scope and issues of the inquiry.[45]

The Tribunal began the wānanga ā-rohe in December 2024 in Ngāruawāhia. Further wānanga will be held in Gisborne, Te Tai Tokerau, Ōtaki, Wairarapa and Te Waiharakeke.[46]

In addition to the process, claimants submitted that the critical starting point for this claim was *He Whakaputanga me te Tiriti The Declaration and the Treaty,* regarding the nature of the agreement between the Crown and Māori contained in te Tiriti.[47] They also submitted that tino rangatiratanga, kāwanatanga, active protection, good governance, consultation and partnership are the most relevant Treaty principles.[48]

Not unlike other kaupapa inquiries, the Waitangi Tribunal has had to pivot from its start-up phase to address government actions that directly impact on the substance of the inquiry. In this case, these are the government's decision to review twenty-eight pieces of legislation with references to the Treaty, known as the Treaty Clause Review, as well as the decision to progress a Treaty Principles Bill.

The Tribunal held two hearings under urgency, one in May 2024 and one in October 2024. The first hearing addressed the Crown's decision to progress a Treaty Principles Bill and a review of existing legislation that contained references to Treaty principles. Following that hearing, in August 2024 the Tribunal released the Ngā Mātāpono interim report. The Tribunal found that the Treaty Clause Review policy breached several Treaty principles.[49]

The second hearing held under urgency took place on 4 October 2024. The focus of that hearing was on whether, since the release of the Ngā Mātāpono interim report, the Crown's approach to the Treaty Principles Bill policy was consistent with existing Treaty principles and what prejudice to Māori would arise if the Bill was enacted.

The Tribunal focused on the Bill drafting process, emphasising the lack of consultation with Māori as well as the absence of a clear basis justifying the Crown's approach given its significance to Māori.[50] The Tribunal also foreshadowed that if the Bill was to pass into law, it would be the most egregious breach of te Tiriti in modern times.[51]

The Tribunal noted that the process adopted by the government demonstrated that existing Treaty principles such as good faith and partnership were being redefined by the Crown separately from and in contradiction to existing jurisprudence. The Tribunal also noted that the draft principles within the Bill bore little relation to the original articles and would significantly undermine tino rangatiratanga.[52]

Analysis

While this inquiry is ongoing, it is possible to glean from the Ngā Mātāpono reports how the Tribunal is approaching this inquiry. For example, the Tribunal's preliminary letter to the government emphasises the constitutional significance of defining Treaty principles in legislation. The Tribunal noted that the Crown's decision to pursue policy change without consultation with Māori, despite staunch opposition, erodes and undermines the reciprocal relationship between Māori and the Crown and is a breach of the principle of good government.[53]

In relation to the Treaty Clause Review, the Tribunal found that the review lacked substantive justification and that the repeal or alteration of existing Treaty references would be an "extremely retrograde step".[54] The Tribunal found evidence of predetermination in that legislative clauses will be either repealed, replaced or limited with no plans to consult with Māori.[55] In addition, the Tribunal found that the policy will reduce the impact and relevance of te Tiriti across different statutes "without regard for the status of the Treaty as the source and constitutional foundation which legitimates the Government itself".[56]

In relation to the content of the Treaty Principles Bill, the Tribunal found the Treaty principle of active protection was breached by the Crown's attempt to unilaterally redefine tino rangatiratanga as applying to individual property rights rather than as a collective right.[57] The Tribunal referred to the Bill as a historical and legal fiction and stated that it was unfair, discriminatory and contrary to rangatiratanga.[58]

The Tribunal also found that the Crown's actions would result in prejudice towards Māori as the Bill would completely alter the meaning and effect of all current Treaty clauses in legislation, would negatively impact relations between the Crown and Māori and would remove existing Treaty obligations.[59] Perhaps most damning is the finding that the Bill would prejudicially and profoundly impact the mana of te Tiriti o Waitangi and its constitutional status.

The Tribunal noted that Treaty principles reaffirm the constitutional significance of te Tiriti and that the principle of partnership creates a duty to consult, particularly where an issue is directly applicable to Māori or affects te Tiriti. The duty to consult in situations such as the drafting of the Treaty Principles Bill places a greater onus on the Crown more akin to negotiation.[60] The Tribunal also noted that if the effect of the Bill and the Treaty Clause

Review was to inhibit access to justice or the exercise of rangatiratanga, and it would be inconsistent with the principle of redress.[61] The Tribunal found that the Bill would have a major constitutional effect on te Tiriti policy and application.

When considering rangatiratanga, the Tribunal referred to a previous Tribunal report, *Te Mana Whatu Ahuru*, which noted the relationship between te Tiriti and tikanga Māori as follows:

> *In Treaty terms, tikanga and tino rangatiratanga cannot be separated, because tikanga guides all relationships with people, the environment, and atua, and because the actions of rangatira are legitimate only if they are tika.*[62]

The Tribunal then went on to explain that the intersection of tikanga and tino rangatiratanga created the constitutional, political and legal landscape in which te ao Māori historically operated and that the exercise of rangatiratanga was undertaken by elders for the benefit of their kin. This, in turn, ensured that Māori retained the right to govern themselves via their own political and legal system.[63] This approach highlights the importance not only of tino rangatiratanga as a realisation of self-determination but also of the way it is intertwined with and underpinned by its own normative system, tikanga Māori.

The Tribunal further noted that the Treaty "was the mechanism whereby Māori leaders in most of the country agreed to share power in exchange for the guarantee of their rangatiratanga"[64] and that the retention of tino rangatiratanga as reaffirmed and guaranteed in te Tiriti provided for Māori political and legal authority to continue.[65]

The Tribunal was scathing in its findings of breach and prejudice. In relation to the Treaty Principles Bill, the Tribunal found that the Crown's pursuit of it was an "unbridled exercise of kāwanatanga power", that there were no policy imperatives to justify it and that it breached Treaty principles of partnership and reciprocity because no consultation took place.[66]

The Tribunal released part two of the Ngā Mātapono report in November 2024. While the Tribunal did not make any further findings, it reaffirmed its recommendation that the Bill be abandoned and the Treaty Clause Review be halted while consultation design was determined with Māori.[67] In addition, the Tribunal recommended that the Crown give notice of a motion to the House of Representatives that it refer the Bill to the Waitangi Tribunal under section 8(2) of the Treaty of Waitangi Act.[68]

The political response to the Tribunal's findings and recommendations were not unsurprising. Prime Minister Christopher Luxon described the release of the Ngā Mātāpono interim reports as "premature", while David Seymour stated he did not accept the findings of the Waitangi Tribunal and that not everything that Ministry of Justice officials said was correct.[69] This response demonstrates how political power can override and ignore fundamental constitutional values such as access to justice, non-discrimination and fairness in addition to Treaty principles and jurisprudence. The findings of the Tribunal should cause the government to pause and rethink its approach the Tribunal could not have been more clear in laying bare all that is wrong and unjust with the Treaty Clause Review and the Treaty Principles Bill.

Despite the two hearings and the reports of those hearings, the Tribunal continues to progress its substantive inquiry. However, given the breadth of this inquiry, it is difficult to see how, even with the demise of the Treaty Principles Bill, the Tribunal will make progress on the nine thematic areas while the government continues to pursue the Treaty Review Clause.

Reflections

In these three inquiries, the Tribunal has approached the interpretation and application of tino rangatiratanga in distinct ways. In the Whaia te Mana Motuhake report, the Tribunal recognised and affirmed the exercise of tino rangatiratanga via entities established under the Māori Community Development Act. The Tribunal challenged executive overreach with reference to the statutory obligations that these entities were charged with carrying out and drew on international law to aid in the interpretation of the scope and content of tino rangatiratanga and kāwanatanga. In addition, the Tribunal set out the consultation and engagement standards that were required of the Crown when legislation providing for the exercise of self-governance was being reviewed.

The TPPA report took a more restrictive approach in its interpretation and application of tino rangatiratanga. This was because the Tribunal accepted as its starting point the Crown's authority to represent New Zealand and engage in international law making. In support of this position, the Tribunal referred to *He Whakaputanga me te Tiriti The Declaration and the Treaty*, highlighting the Crown's obligations to represent Māori in international affairs, *where necessary*. The wording "where necessary" was not elaborated on by the Tribunal, and the direct challenge of claimants to the exercise of kāwanatanga in making international law makes this reasoning less persuasive. While the Tribunal noted that this issue was broader than their inquiry into one trade agreement, and it chose to defer the matter to the future Constitutional Kaupapa Inquiry, the Tribunal could have provided some preliminary views or recognised the tension between their approach and the claimants' pleadings.

The TPPA report also found that the Treaty exception clause was sufficient to protect Māori interests in the TPPA, even though it is the Crown that determines what measures it will adopt to fulfil its Tiriti obligations. Given the findings of the Tribunal in relation to poor engagement with Māori during the negotiation of the TPPA, in my view, the Tribunal's deference to the government to protect Māori rights and interests when it has not fully informed itself of what the concerns and issues are seems misplaced.

The Constitutional Kaupapa Inquiry has the mandate and scope to directly address tino rangatiratanga and its relationship with kāwanatanga in an array of constitutional areas. It could be argued that even the design of this inquiry reflects tino rangatiratanga by enabling claimants to lead a series of regional wānanga and explain their understandings of constitutionalism. This approach, in my view, demonstrates that the Tribunal is looking to claimants themselves to unpack and drill down to the essence of what tino rangatiratanga is and how it might be given the fullest and most expansive interpretation going forward. This is a critically important inquiry as it will undoubtedly address Treaty breaches of past Crown actions and law, but it also clearly wants to map out what Treaty compliant constitutionalism could look like.

However, this inquiry is taking place under the shadow of the Treaty Clause Review, and the now defunct Treaty Principles Bill, which has the ability to radically change the legal landscape in which the Tribunal operates and could significantly impact how this inquiry addresses the nine thematic areas. The vulnerability of te Tiriti within our constitutional arrangements is on full display as the Tribunal navigates this inquiry.

In terms of common themes across all three inquiries, I note the following. First, there is the continually poor approach of the Crown to engagement and consultation with Māori. The Tribunal has, over time, developed its jurisprudence on consultation and engagement, carefully setting out what Tiriti compliant consultation and engagement should look like in different contexts. However, in these three inquiries, there is evidence of the continual failure of the Crown to recognise and implement these standards. This approach is not isolated to one part of government; in the Whaia te

Mana Motuhake report, it was Te Puni Kōkiri, while in the TPPA report, it was the Ministry of Foreign Affairs and Trade. These poor processes continue to reflect negatively on the Crown and, ultimately, diminish the ability of Māori to engage in issues in which their rights and interests are or will be directly impacted.

Second, the relationship between the Crown and Māori as expressed in te Tiriti o Waitangi, is a constitutional relationship. It is a relationship of significant legal importance and must be treated as such. It cannot be redefined by the Crown as affirmed in the Ngā Mātāpono report or reduced to the status of stakeholder, which was the Crown's approach in the TPPA report. Until such time as the Crown truly accepts and acts in accordance with this constitutional understanding, the Tiriti relationship will continue to be strained and undermined.

Third, the Tiriti constitutional relationship defines the scope of kāwanatanga and acts as a restraint on its exercise. The constitutional relationship also recognises and provides for Māori to exercise tino rangatiratanga. This is most evident in the Whaia te Mana Motuhake report with legislation that recognises aspects of Māori self-governance, and it is less pronounced in the TPPA report due to the monopoly that kāwanatanga currently exerts over international law making.

Finally, the Tribunal, whether considering past or future Crown actions, takes pains to articulate the minimum standards required of the Crown to uphold its constitutional relationship with Māori as well as the ways in which kāwanatanga authority is to be exercised in compliance with te Tiriti. The fact that the focus continues to remain squarely on the exercise of kāwanatanga tacitly acknowledges that within these kaupapa inquiries there is little room for the development and realisation of tino rangatiratanga. This is the fundamental tension embedded within all three inquiries – the overreach and misuse of kāwanatanga and its impact on tino rangatiratanga. This is not a new finding, but it highlights the ongoing poor performance of the Crown vis-à-vis its constitutional Tiriti obligations.

Despite these clear themes, it is difficult to ascertain what impact these reports, particularly in the way the Tribunal has engaged with tino rangatiratanga, have on the Crown. This is a result of the weak constitutional protections that exist for te Tiriti as well as the absence of Tiriti accountability measures. While each report is prefaced with a letter of transmittal addressed to specific Crown ministers, for example, the Ngā Mātāpono report was addressed to the Prime Minister, the Minister for Crown Relations, the Minister of Justice and the Associate Minister of Justice, there is no legal requirement for ministers to respond to the substantive findings or recommendations within each report. In the same way, Cabinet is not required to consider and respond to the reports, nor is Parliament. This means that it is left to claimants to advocate for change using the Tribunal's findings as leverage. The lack of constitutional enforceability means the Crown can do as much or as little as it wants.

Finally, the Tribunal's engagement with tino rangatiratanga also impacts more generally on society. Tribunal reports are publicly available. While hefty in length, they are written in plain English and are considered a trusted source of accurate information.[70] Report findings and recommendations assist in reframing public understanding and awareness of the legal and constitutional significance of te Tiriti and in exposing the Crown's breaches of te Tiriti as well as its limited recognition of tino rangatiratanga. This truth telling is important, it raises the bar, underpinning societal expectations that those exercising kāwanatanga do so in ways that are Tiriti compliant, including recognising and providing for the realisation of tino rangatiratanga.

"Despite the limitations of the Tribunal's own ability to promote radical constitutional change, its work is supporting broader conversations of constitutional transformation."

Chapter 15

Whakamana i te Tiriti

— Carwyn Jones

The Māori name for the Waitangi Tribunal is Te Rōpū Whakamana i te Tiriti – the group that gives authority to, or gives effect to, te Tiriti o Waitangi. This aptly and succinctly describes the basic role and function of the Tribunal. One of the aims of this collection has been to explore the way in which the Tribunal has carried out that role across different claims and inquiries into different issues and across the fifty years it has been in existence. Looking across the chapters in this collection, three key themes emerge that I want to draw attention to here: the breadth of the Tribunal's work and the Tribunal's ability to adapt its process according to the claims that come before it and the changing circumstances in which the Tribunal operates; the crucial role of leadership amongst the Tribunal membership, politicians, counsel for claimants and the Crown and, by no means least, leadership and vision of Māori who have brought claims before the

Tribunal; and, the constitutional significance of the Tribunal's work. I address each of these themes briefly in this chapter, and I also consider some of the challenges the Tribunal is facing as we mark its fiftieth anniversary and look forward to the future.

Breadth of the Waitangi Tribunal's Work

The chapters in this collection have examined the Tribunal's engagement with claims about historical land loss, rivers and waterways, freshwater governance, environmental and resource management law and policy, fisheries and the commercial fishing settlement, takutai moana/the foreshore and seabed, the Treaty settlement process, taonga such as te reo Māori and mātauranga Māori, social policy in the areas of health, housing and child welfare, mana wahine, and issues of rangatiratanga in a constitutional context. Even that range of issues really only provides a taste of the work that the Waitangi Tribunal has undertaken over the past fifty years. It has not been possible within the scope of this book to address the Tribunal's reports relating to kōhanga reo, kura kaupapa and wānanga or reports relating to corrections policy and prisoner voting rights, aquaculture, the Māori electoral option, the protection of the Māui's dolphin, the clean-up following the stranding of the MV *Rena*, the proposed reform of Te Ture Whenua Maori Act/the Maori Land Act or many other historical and contemporary issues.

Although this collection does not provide comprehensive coverage of the Waitangi Tribunal's fifty years of inquiries and reports, we have aimed to provide an overview of at least some of the most significant areas of law, policy and practice that the Tribunal has examined. There were two main objectives underpinning that approach. First, we simply wanted to show the breadth of work that the Waitangi Tribunal has undertaken. Recognising the breadth of the Tribunal's work is crucial to understanding the way in which the Tribunal is helping to articulate rights under te Tiriti o Waitangi and fulfilling its role "to make recommendations on claims relating to the practical application of the Treaty and to determine whether certain matters are inconsistent with the principles of the Treaty".[1]

Our second main objective in addressing a selection of key areas of the Tribunal's work was to provide an overview of important findings and recommendations that the Tribunal has made, which we hope will be of practical use to people who are looking to develop Tiriti-centred models of working. For example, if someone is interested in recognising or implementing rights and obligations under te Tiriti within the health sector, they will be able to find the broad topic of health addressed in the relevant chapter and quickly identify some features about the Tribunal's general approach to policy and practice relating to health services and outcomes. They would also be able to see the kinds of recommendations the Tribunal has already made in this area, which may help to progress implementation of those recommendations, avoid unwittingly reinventing the wheel and expending time and energy seeking recommendations already made in a previous inquiry, or help identify where further findings and recommendations would be useful.

Understanding the scope of the Tribunal's work also enables us to see the way in which the Tribunal has adapted in an attempt to meet the needs of claimants in addressing different issues across changing social, political and policy environments. The Tribunal's ability to adapt over its fifty years has been quite remarkable. The opening-up of the Tribunal's historical jurisdiction required the Tribunal to find effective and efficient ways of addressing a large number of claims, all of which were based in detailed and often complex historical evidence. The Tribunal commissioned the Rangahaua Whānui, a national overview report series, to obtain a thorough understanding of the nature and scale of claims that would need to be addressed through its historical inquiry programme. This led the Tribunal to establish its district inquiry programme and historical casebook approach, as considered in Peter Meihana's chapter. This also, incidentally, enabled the Crown to develop its proposal for the systematic negotiation and settlement of historical claims. The Tribunal similarly adjusted its process to meet the needs of claimants in the context of the work of the Office of Treaty Settlements and the desire of claimants to reach negotiated settlements with the Crown. Further adaptations were required through the transition to focusing on the kaupapa inquiry programme.

Leadership and the Waitangi Tribunal

The leadership in and around the Waitangi Tribunal has played an important role in its ability to adjust and adapt. As a commission of inquiry, the Tribunal has considerable flexibility in setting its own procedure, which has enabled it to respond to changing circumstances and different needs. But the vision, leadership skills and experience of the Tribunal members and staff have also been essential. There have been big procedural changes, such as developing the district inquiry programme, adapting that to the environment of direct negotiations and the systematic settlement of historical claims, and then transitioning to the kaupapa inquiry programme. Those changes have also been supported and supplemented by innovative procedural developments, sometimes in response to distinctive issues that have arisen in a particular inquiry. These include practices such as holding hearings on marae and incorporating tikanga Māori or ensuring that each Tribunal panel includes men and women. They also include measures such as addressing accessibility and other associated issues as part of the practice in the Health Services and Outcomes inquiry, tailoring procedure in a way that aligns with the nature of the claims in kaupapa inquiries, adapting urgent inquiries to make certain that recommendations can be made in a timely way, or utilising interim recommendations to allow opportunities for further discussion or information to be provided before being finalised.

The Tribunal's role in nation-building is significant. It has been described as the conscience of the nation and its function being to work towards truth and reconciliation. Due to the nature of its work, the Tribunal has often found itself in the middle of political debate. The Tribunal leadership and membership have been vital in navigating the political waves (and, sometimes, storms) that surround it. As a body with only limited binding powers, the Tribunal must persuade rather than being able to order compliance with its recommendations. This may be as much about persuading the public of the justice of the case as it is about persuading an individual minister. Part of the way in which the Tribunal does this is by ensuring that its findings and recommendations are grounded in solid evidence and robust analysis. The role of individual Tribunal members is also important in establishing credibility and legitimacy with the community. For the Tribunal to work, it is certainly important that Māori see ourselves reflected among the membership of the Tribunal. But also important are the Pākehā members of the Tribunal and the communities they reflect. Throughout the fifty years of the Waitangi Tribunal, in both historical and contemporary inquiries, the experiences and perspectives of Pākehā farming, business, public service and political communities have been vital. Just as Māori need to see that the concerns and experiences of our various communities are being brought to bear on the claims before the Tribunal, Pākehā communities need to see the same. That is not to say that the Tribunal members have a representative role, there to promote the interests of one particular community. One of the things that has made the Tribunal a success in its role as a truth and reconciliation commission is that the members have been people of mana, whether Māori or Pākehā. They are leaders within their own communities in different ways, joined in the common purpose of developing, in good faith, measures for the practical application of Treaty principles to address past breaches and create a more just future for Aotearoa. The structure of the Tribunal is important, but its effectiveness also depends on the people who comprise its membership.

Constitutional Dimensions of the Waitangi Tribunal's Work

Perhaps the overarching theme that runs through the chapters in this collection is the constitutional nature of the Waitangi Tribunal's work. In some senses, this is unsurprising. The Tribunal has been established as a quasi-judicial body to assess whether the Crown is meeting its obligations under the country's founding document. But there is a second, perhaps more subtle, strand of constitutional development that is at work across the Tribunal's inquiries and reports, which is potentially transformational.

First, there needs to be a brief note on the constitutional significance of the establishment of the Waitangi Tribunal. The passing of the Treaty of Waitangi Act was an important constitutional moment. Prior to 1975, the Crown side of the Tiriti relationship had largely ignored the obligations that it signed up to in 1840. While acknowledgements of the Treaty had been included in various statutes prior to 1975, the Crown had not shown any desire to give effect to te Tiriti and had established a colonial system of government here without any consideration of te Tiriti and the relationship it created between kāwanatanga and tino rangatiratanga. The colonial courts, whose own authority was and is sourced in the institutions of the Crown, reinforced the legal and constitutional authority of the Crown. In the case of *Wi Parata v The Bishop of Wellington* in 1877, the Chief Justice infamously declared te Tiriti to be "a simple nullity" and that, so far as any moral obligation existed for the Crown to fulfil promises it entered into in 1840, these were not matters that the courts could enforce, and it was therefore up to the Crown to determine what was appropriate as "the arbiter of its own justice". Although aspects of that judgment were challenged almost immediately and the decision was finally overruled in 2003, the core idea that te Tiriti o Waitangi is not, by itself, able to be legally enforced in the New Zealand courts has remained.

The Waitangi Tribunal was established to provide a legal forum where claims alleging breaches of the principles of the Treaty could be brought. It came as a response, not only to the fact that the courts could not be used to address Tiriti issues without some other legal hook, but also as a response to increasing direct protest action about te Tiriti rights. The Waitangi Tribunal was something of a safety valve to enable Tiriti issues to be dealt with through legal means rather than leaving the civil and political pressure to build through direct action. The enactment of the Treaty of Waitangi Act was, therefore, a major step in New Zealand's constitutional development. Through establishing the Waitangi Tribunal, Parliament had recognised that there ought to be a mechanism within the institutions of government to address Tiriti issues. That, in itself, is an acknowledgement of the constitutional status and significance of te Tiriti. While this may be filtered through the compromise statutory language of 'the principles of the Treaty', the Act undoubtedly marked a major shift in that the Crown would now be subject to some accountability for its obligations under te Tiriti.

A more subtle shift can also be discerned arising from the Tribunal's work over the past fifty years. That is, the fundamentally constitutional nature of the Tiriti relationship has been articulated by the Tribunal and made plainly visible. Despite the limitations of the Tribunal's own ability to promote radical constitutional change, its work is supporting broader conversations of constitutional transformation. As reflected in the chapters in this collection, whether the particular issues in question relate to whenua, awa, ika, takutai moana, settlements, te reo Māori, mātauranga Māori, areas of social policy and well-being, the rights of Māori women or conduct in international relations, giving effect to the relationship between the spheres of tino rangatiratanga and kāwanatanga, as envisaged in te Tiriti, will require constitutional transformation. The Tribunal's consideration of that relationship, albeit through its jurisdictional lens of Treaty principles, will continue to help us navigate the path ahead.

Toitū Te Tiriti: Current Challenges in 2025

On the eve of its fiftieth anniversary, the Waitangi Tribunal does face some significant and immediate political challenges. In the Tribunal's fiftieth anniversary year, Parliament has already considered the Principles of the Treaty of Waitangi Bill, which, if enacted, would have effectively put an end to the Waitangi Tribunal. The Bill had sought to redefine 'the principles of the Treaty' in such a way as to ensure that te Tiriti could not be recognised as a source of Māori rights. It is difficult to see what the role of the Tribunal would have been if the Bill had passed. That Bill was ultimately rejected, but the government is pursuing other mechanisms that will limit the ability to use 'Treaty principles' to influence law and policy, and a formal review of the Treaty of Waitangi Act is also underway.[2]

Aside from those measures that are directly targeted at Treaty principles, the coalition government also seems intent on undermining the Waitangi Tribunal in other ways. Government ministers have made public statements that have questioned the impartiality of judges serving on the Tribunal. These statements prompted the co-presidents of Te Hunga Rōia Māori (the Māori Law Society) to write to the Prime Minister, expressing their concerns and also led to a rebuke from the Attorney-General.

But perhaps of more concern is the irrational approach to creating policy that has been adopted by the government, which makes it very difficult to hold the Crown to account for, amongst other things, consistency with Treaty principles. Since the formation of the coalition government, the Waitangi Tribunal has held a number of urgent inquiries focused on policies arising from the coalition agreements. These have included inquiries into the disestablishment of the Māori Health Authority, changes to the establishment of Māori wards, the removal of section 7AA of the Oranga Tamariki Act, and the Treaty Principles Bill. In each of these instances, the normal policy development processes have been abandoned. There has been no work done to identify or define the policy problem that needs to be addressed, no discussion of possible policy options, no consultation with Māori, no evidence-based assessment of the consequences of the policy and, often, a rejection of official advice. That is, these policies are driven by political whim rather than rational policy development. Consideration of the impact of policy (in general, but on Māori in particular, in this context) and consistency with Treaty principles form part of the orthodox approach to policy development. If the political leadership is determined to act outside these norms, then conventional accountability mechanisms and the checks and balances on which the constitution relies, including the Waitangi Tribunal and the courts, are severely undermined.

However, as has been noted above, this is not the first time that the Waitangi Tribunal has been the subject of political attacks. The Tribunal has endured for fifty years, adapting to changing policy settings and political circumstances to maintain its important role in assisting the Crown to make good on its obligations under te Tiriti and to help Māori and the Crown realise the promise of the Tiriti relationship. The reports of the Waitangi Tribunal, their findings, recommendations and analyses of Treaty principles have greatly enhanced New Zealanders' understanding of our shared history and the vision of our ancestors who entered into te Tiriti o Waitangi. In the face of challenging political times, Moana Jackson would sometimes refer to Martin Luther King Jr.'s well known statement that "the arc of the moral universe is long, but it bends towards justice". The first fifty years of the Tribunal have not been free of criticism and challenges. Some have suggested the Tribunal is toothless; others have attacked it for having too much influence. I hope that the essays in this collection show the important contribution that the Waitangi Tribunal has made to date, set out the progress that has been made since 1975 and prompt more thinking about the work still to be done and the path ahead. Whatever role the Tribunal plays over the next fifty years, it has already provided a strong foundation for us to take conversations about te Tiriti and constitutional transformation forward. Reflecting on the Tribunal's own history should give us confidence that, no matter the politics of the day, the ability to find ways to meet the challenge and opportunities of just Tiriti relationships – ki te whakamana i te Tiriti – cannot be resisted.

Endnotes

Chapter 3 | Historical Claims and District Inquiries

1 David Williams "Historians' context and lawyers' presentism: Debating historiography or agreeing to differ" (2014) 48(2) New Zealand Journal of History.

2 Michael Belgrave "The Politics of Māori history in the age of protest" (2014) 2(2) Journal of New Zealand and Pacific Studies at 140.

3 Belgrave, above n 2, at 141.

4 Keith Sinclair "Why are race relations in New Zealand better than in South Africa, South Australia or South Dakota?" (1971) 5(2) New Zealand Journal of History.

5 Alan Ward *A Show of Justice – Racial 'amalgamation' in nineteenth century New Zealand* (Auckland University Press, Auckland, 1974) at 308.

6 Claudia Orange *The Treaty of Waitangi* (2nd edition, Bridget Williams Books, Wellington, 2011) at 228.

7 Rachael Bell "Ruth Ross – New Zealand Scholar/Treaty Scholar" (Master's Thesis, Massey University, 2005).

8 Ruth Ross "The Treaty of Waitangi: Texts and Translations" (1972) 6(2) New Zealand Journal of History.

9 Ranginui Walker *Ka Whawhai Tonu Matou Struggle Without End* (2nd edition, Penguin Books, Auckland, 2004) at 90.

10 Ned Fletcher *The English Text of the Treaty of Waitangi* (Bridget Williams Books, Wellington, 2022).

11 M.P.K. Sorrenson "Towards a Radical Reinterpretation of New Zealand History: The Role of the Waitangi Tribunal" (1987) 21(1) New Zealand Journal of History at 173–188.

12 Alan Ward "History and Historians Before the Waitangi Tribunal" (1990) 24(2) New Zealand Journal of History at 155.

13 Michael Belgrave "Looking Forward: Historians and the Tribunal" (2006) 40(2) New Zealand Journal of History at 232–234.

14 W.H. Oliver "The Future Behind Us: The Waitangi Tribunal's Retrospective Utopia" in Andrew Sharp and Paul McHugh (eds) *Histories, Power and Loss: Uses of the Past—A New Zealand Commentary* (Bridget Williams Books, Wellington, 2001) at 9–29.

15 Belgrave, above n 13, at 230.

16 Giselle Byrnes *The Waitangi Tribunal and New Zealand History* (Oxford University Press, Auckland, 2004).

17 Jim McAloon "By Which Standards? History and the Waitangi Tribunal" (2006) 40(2) New Zealand Journal of History at 194–197.

18 McAloon, above n 17, at 196–197

19 Above n 17, at 201–202.

20 E.T. Durie "Chairperson's Foreword" in Professor Alan Ward and Waitangi Tribunal (eds) *National Overview Volume 1*, Waitangi Tribunal Rangahaua Whanui Series (Wellington, 1997) at xiii–xiv.

21 Chairperson "Practice Note" in Michael Belgrave (ed) *Rangahaua Whanui District 1 Auckland Counting the Hectares: Quantifying Maori Land Loss in the Auckland District, 1865–1908* (Waitangi Tribunal, 1997) at 65.

22 Waitangi Tribunal "Rangahaua Whānui" (n.d.) https://www.waitangitribunal.govt.nz/en/publications/general/rangahaua-whanui.

23 Chairperson, above n 21, at 65.

24 Waitangi Tribunal "New Report Streamlines Claims Process" *Te Manutukutuku* [41] (pdf copy, Wellington, June/July 1997) at 1 https://www.waitangitribunal.govt.nz/assets/Te-Manutukutuku/Te-Manutukutuku-Issue-41.pdf.

25 Therese Crocker "Settling Treaty Claims: The Formation of Policy on Treaty of Waitangi Claims in the Pioneering Years, 1988–1998" (Doctoral Thesis, Victoria University of Wellington, 2016) at 111.

26 Waitangi Tribunal *Mohaka ki Ahuriri Report* (Wai 201, 2004) at 5.

27 Above n 26, at 5.

28 Above n 26, at 5–6.

29 Above n 26, at xxiii–xxiv.

30 Above n 26, at xxiv.

31 Above n 26, at 8–9.

[32] Waitangi Tribunal "Te Manutukutu Issue 65" https://www.waitangitribunal.govt.nz/assets/Te-Manutukutuku/Te-Manutukutuku-Issue-65.pdf
[33] Waitangi Tribunal "Te Manutukutu Issue 63" https://www.waitangitribunal.govt.nz/assets/Te-Manutukutuku/Te-Manutukutuku-Issue-63.pdf
[34] Waitangi Tribunal, above n 33.
[35] Waitangi Tribunal *Te Urewera* vol 1 (Wai 894, 2017) at xxxiii–xxxvi.
[36] Waitangi Tribunal, above n 35, at 330.
[37] Above n 35, at 333–334.
[38] Above n 35, at 335–336.
[39] Above n 35, at 335–337
[40] Above n 35, at 337–338
[41] Above n 35, at 337–338
[42] Above n 35, at 341.
[43] Above n 35, at 337–338.
[44] Above n 35, at 343–344.
[45] Above n 35, at 344.
[46] Waitangi Tribunal *Te Tau Ihu o te Waka a Maui* vol 1 (Wai 785, 2008) at 6–7. Note: All iwi submitted claims except Ngāti Waikauri.
[47] Waitangi Tribunal, above n 46, at 7.
[48] Waitangi Tribunal *Te Tau Ihu o te Waka a Maui: Preliminary Report on Customary Rights in the Northern South Island* (Wai 785, 2007).
[49] Waitangi Tribunal "Te Manutukutu Issue 61" (December 2007 January 2008) https://www.waitangitribunal.govt.nz/assets/Te-Manutukutuku/Te-Manutukutuku-Issue-61.pdf.
[50] *Te Tau Ihu*, above n 46, at before xix.
[51] *Te Tau Ihu Customary*, above n 48, at 17.
[52] Above n 48, at 20.
[53] Waitangi Tribunal *Rekohu: A Report on Moriori and Ngati Mutunga Claims in the Chatham Islands* (Wai 64, 2001).
[54] *Te Tau Ihu Customary*, above n 48, at 21.
[55] Waitangi Tribunal *The Ngai Tahu Report* vol 1 (Wai 27, 1991) at 3.
[56] *Ngai Tahu*, above n 55, at 23–24.
[57] *Ngai Tahu*, above n 55, at 23–24.
[58] *Te Tau Ihu Customary*, above n 48, at 12.
[59] Waitangi Tribunal *Te Tau Ihu o te Waka a Maui: Preliminary Report on Te Tau Ihu Customary Rights in the Statutory Ngai Tahu Takiwa* (Wai 785, 2007) at 7.
[60] *Te Tau Ihu o te Waka a Maui*, above n 59, at 13.
[61] *Te Tau Ihu o te Waka a Maui*, above n 59, at 13–14.
[62] Grant Phillipson "2001, A Waitangi Tribunal Odyssey: the Tribunal's response to the 'presentism' critique (2012) 40 Melbourne Historical Journal at 21–23.
[63] Phillipson, above n 62, at 22–25.
[64] Phillipson, above n 62, at 24–26.
[65] Cited in Phillipson, above n 62, at 30.
[66] Waitangi Tribunal The Hauraki Report (Wai 686, 2006) at 1206–1207.
[67] Phillipson, above n 62, at 27–28.
[68] Michael Bassett "Minority Opinion" *Te Raupatu o Tauranga Moana* Waitangi Tribunal (Wai 215, 2004) at 413–417.
[69] David Williams, above n 1, at 136.
[70] Williams, above n 1, at 147–148.
[71] Waitangi Tribunal *Te Tau Ihu o te Waka a Maui: Preliminary Report on Customary Rights in the Northern South Island* (Wai 785, 2007), above n 48, at 4.
[72] Waitangi Tribunal *Te Tau Ihu o te Waka a Maui: Preliminary Report on Customary Rights in the Northern South Island* (Wai 785, 2007), above n 48, at 111–142.
[73] Michael Belgrave Unraveling Historical Narratives and Customary Disputes: The Himatangi Hearings 2024 Evidence for the High Court, at 19–23.
[74] Williams, above n 1, at 141.
[75] Waitangi Tribunal *Te Urewera* vol 1 (Wai 894, 2017), above n 35, at 21.
[76] Michael Belgrave Unraveling Historical Narratives and Customary Disputes: The Himatangi Hearings 2024 Evidence for the High Court, above n 73, at 39.
[77] Waitangi Tribunal *Horowhenua The Muaūpoko Priority Report* (Wai 2200, 2017) at 658.
[78] Waitangi Tribunal *Horowhenua The Muaūpoko Priority Report*, above n 77, at 4–7.

Chapter 4 | Awa

[1] The inspiration for the title of this chapter comes from the elevation of Te Arikinui Kuīni Nga wai hono i te po in 2024 and a statement of the late Canon Huata in Waitangi Tribunal *The Mohaka River Report* (Wai 119, 1992) at 17.
[2] Treaty of Waitangi Act 1975.

[3] Te Tiriti o Waitangi guarantees protection of "taonga", often translated as treasures. The nature of taonga is discussed more fully below.

[4] Proposed changes to resource management law and policy are described by the Environmental Defence Society as a "war on nature". See Environmental Defence Society "The government's war on nature goes nuclear" (6 March 2024) https://eds.org.nz/resources/documents/media-releases/2024/fast-track-bill/.

[5] Recognising that tikanga in the state legal system is growing, the Law Commission has produced a report titled *He Poutama*, itself a valuable resource, which, among other things, draws heavily on this type of tikanga evidence. Law Commission *Pūrongo Rangahau He Poutama* (NZLC SP24, 2023).

[6] New Zealand National Party and New Zealand First *Coalition Agreement* (2023) at 10.

[7] *Coalition Agreement*, above n 6, at 10.

[8] See Linda Te Aho "The 'False Generosity' of Treaty Settlements" in Andrew Erueti (ed) *International Indigenous Rights in Aotearoa New Zealand* (Te Herenga Waka University Press, Wellington, 2017), at 99.

[9] Cordry Huata defined taonga as "treasures, precious and prized" in Waitangi Tribunal *The Mohaka River Report* (Wai 119, 1992) at 10.

[10] Waitangi Tribunal *Motunui–Waitara Report* (Wai 6, 1983). While the Motunui–Waitara claim concerned the gross pollution of coastal reefs in Taranaki, the Tribunal took the view that the discussion of impacts also applied to the Waitara River, a natural discharge to the ocean reefs, and considered the impact of extraction from the river for industrial needs and the impact of that on freshwater biota.

[11] *Mohaka River Report*, above n 1, at 50.

[12] *Mohaka River Report*, above n 1, at 10–11.

[13] In above n 1, the late Canon Huata spoke of the healing powers of the river for the body and mind, as well as for the spirit, at 13.

[14] Waitangi Tribunal *Manukau Report* (Wai 8, 1985) at 51 and 72. Although the claim relates to the Manukau Harbour, the Tribunal was clear that impacts on the river flowed into the harbour. See also *The Pouakani Report* (Wai 33, 1993), Part 2, Ch 16 for extensive historical information about the Waikato River.

[15] *Manukau Report*, above n 14, at 70.

[16] Waitangi Tribunal *Turangi Township Report* (Wai 84, 1995) at 133.

[17] Para 3.18; the original report has kiakia, I have corrected to kiekie, a weaving material.

[18] The reports clearly indicate the value and importance of rivers as food baskets.

[19] *The Mohaka River Report*, above n 1, at 8 and 11.

[20] *The Mohaka River Report*, above n 1, at 17.

[21] Kenehihi, An early translation of the Lord's Prayer into Māori by missionaries, 1827 as cited in Betsan Martin and New Zealand Māori Council with Linda Te Aho *Ka Māpuna: Towards a Rangatiratanga Framework for the Governance of Waterways* (Response Trust, Wellington, 2021).

[22] Archives New Zealand "He Whakaputanga o te Rangatiratanga o Nu Tireni, The Declaration of the Independence of New Zealand" (11 June 2024) archives.govt.nz/ discover-our-stories/the-declaration-of-independence-of-new-zealand.

[23] *Motunui–Waitara Report*, above n 10, at 51.

[24] *Motunui–Waitara Report*, above n 10, at 51.

[25] *Motunui–Waitara Report*, above n 10, at 51.

[26] Waitangi Tribunal *Kaituna River Report* (Wai 4, 1984).

[27] Waitangi Tribunal *Te Ika Whenua Rivers Report* (Wai 212, 1998) at 15.

[28] Marama Muru-Lanning *Tupuna Awa: People and Politics of the Waikato River* (Auckland University Press, Auckland, 2016).

[29] *R v Symonds* [1847] NZPCC 387.

[30] *Embrey v Owen* [1851] 6 Exch at [353, 372–73].

[31] *The Mohaka River Report*, above n 1, at 33–38.

[32] See Linda Te Aho "Ngā Whakataunga Waimāori: Freshwater settlements" in Nicola Wheen and Janine Hayward (eds) *Treaty of Waitangi Settlements* (Bridget Williams Books, Wellington, 2012) at 104–105.

[33] Waitangi Tribunal *The Pouakani Report* Part 2 (Wai 33,1993), at 295–297.

[34] *Kaituna River Report*, above n 26, at 37.

[35] *The Mohaka River Report*, above n 1, at 21.

[36] *The Mohaka River Report*, above n 1, at 78.

[37] See Jane Kelsey "Submission on the Principles of the Treaty of Waitangi Bill January 2025" at [19]. https://www.parliament.nz/resource/

enNZ/54SCJUST_EVI_227e6d0b-e63242eb-cffe -08dcfeb826c6_JUST50483/ce798408 fab 8338633c16 b38f94787071f00ffa7. Accessed 18th August 2025.

38 Andrew Erueti "Māori Rights to Freshwater: The Three Conceptual Models of Indigenous Rights" (2016) 6 Waikato Law Review at 58.

39 Te Maire Tau *Water Rights for Ngāi Tahu: A discussion paper* (Canterbury University Press, Christchurch, 2017).

40 Waikato-Tainui Raupatu Claims (Waikato River) Settlement Act 2010, ss 64, 65.

41 Te Rūnanga o Ngāi Tahu "Enough is enough why Ngāi Tahu is suing the Crown over its waterways" (20 December 2020) https://ngaitahu.iwi.nz/opportunities-and-resources/publications/te-karaka/enough-is-enough-why-ngai-tahu-is-suing-the-crown-over-its-waterways-tk87/.

42 Waitangi Tribunal "National Freshwater and Geothermal Resources" (n.d.) https://www.waitangitribunal.govt.nz/en/inquiries/kaupapa-inquiries/freshwater.

43 Refer iwi leaders' letter to King Charles, December 2024 https://tiaki.natlib.govt.nz/#details =ecatalogue.1118165. Accessed 18 August 2025, and proposals to review the scope of the Waitangi Tribunal, above, n 7.

44 EDS media statement, above n 4.

45 *Motunui–Waitara Report*, above n 10, at 20.

46 *Manukau Report*, above n 14, at 53.

47 *Manukau Report*, above n 14, at 91.

48 *Manukau Report*, above n 14, at 98.

49 Waikato-Tainui Raupatu Claims (Waikato River) Settlement Act 2010, s 3; and see Linda Te Aho "Freshwater Settlements" in Nicola Wheen and Janine Hayward (eds) *Treaty of Waitangi Settlements* (Bridget Williams Books, Wellington, 2012) at 109–112.

50 Waipā District Council "Cambridge Wastewater Treatment Plant wins special award" (25 October 2024) https://www.waipadc.govt.nz/our-council/news?item=id:2rxo9idq617q9ssgc18f. The Kaitiaki Group, established by the Waipā District Council won an award for its commitment to collaboration, embracing indigenous knowledge and honouring the principles of kaitiakitanga and te Tiriti o Waitangi.

51 Waikato-Tainui Raupatu Claims (Waikato River) Settlement Act 2010, preamble s 17 and Schedule 1.

52 Following the Waikato River settlement, Tā (Eddie) Taihākurei Durie and the New Zealand Māori Council introduced the idea of a hierarchy of interests to be recognised in water governance, with the well-being of freshwater being the primary interest. These became known as Te Mana o te Wai through the work of iwi leaders, though Tā Taihākurei often speaks of his preference for Te Mauri o te Wai.

53 Ministry for the Environment "National Policy Statement for Freshwater Management" (November 2024) https://environment.govt.nz/publications/national-policy-statement-for-freshwatermanagement-2020-amended-october-2024/.

54 Waitangi Tribunal *The Whanganui River Report* (Wai 167, 1999) at 343.

55 Te Awa Tupua (Whanganui River Claims Settlement) Act 2017, s 14.

56 Te Awa Tupua, above n 55, at s 34 provides for collaborative freshwater planning.

57 Te Awa Tupua, above n 55, at s 12.

58 Te Awa Tupua, above n 55, at s 13(c.) "*Ko Te Kawa Tuatoru Ko au te Awa, ko te Awa ko au*: I am the River and the River is me: The iwi and hapū of the Whanganui River have an inalienable connection with, and responsibility to, Te Awa Tupua and its health and well-being."

59 *Motunui–Waitara Report*, above n 10, at 21.

60 Taane Aruka Te Aho, Rangatahi and Kaitiaki Representative, Pohara Poukai, 2024.

61 Ella Cameron-Smith, PhD student, Ngaati Koroki Kahukura Rangatahi, 2024.

62 This whakataukī derives from a tongikura (saying) of King Tāwhiao "Kohikohia ngā maramara o te waka kia topu ai ki to aroaro. Waiho mā waho hei wherawhera he kokopi tau – Gather the chips of the canoe together and confront the challenges before us". It is a call to people to come together in trying times.

63 This is not to mention the contradictory views of parliamentary representatives. For example, refer to an interview of Māori representatives from the Labour, Green and Māori parties, Te Ao with Moana, Who owns waters? 15 August 2020. https://www.facebook.com/watch/?v=241411126985539. Accessed 18 August 2025. Accessed 18 August 2025.

64 Te Aho, above n 49, at 113.

65 Te Maire Tau, above n 39, at 58.

Chapter 5 | Wai me Te Taiao

*The authors would like to thank Waitapu Beach and Angel Stewart for their research and proofing assistance. Responsibility for all views and/or errors rest with the authors.

1 Joseph Williams, Justice of New Zealand "He Pūkenga Wai" (Salmon Lecture 2019, Resource Management Law Association, 12 September 2019) at 1. As acknowleged.

2 Associate Professor Linda Te Aho has contributed a chapter to this collection entitled "Awa: Ngā Wai Honohono – The Rivers that Join Us" that examines the Waitangi Tribunal's rivers reports. Some of these reports are referred to in this chapter, but they are not a focus.

3 Noting Associate Professor Te Aho's chapter.

4 Linda Te Aho "Nga Whakataunga Waimāori: Freshwater Settlements" in Nicola R. Wheen and Janine Hayward (eds) *Treaty of Waitangi Settlements* (Bridget Williams Books, Wellington, 2012) at 102.

5 Some of the material from this chapter has drawn on earlier work of the authors, including a literature review prepared for the Freshwater Iwi Leaders Group that was filed with the Waitangi Tribunal in the Wai 2358 hearing: Horiana Irwin-Easthope and others *Iwi/Hapū Rights And Interests In Fresh Water: Recognition Work-Stream Research Report Literature Review prepared for Iwi Advisory Group* (2015).

6 Edward T. Durie "Custom Law: Address to the New Zealand Law Society for Legal and Social Philosophy" (1994) 24 VUWLR 325 at 328.

7 Waitangi Tribunal *The Mōhaka River Report* (Wai 119, 1992) at [2.6].

8 Durie, above n 6, at 328.

9 Waitangi Tribunal Ko Aotearoa Tēnei: *A Report into Claims Concerning New Zealand Law and Policy Affecting Māori Culture and Identity – Te Taumata Tuarua* (Wai 262, 2011) vol 1.

10 *Ko Aotearoa Tēnei* above n 9, at chapter 3.

11 *Ko Aotearoa Tēnei* above n 9, at 235.

12 *Ko Aotearoa Tēnei* above n 9, at 235.

13 *Ko Aotearoa Tēnei* above n 9, at 239.

14 Following the passing of the original presiding officer, Judge Richard Kearney, in 2005.

15 Joseph Williams "Lex Aotearoa: An Heroic Attempt to Map the Māori Dimension in Modern New Zealand Law" (2013) 21 Wai L Rev 1 at 4.

16 Joseph Williams, Justice of New Zealand "He Pūkenga Wai" (Salmon Lecture 2019, Resource Management Law Association, 12 September 2019) at 7.

17 Waitangi Tribunal *He Maunga Rongo: Report on Central North Island Claims* (Wai 1200, 2008).

18 Waitangi Tribunal *He Maunga Rongo: Report on Central North Island Claims* (Wai 1200, 2008), vol 4, above n 17, at 1251.

19 Waitangi Tribunal *The Stage 1 Report on the National Freshwater and Geothermal Resources Claim* (Wai 2358, 2012) at 35.

20 Waitangi Tribunal *Te Ika Whenua Energy Assets Report* (Wai 212, 1993) at [2.4].

21 *Te Ika Whenua Energy* above n 20, at [2.4].

22 Waitangi Tribunal *Report on the Manukau Claim* (Wai 8, 1985) at [7.2].

23 Freshwater Report above n 19, at 55.

24 Freshwater Report above n 19, at 55.

25 Waitangi Tribunal *Report of the Waitangi Tribunal on the Kaituna River Claim* (Wai 4, 1984); *The Pouakani Report* (Wai 33, 1993); *The Mohaka River Report* (Wai 119, 1992); *The Whanganui River Report* (Wai 167, 1999); and *Te Ika Whenua Rivers Report* (Wai 212, 1998).

26 Freshwater Report above n 19, at 49.

27 Waitangi Tribunal *Te Ika Whenua Rivers Report* (Wai 212, 1998) at 84.

28 Waitangi Tribunal *The Mohaka River Report* (Wai 119, 1992) at 10.

29 Waitangi Tribunal: *Report of the Waitangi Tribunal on the Kaituna River Claim* (Wai 4, 1984) at 31.

30 *Kaituna River Claim* above n 29, at 34–37.

31 *Kaituna River Claim above n 29, at 33.*

32 *Mohaka River* above n 28, at 64.

33 Waitangi Tribunal *Te Ika Whenua Rivers Report* (Wai 212, 1998) at 135–136; The Whanganui River Report (Wai 167, 1999) at 338–339. See also, Associate Professor Linda Te Aho's chapter in this book.

34 Waitangi Tribunal *Te Ika Whenua Rivers Report* (Wai 212, 1998), above n 27, at 84.

35 *Te Ika Whenua* above n 27, at 86.

36 *Te Ika Whenua* above n 27, at 86.

37 *Te Ika Whenua* above n 27, at 126.
38 *Te Ika Whenua* above n 27, at 131–132.
39 *Te Ika Whenua* above n 27, at 132.
40 *He Maunga Rongo* above n 17, at 1286.
41 *He Maunga Rongo* above n 17, at 1286.
42 *Freshwater Report* above n 19, at 101.
43 *Freshwater Report* above n 19, at 72.
44 *Freshwater Report* above n 19, at 72.
45 *Freshwater Report* above n 19, at 72.
46 *Freshwater Report* above n 19.
47 He Whakaputanga o te Rangatiratanga o Niu Tireni – the Declaration of Independence of the United Tribes of New Zealand (1835).
48 Hugh Kawharu *Translation of Te Tiriti | The Treaty of Waitangi* (2021) at 2.
49 *Ko Aotearoa Tēnei* above n 9, at 249.
50 *Ko Aotearoa Tēnei* above n 9, at 17.
51 Carwyn Jones "Ko Aotearoa Tēnei: A Report into Claims Concerning New Zealand Law and Policy Affecting Māori Culture and Identity" (2020) 10(19) Māori Law Review at 4.
52 Waitangi Tribunal *The Stage 2 Report on the National Freshwater and Geothermal Resources Claims* (Wai 2358, 2019) at 101.
53 Freshwater Report above n 19, at 69.
54 Waitangi Tribunal *The Stage 2 Report on the National Freshwater and Geothermal Resources Claims* (Wai 2358, 2019), above n 52, at 526.
55 Waitangi Tribunal *The Stage 2 Report on the National Freshwater and Geothermal Resources Claims* (Wai 2358, 2019), above n 52, at 527.
56 Waitangi Tribunal *The Interim Report on Māori Appointments to Regional Planning Committees* (Wai 2358, 2022) at 105.
57 *Māori Appointments* above n 56, at 104–105.
58 *Māori Appointments* above n 56, at 104.
59 *Ko Aotearoa Tēnei* above n 9, vol 1.
60 Waitangi Tribunal *The Stage 2 Report on the National Freshwater and Geothermal Resources Claims* (Wai 2358, 2019), above n 52, at 101.
61 Waitangi Tribunal *National Freshwater and Geothermal Resources* (n.d.) Waitangi Tribunal https://www.waitangitribunal.govt.nz/en/inquiries/kaupapa-inquiries/freshwater at 1.
62 Freshwater Report above n 19.
63 Waitangi Tribunal *The Stage 2 Report on the National Freshwater and Geothermal Resources Claims* (Wai 2358, 2019), above n 52.
64 Waitangi Tribunal *The Stage 2 Report on the National Freshwater and Geothermal Resources Claims* (Wai 2358, 2019), above n 52, at 66.
65 Freshwater Report above n 19, at 75.
66 Freshwater Report above n 19, at 10 and 31.
67 Freshwater Report above n 19, at 10.
68 Freshwater Report above n 19, at 76.
69 Freshwater Report above n 19, at 76.
70 Freshwater Report above n 19, at 77.
71 Freshwater Report above n 19, at 81.
72 Freshwater Report above n 19, at 31 and 33.
73 Freshwater Report above n 19, at 32.
74 Freshwater Report above n 19, at 87.
75 Waitangi Tribunal *Stage 1 Report on the National Freshwater and Geothermal Resources Claim* (Wai 2358, 2012), above n 19, at 75.
76 Freshwater Report above n 19, at 77–79.
77 Freshwater Report above n 19, at xx.
78 Freshwater Report above n 19, at xxi.
79 Waitangi Tribunal *The Stage 2 Report on the National Freshwater and Geothermal Resources Claims* (Wai 2358, 2019), above n 52, at 66.
80 Stage 2 Freshwater Report above n 52, at 524.
81 Stage 2 Freshwater Report above n 52, at 524
82 Stage 2 Freshwater Report above n 52, at 524.
83 Stage 2 Freshwater Report above n 52, at 524.
84 Stage 2 Freshwater Report above n 52, at 320 and 543.
85 Stage 2 Freshwater Report above n 52, at 529.
86 Stage 2 Freshwater Report above n 52, at 114.
87 Stage 2 Freshwater Report above n 52, at 526.
88 Aside from the Tribunal's resumptive jurisdiction.
89 For example, it took at least eight years for the then Labour-led Government to propose Te Pae Tawhiti work programme in 2019. Its proposal was for the programme to address the Crown breaches of its Treaty guarantee to allow Māori to exercise rangatiratanga over mātauranga Māori and taonga.
90 For example, see the work of Associate Professor Linda Te Aho and Professor Jacinta Ruru in particular.

91 We have not included the Tribunal's stage one Freshwater Report recommendations in this section as the recommendations related solely to the context at that time of the reorganisation of state-owned enterprises into mixed ownership model entities.

92 *Ko Aotearoa Tēnei* above n 9, at 286.

93 *Ko Aotearoa Tēnei* above n 9, at 286.

94 *Ko Aotearoa Tēnei* above n 9, at 286.

95 *Ko Aotearoa Tēnei* above n 9, at 286.

96 Stage 2 Freshwater Report above n 52, at 527 and 559.

97 Stage 2 Freshwater Report above n 52, at 527 and 559.

98 Stage 2 Freshwater Report above n 52, at 560.

99 Stage 2 Freshwater Report above n 52, at 561.

100 Stage 2 Freshwater Report above n 52, at 527 and 560.

101 Stage 2 Freshwater Report above n 52, at 560.

102 Stage 2 Freshwater Report above n 52, at 560–561.

103 Stage 2 Freshwater Report above n 52, at 561.

104 Stage 2 Freshwater Report above n 52, at 561.

105 Stage 2 Freshwater Report above n 52, at 561.

106 Stage 2 Freshwater Report above n 52, at 561.

107 Stage 2 Freshwater Report above n 52, at 563.

108 Stage 2 Freshwater Report above n 52, at 563.

109 Stage 2 Freshwater Report above n 52, at 563.

110 Stage 2 Freshwater Report above n 52, at 564.

111 Stage 2 Freshwater Report above n 52, at 563.

112 Stage 2 Freshwater Report above n 52, at 564.

113 Stage 2 Freshwater Report above n 52, at 560.

114 Stage 2 Freshwater Report above n 52, at 562.

115 Stage 2 Freshwater Report above n 52, at 562.

116 Stage 2 Freshwater Report above n 52, at 564.

117 Stage 2 Freshwater Report above n 52, at 564.

118 *New Zealand Māori Council v Attorney-General* [2013] 3 NZLR 31 (SC).

119 *New Zealand Māori Council v Attorney-General* [2013] 3 NZLR 31 (SC), above n 118, at [83].

120 *New Zealand Māori Council v Attorney-General* [2013] 3 NZLR 31 (SC), above n 118, at [11].

121 *New Zealand Māori Council v Attorney-General* [2013] 3 NZLR 31 (SC), above n 118, at [11].

122 *New Zealand Māori Council v Attorney-General* [2013] 3 NZLR 31 (SC), above n 118, at [85].

123 *New Zealand Māori Council v Attorney-General* [2013] 3 NZLR 31 (SC), above n 118, at [113].

124 Simon William English, affidavit, 7 November 2012.

125 *New Zealand Māori Council v Attorney-General* [2013] 3 NZLR 31, above n 118, at [145].

126 Stage 2 Freshwater Report above n 79, above n 52, at 178.

127 Treaty of Waitangi Act 1975, s 81.

128 Hon Chris Bishop and Simon Court "Speech on replacing the Resource Management Act" (20 September 2024) Beehive.govt.nz Speech on replacing the Resource Management Act | Beehive.govt.nz.

129 "Environmental Legal Assistance Fund" (7 June 2024) Ministry for the Environment Environmental Legal Assistance Fund | Ministry for the Environment.

130 Acknowledging Fat Freddy's Drop *Hope for a Generation* EP that was released in 2003.

131 Waitangi Tribunal *He Maunga Rongo: Report on the Central North Island Claims Part V Te Taiao The Environment and Natural Resources* (WAI 1200, 2008) at 1240.

132 Michael King (ed) *Te Ao Hurihuri: Aspects of Māoritanga* (2nd ed, Reed, Auckland, 1992).

133 For example, there were seven claims that the Tribunal heard and reported on under urgency in 2024: Waitangi Tribunal *Kāinga Kore: The Stage One Report of the Housing Policy and Services Kaupapa Inquiry on Māori Homelessness* (Wai 2750, 2024); Waitangi Tribunal *Ngā Mātāpono/The Principles: The Interim Report of the Tomokia Ngā Tatau o Matangirea – The Constitutional Kaupapa Inquiry Panel on The Crown's Treaty Principles Bill and Treaty Clause Review Policies* (WaiI 3300, 2024); Waitangi Tribunal *Te Oranga Tamariki (Section 7AA) Urgent Inquiry Report* (Wai 3350, 2024); Waitangi Tribunal *The Māori Wards and Constituencies Urgent Inquiry Report* (Wai 3365, 2024); Waitangi Tribunal *The Takutai Moana Act 2011 Urgent Inquiry Stage 1 Report* (Wai 3400, 2024); Waitangi Tribunal *Te Reo I te Kāwanatanga – Te Reo in the Public Sector Urgent Inquiry* (Wai 3327, 2024); and Waitangi Tribunal *Kura Kaupapa Māori Urgent Inquiry* (Wai 1718, 2024).

134 Russel Palmer "Line by line: The coalition's Budget cuts in one list" (1 June 2024) RNZ

https://www.rnz.co.nz/news/political/518376/line-by-line-the-coalition-s-budget-cuts-in-one-list.

[135] For example, those comments made by the Hon David Seymor and the Hon Shane Jones in 2024 reported by Marc Daalder "Ministers accused of Cabinet Manual breach with threats to Waitangi Tribunal" (19 April 2024) Newsroom https://newsroom.co.nz/2024/04/19/ministers-accused-of-cabinet-manual-breach-with-threats-to-waitangi-tribunal/.
See Checkpoint "Hīkoi not representative of New Zealand, David Seymour says" (19 November 2024) RNZ https://www.rnz.co.nz/news/political/534223/hikoi-not-representative-of-new-zealand-david-seymour-says.

[136] Treaty of Waitangi Act 1975, s 6.

Chapter 6 | Takutai Moana

*The title of this chapter is a revision of a comment from the Waitangi Tribunal's report "we proceed in the expectation that governments in New Zealand want to be good governments, whose actions although carried by power are mitigated by fairness."

[1] Ruth Berry "Tribunal call for 'fruitful' seabed talks" *The New Zealand Herald* (online ed, Auckland, 12 September 2003).

[2] Waitangi Tribunal *Report on the Crown's Foreshore and Seabed Policy* (Wai 1071, 2004).

[3] See Boast "Legal history Ownership and Management of the Forseshore and Seabed" in *Pākia ki Uta Pākia ki Tai: Ministerial Review of the Foreshore and Seabed Act 2004 Vol 2 Appendices* (Minsterial Review Panel, 2009) at 8.

[4] Jamie Tahana "A new generation of activism: Marking 20 years since the foreshore and seabed hīkoi" *The Spinoff* (online ed, Auckland, 2 May 2024).

[5] Kahurangi Dame Tariana Turia DNZM, (8 April 1944–3 January 2025).

[6] *Ngati Apa v Attorney-General* [2003] NZCA 117; [2003] 3 NZLR 643 (CA).

[7] Andrew Erueti "Ngāti Apa and the Environmental Managment of New Zealand's Coastal Marine Area" (2005) Hors Serie Volume V Essays on Environmental Law in the Pacific: International and Comparative Perspectives 235 at 241.

[8] Erueti, above n 7, at 241. For example, Ngāti Tama had made thirty-five unsuccessful applications.

[9] Wai 1071, above n 2, at 41.

[10] Specifically section 129(2)(a) Te Ture Whenua Maori Act 1993.

[11] Erueti, above n 7, at 244.

[12] *Ngati Apa,* above n 6, at [4] with reference to *In Re the Ninety-Mile Beach* [1963] NZLR 461 (CA).

[13] *In Re Marlborough Sounds Foreshore and Seabed* 22A Nelson MB1, 22 December 1997 per Hingston J.

[14] *Ngati Apa,* above n 6, at [5].

[15] *In Re Marlborough Sounds Foreshore and Seabed*, above n 13, at 5.

[16] For a critique of *In Re Ninety-Mile Beach* see Richard Boast "In Re Ninety Mile Beach Revisited: The Native Land Court and the Foreshore in New Zealand Legal History" (1993) 23 VUWLR 145.

[17] See Jacinta Ruru "A Politically Fuelled Tsunami:The Foreshore/Seabed Controversy in Aotearoa Me Te Wai Pounamu New Zealand" (2004) 113(1) NZJPS at 57–72 for a detailed description of the legal history.

[18] *Crown Law Office v Maori Land Court (Marlborough Sounds)* 1998/3-9 Te Waipounamu ACMB, 19 October 1998, Durie CJ, Smith, Carter, Isaac JJ.

[19] *Ngati Apa v Attorney-General* [2002] 2 NZLR 661 (HC).

[20] *Ngati Apa,* above n 6, at [13].

[21] *Ngati Apa,* above n 6, at [31].

[22] Tom Bennion, Malcolm Birdling and Rebecca Paton *Making Sense of the Foreshore and Seabed: A Special Edition of the Māori Law Review* (The Māori Law Review, Wellington, 2004) at i.

[23] For example see Jonathon Milne "Civil war on Foreshore Bill" *The Dominion Post* (Wellington, 1 August 2024).

[24] Wai 1071, above n 2, at 122–124.

[25] Wai 1071, above n 2, at 139.

[26] Wai 1071, above n 2, at 3.

[27] Wai 1071, above n 2, at 3.

[28] Wai 1071, above n 2, at 4.

[29] Wai 1071, above n 2, at 6.

[30] Wai 1071, above n 2, at 7.

[31] Wai 1071, above n 2, at 7.

[32] Wai 1071, above n 2, at 8.

33 Wai 1071, above n 2, at 9.
34 Wai 1071, above n 2, at 10.
35 Wai 1071, above n 2, at 10.
36 Wai 1071, above n 2, at 11.
37 Wai 1071, above n 2, at 18–19.
38 Wai 1071, above n 2, at 18.
39 Wai 1071, above n 2, at ix.
40 At xiii.
41 Wai 1071, above n 2, at xii.
42 Wai 1071, above n 2, at 83.
43 Wai 1071, above n 2, at 87.
44 Wai 1071, above n 2, at 85.
45 Wai 1071, above n 2, at 31.
46 Wai 1071, above n 2, at 83.
47 Wai 1071, above n 2, at 84.
48 Wai 1071, above n 2, at 86.
49 Hon Michael Cullen "Government proposals on foreshore and seabed" (press release, 18 December 2003). www.beehive.govt.nz/release/government-proposals-foreshore-seabed.
50 Wai 1071, above n 2, at 86.
51 Wai 1071, above n 2, at 87.
52 Wai 1071, above n 2, at 108.
53 Wai 1071, above n 2, at 95.
54 Wai 1071, above n 2, at 96.
55 Wai 1071, above n 2, at 127.
56 Wai 1071, above n 2, at 128.
57 Wai 1071, above n 2, at 128.
58 Wai 1071, above n 2, at 131.
59 Wai 1071, above n 2, at 134.
60 Wai 1071, above n 2, at 135.
61 Wai 1071, above n 2, at 136.
62 Wai 1071, above n 2, at 136.
63 Wai 1071, above n 2, at 139–141.
64 Wai 1071, above n 2, at 140.
65 *New Zealand Maori Council v Attorney-General* [1987] 1 NZLR 641, (1987) 6 NZAR 353 (the 'Lands' case); *New Zealand Maori Council v Attorney-General* [1989] 2 NZLR 142 (the 'Forests' case); *New Zealand Maori Council v Attorney-General* [1991] 2 NZLR 129 (the 'Spectrum' case) and *New Zealand Maori Council v Attorney-General* [1994] 1 NZLR 513 (the 'Broadcasting' case).
66 See Office of Treaty Settlements Ka tika ā muri, ka tika ā mua – Healing the past, building a future – A Guide to Treaty of Waitangi Claims and Negotiations with the Crown (Wellington, 2018).
67 For example, in 1994 the government proposed a "fiscal envelope" for all Treaty settlements limiting compensation to $1 billion. The cap was fiercely opposed by Māori, and the proposal was eventually dropped. As at 2023, there have been over eighty settlements with reparations valued at over $2 billion. Office of the Minister in Charge of Treaty of Waitangi Negotiations *Policy papers for Crown proposals for the settlement of Treaty of Waitangi claims* (Wellington, 1995). For a full discussion of the Māori opposition see Margaret Mutu *The State of Māori Rights* (Huia Publishers, Wellington, 2011); Research Unit for Maori Education *The Fiscal Envelope: economics, politics & colonisation – Volume one: a series of readers examining critical issues in contemporary Māori Society* (University of Auckland, Auckland, 1995).
68 Waikato Raupatu Claims Settlement Act 1995; Ngāi Tahu Claims Settlement Act 1998.
69 Waitangi Tribunal *The Petroleum Report* (Wai 796, 2003).
70 See Craig Coxhead "Māori title to petroleum: The Waitangi Petroleum report" [2004] NZYbkNZJur 6.
71 Tracy Watkins "Treaty finding on oil upsets" *The Press* (Christchurch, 22 May 2003).
72 Wai 1071, above n 2, at 75.
73 Metiria Turei "Litigation is an Evil" (1998) 8(3) Auckland U LRev 900 at 900–901.
74 The Maori Commercial Aquaculture Claims Settlement Act 2004 was divided from the Aquaculture Reform Bill at its third reading on 14 December 2004. See for commentary Vernon Small "Flexing muscles in marine farm goldrush" *The Dominion Post* (Wellington, 21 September 2003).
75 For more on the consequences of the Foreshore and Seabed Act 2004 on commercial exploitation of seabed mineral resources see Maria Bargh "Changing the game plan: The Foreshore and Seabed Act and constitutional change" (2006) 1(1) Kōtuitui: New Zealand Journal of Social Sciences Online at 13–24. https://doi.org/10.1080/1177083X.2006.9522408
76 Wai 1071, above n 2, at 138.
77 The Young Māori Party was not a political party with its own representation. Its members joined other parties. Mana Motuhake contested five elections between 1980 and

1990, but its only member of Parliament was Sandra Lee elected in 1993 under the Alliance banner. Mana Wāhine Te Ira Tangata was established by sitting MP Alamein Kopu but did not win sufficient votes in the 1999 election to gain a seat. Hone Harawira won his seat of Tai Tokerau in the 2011 general election under the Mana Party.

78 Marine and Coastal Area (Takutai Moana) Act 2011, section 5.

79 Sections 6 and 11.

80 Waitangi Tribunal Takutai Moana Act 2011 Urgent Inquiry Stage 1 Report (Wai 3400, 2024).

81 Hon Paul Goldsmith "Test for Customary Marine Title being restored" (25 July 2024) Beehive Government of New Zealand www.beehive.govt.nz/release/test-customary-marine-title-being-restored. This announcement was made in response to give effect to the provisions of the coalition agreement with New Zealand First.

82 *Whakatōhea Kotahitanga Waka (Edwards) & Ors v Te Kāhui and Whakatōhea Māori Trust Board & Ors* [2003] NZCA 504 (18 October 2023). This case was appealed in 2024, and the Supreme Court upheld the appeal, narrowing the Court of Appeal's approach but maintaining a strong focus on the reconciliatory intent of the MACA Act. See *Whakatōhea Kotahitanga Waka (Edwards) and Ors v Te Kāhui and Ors* [2024] NZSC 164.

83 Marine and Coastal Area (Takutai Moana) (Cutomary Marine Title) Amendment Bill 2024 No 83-2, clause 7. The Bill is due to be passed into law in mid 2025.

84 Clause 7.

85 Wai 3400, above n 80, at 57 and 62.

86 At 67.

87 At 71.

Chapter 7 | Ika

1 These iwi include Te Ātiawa (Taranaki), Te Ātihaunui a Pāpārangi, Taranaki, Ngāti Ruanui, Rangitāne (North Island), Ngā Rauru, Ngā Ruahine, Ngāti Apa (North Island), Muaupoko, Ngāti Mutunga (Taranaki), Ngāti Hauiti and Ngāti Maru (Taranaki).

2 Ngāti Raukawa (ki te Tonga), Ngāti Toa Rangatira, Te Ātiawa (Wellington), Te Ātiawa (Te Tau Ihu), Ngāti Kuia, Rangitāne (Te Tau Ihu), Ngāti Koata, Ngāti Rarua, Ngāti Apa ki te Waipounamu, Ngāti Tama (Te Tau Ihu) and Ātiawa ki Whakarongotai.

3 See Schedule 3 of the Maori Fisheries Act 2004.

4 The government's 2022 agreement with Māori on the radio spectrum, while entered into on behalf of all Māori and recognising Māori interests in the management of the spectrum, is not a Treaty settlement in the ordinary sense. The memorandum of understanding, for example, provides that the Crown does not accept the spectrum as a taonga protected by te Tiriti. See the *Memorandum of Understanding on Radio Spectrum* (Ministry of Business, Innovation and Employment, 2022) at 4, which provides that "The Crown does not accept the conclusions and recommendations of the Wai 776 report, and in particular does not accept that radio spectrum is a taonga".

5 "The Treaty of Waitangi and Maori Fisheries – Mataitai Nga Tikanga Maori me te Tiriti o Waitangi" (The Law Commission, A Background Paper NZLC PP9, 1989) at 11.

6 The Fisheries Act 1983 was repealed by section 22 of the Fisheries Amendment Act 2022 (2022 No 56), but the rights of holders of section 28N rights are still the subject of extant litigation.

7 See *Te Ohu Kai Moana Trustee Ltd v Attorney-General* [2016] NZHC 1798.

8 Fish Protection Act 1877, at s 8.

9 Sea-fisheries Amendment Act 1903, at s 14.

10 Waitangi Tribunal *Muriwhenua Fishing Report* (Wai 22, 1988) at [5.4.6] [*Muriwhenua Fishing Report*].

11 See the discussion in the *Muriwhenua Fishing Report* at [6.2.1].

12 *Baldick and Others v Jackson* [1910] All ER 343 (SC) Stout CJ.

13 At 344–345. See also Alex Frame and Joeliee Seed-Pihama "Some Customary Legal Concepts in Traditional Māori Migration Accounts" in 2 RJP/NZACLYEARBOOK11.

14 *Waipapakura v Hempton* (1914) 33 NZLR 1065 (Full Court of the Supreme Court).

15 See Richard Boast "Sir John Salmond and Māori Land Tenure" (2007) 38(4) VUWLR 831 at 849. See also Mark Hickford "John

Salmond and Native Title in New Zealand: Developing a Crown Theory on the Treaty of Waitangi, 1910–1920" (2007) 38(4) VUWLR 853.

[16] *Keepa and Wiki v Inspector of Fisheries* [1965] NZLR 322 (HC).

[17] For a discussion, see *Muriwhenua Fishing Report* at 99. See also Justine Munro "The Treaty of Waitangi and the Sealord Deal" (1994) 24(4) VUWLR at 399.

[18] *Keepa and Wiki v Inspector of Fisheries* [1965] NZLR 322.

[19] *Te Weehi v Regional Fisheries Officer* [1986] 1 NZLR 680 at 692.

[20] At 692.

[21] At 691–692.

[22] *Green v Ministry of Agriculture and Fisheries* [1990] 1 NZLR 411.

[23] *R v Saxton* [2009] NZCA 498; *R v Gorrie* [2007] NZCA 144; *Taranaki Fish & Game Council v McRitchie* HC Whanganui AP19/97, 14 May 1998, HC; *Green v Ministry of Agriculture and Fisheries* HC Whanganui M54/87, 3 June 1988.

[24] *Ngati Apa v Attorney General* [2003] NZCA 117 at [149].

[25] *Takamore v Clarke* [2012] 1 NZLR 573 at [118].

[26] *In Re Tipene* [2016] NZHC 3199 at [17].

[27] Te Kerēme and the Ngāi Tahu Settlement Workshop Series 2022 "Ngāi Tahu and the Fisheries Settlement" panel discussion with Tā Tipene O'Regan, Craig Ellison and David Higgins (9 June 2022) https://www.youtube.com/watch?v=LnAiv81dI1A&t=5065s.

[28] See Kathryn Cammell "A 'Cornerstone Decision': The Historical Significance of the Motunui-Waitara (Wai 6) Report" (MA Thesis, University of Auckland, 2020).

[29] Waitangi Tribunal *Report of the Waitangi Tribunal on the Waiau Pa Power Station Claim* (Wai 2, 1978).

[30] At 12–13.

[31] Waitangi Tribunal *Report of the Waitangi Tribunal on the Kaituna River Claim* (Wai 4, 1984) at 31.

[32] At 31.

[33] Waitangi Tribunal *Report of the Waitangi Tribunal on the Motunui–Waitara Claim* (Wai 6, 1983) [*Motunui–Waitara Claim*].

[34] See Appendix 1 "The Original Claim" in Waitangi Tribunal *Report of the Waitangi Tribunal on the Motunui–Waitara Claim* (Wai 6, 1983) at 65.

[35] Waitangi Tribunal *Report of the Waitangi Tribunal on the Motunui–Waitara Claim* (Wai 6, 1983), above n 33, at 70.

[36] See *New Zealand Māori Council v Attorney-General* HC Wellington CP942/88, 3 May 1991 at 17; *New Zealand Māori Council v Attorney-General* [1992] 2 NZLR 576 (CA) at 578 per Cooke P; *New Zealand Māori Council v Attorney-General* [1994] 1 NZLR 513 (PC) at 517.

[37] *Motunui–Waitara Claim,* above n 33, at 70.

[38] At 52.

[39] At 52.

[40] Prime Minister Robert Muldoon initially called for tenders for the Motunui outfall to ensure that the project would be completed on time. See Paul James "Occurrence and Resolution of the Motunui-Waitara Resource Conflict (Wai 6)" (MSc Thesis, University of Canterbury, 1993) at 67–68.

[41] See Kathryn Cammell "A 'Cornerstone Decision': The Historical Significance of the Motunui-Waitara (Wai 6) Report" (MA Thesis, University of Auckland, 2020).

[42] Paul James and Eric Pawson "Contested Places: The Significance of the Motunui-Waitara Claim to the Waitangi Tribunal" (1995) 19 Aboriginal History at 111–125.

[43] *Greenpeace Aotearoa Inc v Hiringa Energy* Ltd 21 December [2023] NZCA 672. See also *Carter Holt Harvey Limited v Te Runanga o Tuwharetoa ki Kawerau* [2003] 2 NZLR 349 at [27].

[44] *Greenpeace Aotearoa Inc v Hiringa Energy* Ltd 21 December [2023] NZCA 672 at [195]–[204].

[45] At [194].

[46] *Muriwhenua Fishing Report*, above n 10, at 290.

[47] Stephanie Milroy "The Fisheries Reports" in Janine Hayward and Nicola R. Wheen (eds) *The Waitangi Tribunal – Te Roopu Whakamana i te Tiriti o Waitangi* (Bridget Williams Books, Wellington, 2004) at 85.

[48] *Ngai Tahu Māori Trust Board v Attorney General* HC Wellington CP559/87, 2 November 1987 at 6.

[49] At 6.

[50] *Muriwhenua Fishing Report*, above n 10, at 228.

[51] Waitangi Tribunal *The Ngai Tahu Sea Fisheries Report 1992* (Wai 27, 1992) at [13.11.2] [*Ngai Tahu Sea Fisheries Report*].

[52] *Muriwhenua Fishing Report,* above n 10, at 298.

[53] *Ngai Tahu Sea Fisheries Report*, above n 51, at [13.11.1].

[54] At 309. See also the *Muriwhenua Fishing Report*, above n 10, at [1.2.1]: "The report therefore makes findings of fact and interpretation on the fisheries questions. It then urges that negotiations proceed in the light of our findings; but the question of specific recommendations is reserved in case an agreement should not be reached. We have adopted this approach because, in our view, reasonable discussions and a committed search for solutions are essential in a case like this, if the Treaty is still to work well."

[55] The Tribunal noted in the *Muriwhenua Fishing Report*, above n 10, at 228 that "The Quota Management System places severe restrictions on Maori seeking to enter the industry; it makes no allowance for the ancient Muriwhenua practice of working land and seas together, fishing if need be on part-time basis and it leads to concentration of processing plants away from the local district. It is directed to the industry with insufficient regard for Maori communities and is therefore contrary to the Maori interest that was guaranteed."

[56] See Lynne Hale and Jeremy Rude (eds) "The Central Role of the Quota Management System in the Settlement of Māori Treaty Rights" (2017) *The Nature Conservancy* new-zealand-fisheries-quota-management.pdf at 62.

[57] Te Aka Matua o te Ture – Law Commission "The Treaty of Waitangi and Māori Fisheries – Mataitai Nga Tikanga Māori me te Tiriti o Waitangi (NZLC PP9)" (7 March 1989) Māori fisheries www.lawcom.govt.nz/our-work/maori-fisheries/tab/preliminary-paper at Preface.

[58] *Taranaki Fish & Game Council v McRitchie* [1997] DCR 446 at 5.

[59] At 54–55.

[60] At 55.

[61] At 55.

[62] At 55.

[63] *Takamore v Clarke* [2012] 1 NZLR 573.

[64] See for example *Te Ohu Kaimoana Trustee Limited v Te Rūnanga nui o te Aupōuri* MLC Taitokerau (2015) 102 Taitokerau MB 1, 1 May 2015; *Henare Rakiihia Tau and the Ngai Tahu Trust Board v R* BC 1989200004; *Perry v West* 23 FRNZ 204 HC Laurenson J; *Mahuta and Tainui Māori Trust Board v Attorney General* [1989] 2 NZLR 513.

[65] The exceptions being the East Coast iwi (Ngāti Tai, Te Whānau a Apanui, Ngāti Porou, Te Aitanga a Māhaki and Rongowhakaata), Ngāti Maniapoto and Ngāti Tama, Ngāti Raukawa ki te Tonga, Rangitāne and Muaupoko and Rangitāne (Te Tau Ihu), Ngāti Toa Rangatira and Ngāi Tahu.

[66] The strategic pou are set out in Te Ohu Kaimoana *Rima Tau Rautaki – Te Ohu Kaimoana Five-Year Strategy 2021–2026* available at www.teohukaimoana.nz.

[67] Te Kerēme and Ngāi Tahu Settlement Workshop Series 2022 "Ngāi Tahu and the Fisheries Settlement" panel discussion with Tā Tipene O'Regan, Craig Ellison and David Higgins (5 July 2022) https://www.youtube.com/watch?v=LnAiv81dI1A.

[68] Te Aka Matua o te Ture – Law Commission "The Treaty of Waitangi and Māori Fisheries – Mataitai Nga Tikanga Māori me te Tiriti o Waitangi (NZLC PP9)" (7 March 1989) Māori fisheries www.lawcom.govt.nz/our-work/maori-fisheries/tab/preliminary-paper at Appendix E Report of the Maori Representatives on the Fisheries Working Group, at [1.3].

[69] At [1.8].

[70] At [1.11].

[71] At [4.1].

[72] At [5.3].

[73] At [13].

[74] At [19].

[75] See for example: "Legal challenge to Kermadec Ocean Sanctuary" RNZ (Online ed, New Zealand, 20 March 2016) https://www.rnz.co.nz/news/national/299413/legal-challenge-to-kermadec-ocean-sanctuary.

[76] See for example the judgment of the High Court in *Te Ohu Kai Moana Trustee Limited v Attorney General* [2016] NZHC 1798 [4 August 2016].

[77] See *Te Ohu Kai Moana Trustee Ltd v Minister of Oceans and Fisheries* CIV-2021-485-535 [2021] NZHC 2573.

[78] *Te Ohu Kai Moana Trustee Limited v Attorney-General* [2025] NZHC 657 at [167].
[79] At [186].
[80] At [187].
[81] At [195].

Chapter 8 | Issues Relating to Treaty Settlements

[1] David Baragwanath "Arguing the Case for the Appellants" in Jacinta Ruru (ed) *In Good Faith: Symposium proceedings marking the 20th anniversary of the* Lands *case* (New Zealand Law Foundation and Faculty of Law, University of Otago, 2008) at 23.
[2] David V. Williams "Unique Treaty-Based Relationships Remain Elusive" in Michael Belgrave, Merata Kawharu and David V. Williams (eds) *Waitangi Revisited: Perspectives on the Treaty of Waitangi*, (2nd ed, Oxford University Press, Melbourne, 2005) at 367; *New Zealand Maori Council v Attorney-General* [1987] 1 NZLR 641 (CA).
[3] *New Zealand Maori Council v Attorney-General* at [719].
[4] Williams "Unique Treaty-Based Relationships Remain Elusive" above n 2.
[5] Douglas Graham *Trick or Treaty?* (Institute of Policy Studies, Wellington, 1997) at 41.
[6] Robert J. Miller, Jacinta Ruru, Larissa Behrendt and Tracey Lindberg *Discovering Indigenous Lands: The Doctrine of Discovery in the English Colonies* (Oxford University Press, Oxford, England, 2010) at 246.
[7] Tiopira McDowell "Diverting the Sword of Damocles: Why did the Crown Choose to Settle Māori Historical Treaty Claims?" (2018) 64(4) Australian Journal of Politics and History at 592; Margaret Mutu "Behind the Smoke and Mirrors of the Treaty of Waitangi Claims Settlement Process in New Zealand: No Prospect for Justice and Reconciliation for Māori without Constitutional Transformation" (2018) 14(2) Journal of Global Ethics at 208; Baden Vertongen "Legal Challenges to the Treaty Settlement Process" in Nicola R. Wheen and Janine Hayward (eds) *Treaty of Waitangi Settlements* (Bridget Williams Books, Wellington, 2012) at 65.
[8] Office of Treaty Settlements *Crown Proposals for the Settlement of Treaty of Waitangi Claims – Detailed Proposals; Crown Proposals for the Settlement of Treaty of Waitangi Claims – Summary; Crown Proposals for the Settlement of Treaty of Waitangi Claims – Consultation with Māori* (Office of Treaty Settlements, Wellington, 1994). Although the government claimed to have dropped the policy in 1996, it has remained *de facto* to the present day.
[9] Office of Treaty Settlements *'Ka tika ā muri, ka tika ā mua — Healing the past, building a future': A Guide to Treaty of Waitangi Claims and Negotiations with the Crown* (Office of Treaty Settlements, Wellington, 1999 (revised 2018)), commonly referred to as the *Red Book*.
[10] Sid Dymond "Treaty-based judicial review: The treaty settlement negotiation process and legitimate expectation" (2018) 6 Te Tai Haruru: Journal of Māori and Indigenous Issues at 31.
[11] McDowell "Diverting the Sword of Damocles"; Mutu, "Behind the Smoke and Mirrors" above n 7. Only one of the more than 150 interviewees for the research project into the Treaty claims settlement process was aware of the Crown's true intentions (Interview with counsel for claimant group (the author, by phone, 29 March 2017)).
[12] John Dawson and Abby Suszko "Courts and Representations Disputes in the Treaty Settlement Process" (2012) 1 NZLR 35 at 46.
[13] Vertongen "Legal Challenges" above n 7; Dymond "Treaty-based judicial review" above n 10; *Mita Michael Ririnui v Landcorp Farming Ltd* [2016] NZSC 62, [2016] 1 NZLR 1056 at [89].
[14] McDowell "Diverting the Sword of Damocles" above n 7.
[15] Malcolm Birdling "Healing the Past or Harming the Future? Large Natural Groupings and the Waitangi Settlement Process" (2004) 2(2) NZJPIL 259; Interview with counsel for several claimants (the author, Hastings, 21 February 2017).
[16] Interviews with many counsels for claimants (the author and Tiopira McDowell, by phone or in several New Zealand locations, various dates between 2015 and 2020); Waitangi Tribunal *The Ngāti Tūwharetoa ki Kawerau Settlement Cross-Claim Report* (Wai 996, 2003) at 19–21 and 59.
[17] Margaret Mutu "'To Honour the Treaty,

We Must First Settle Colonisation' (Moana Jackson 2015): The Long Road from Colonial Devastation to Balance, Peace and Harmony" (2019) 49(sup1) Journal of the Royal Society of New Zealand at 8; McDowell "Diverting the Sword of Damocles", above n 7, at 601–602.

18 Margaret Mutu, Lloyd Pōpata, Te Kani Williams, Ānahera Herbert-Graves, Reremoana Rēnata, JudyAnn Cooze, Zarrah Pineaha, Tania Thomas, Te Ikanui Kingi-Waiaua, Te Rūnanga-ā-Iwi o Ngāti Kahu, Wackrow Williams and Davies Ltd *Ngāti Kahu: Portrait of a Sovereign Nation* (Huia, Wellington, 2017) at 290–291.

19 Mutu "To Honour the Treaty We Must First Settle Colonisation" above n 17, at 8.

20 Miriama Jordan Cribb and Jason Paul Mika "The Design and Operation of Post-Settlement Governance Entities" (2023) 12(2) MAI Journal 111; *Nikora v Kruger* [20024] NZSC 130.

21 Ani Mikaere "Settlement of Treaty Claims: Full and Final, or Fatally Flawed?" (1997) 17(4) NZULR at 452–454; Richard Boast "Negotiations for Reconciliation: How they can exacerbate division as well as promote reconciliation" in Peter Adds, Brigitte Bonisch-Brednich, Richard S. Hill, Graeme Whimp (eds) *Reconciliation, Representation and Indigeneity: 'Biculturalism' in Aotearoa New Zealand*, (Universitätsverlag Winter: Heidelberg, Germany, 2016) 95 at 99.

22 Mutu "Behind the Smoke and Mirrors" above n 7; Ex-staff of the Office of Treaty Settlements confirm that they are instructed to apply the Doctrine of Discovery to extinguish Treaty claims and not to adhere to te Tiriti o Waitangi.
The Human Rights Commission provides the following: "The Doctrine of Discovery is both a legal doctrine and an ideology that has its origins in Catholic Papal canonical law in the 15th and early 16th centuries. From its inception, and as it evolved over the centuries, it underpinned European colonial claims to sovereignty over Indigenous peoples and their territories, including the British Crown's claim to New Zealand. Today, the Doctrine of Discovery has been exposed as racist, genocidal in impact, unjust and illegitimate." (Human Rights Commission *The Doctrine of Discovery: Some Basic Facts* (September 2023)).

23 Metiria Turei "A Modern-day Muru: The Saga of the Wairarapa Moana and Pouākani Whenua" in Metiria Stanton Turei, Nicola R. Wheen and Janine Hayward (eds) *Te Tiriti o Waitangi Relationships: People, Politics and Law* (Bridget Williams Books, Wellington, 2024) at 98–114; McDowell "Diverting the Sword of Damocles" above n 7; Mutu "Behind the Smoke and Mirrors" above n 7.

24 United Nations Special Rapporteur in the field of cultural rights, Special Rapporteur on the independence of judges and lawyers and Special Rapporteur on the rights of Indigenous Peoples *Mandate of the Special Rapporteurs* AL NZL 1/2024, Geneva, United Nations (1 July 2024).

25 Mutu et al. *Ngāti Kahu: Portrait of a Sovereign Nation*, above n 18, at 296–297.

26 Turei "A Modern-day Muru", above n 23; United Nations Special Rapporteurs *Mandate*, above n 24; *Attorney-General v Haronga* [2016] NZCA 626, [2017] 2 NZLR 394 (CA).

27 A significant number of interviewees who participated in the research project on the Treaty claims settlement process (funded by the Royal Society of New Zealand's Marsden Fund), most notably government employees, lawyers and judges, asked to remain anonymous for fear of either losing their jobs or being the subject of retribution from the Office of Treaty Settlements or their post-settlement governance entity. As such, all remain anonymous. All interviews were transcribed by the What Do the Claimants Say? research project team (Kaitāia).

28 Tiopira McDowell "Screaming from the Shadows: Māori Views on the Treaty Claims Settlement Process" (2016) 8 Te Pouhere *Kōrero: Māori History, Māori People* 26.

29 Interview with negotiator (Tiopira McDowell and the author, by phone, 30 June 2016).

30 Almost all interviewees provided details of the divisions and trauma caused in their communities; Mutu "Recovering Fagin's Ill-gotten Gains: Settling Ngāti Kahu's Treaty of Waitangi claims against the Crown" in Michael Belgrave, Merata Kawharu and David Williams (eds) *Waitangi Revisited: Perspectives on the Treaty of Waitangi* (Oxford University Press,

Melbourne, 2005) 187 at 202–203.

31 Mutu "Behind the Smoke and Mirrors" above n 7.

32 Dion Tuuta *Māori Experiences of the Direct Negotiations Process* (Crown Forestry Rental Trust, Wellington, 2003); many interviewees; McDowell "Screaming from the Shadows" above n 28, at 33–35.

33 Many interviewees; McDowell "Screaming from the Shadows" above n 28, at 36.

34 Mikaere "Full and Final or Fatally Flawed?" above n 21, at 447; McDowell "Diverting the Sword of Damocles" above n 7; Mutu "Behind the Smoke and Mirrors" above n 7; Ken Taiapa, Helen Moewaka Barnes and Tim McCreanor "Tension without tikanga: the damaging face of the treaty claims settlement system" (2021) 17(2) AlterNative at 317; Dymond "Treaty-based judicial review" above n 10, at 45; Matiu Dickson "Ngāiterangi Negotiations: A Personal Perspective (2017) 5 Te Tai Haruru Journal at 91.

35 Boast "Negotiations for Reconciliation" above n 21, at 101; Mutu "Behind the Smoke and Mirrors" above n 7, at 247; several interviewees.

36 Mutu et al. *Ngāti Kahu: Portrait of a Sovereign Nation* above n 18, at 286; Craig Coxhead "Where are the Negotiations in the Direct Negotiations of Treaty Settlements?" (2002) 10 WLR 13; most interviews with negotiators; Office of Treaty Settlements *Healing the Past, Building a Future* above n 9, at 51–53.

37 Mutu "Behind the Smoke and Mirrors" above n 7, at 215–216; Waitangi Tribunal *The Tāmaki Makaurau Settlement Process* (Wai 1362, 2007) at 3, 4, Ch 4; many interviewees.

38 Interviews with several counsels (the author, 2015–2020); Margaret Mutu "Unconscionable Fraud? The Role of Whiteness and Race in the treaty claims settlement process in New Zealand" (paper presented to Race, Whiteness and Indigeneity International Conference, Surfers Paradise, June 2017).

39 Mutu "Behind the Smoke and Mirrors" above n 7, at 215.

40 Tuuta *Māori Experiences of the Direct Negotiations Process* above n 32; interview with negotiator (Tiopira McDowell and the author, by phone, 30 June 2016).

41 Mutu "Behind the Smoke and Mirrors" above n 7, at 215; many interviewees.

42 Mutu et al. *Ngāti Kahu: Portrait of a Sovereign Nation* above n 18, at 125–127, 265 footnote 23, 325–326.

43 Many interviewees.

44 Mutu et al. *Ngāti Kahu: Portrait of a Sovereign Nation* above n 18, at 190, 289–299; Carwyn Jones *New Treaty New Tradition: Reconciling New Zealand and Māori Law* (University of British Columbia Press, Vancouver, Canada, 2016) at 87–114.

45 Boast "Negotiations for Reconciliation" above n 21, at 104–108

46 Waitangi Tribunal "Decision of the Tribunal in an urgent claim by Kingi Smiler et al re: the Ngāti Kahungunu ki Wairarapa Tāmaki nui-ā-Rua settlement" (Wai 863, 2021) at [77].

47 Boast "Negotiations for Reconciliation" above n 21, at 104.

48 See for example Waitangi Tribunal *The Tāmaki Makaurau Settlement Process Report* (Wai 1362, 2007) at 3; *The Te Arawa Settlement Process Reports* (Wai 1353, 2007) at 220.

49 United Nations Special Rapporteurs *Mandate* above n 24.

50 Treaty of Waitangi Act 1975, s 5.2.

51 Waitangi Tribunal *Muriwhenua Land Report* (Wai 45, 1997) at 388.

52 Waitangi Tribunal *Tāmaki Makaurau* above n 48, at 8.

53 Waitangi Tribunal *He Whakaputanga me Te Tiriti: The Declaration and the Treaty: The Report on Stage 1 of the Te Paparahi o Te Raki Inquiry* (Wai 1040, 2014).

54 Many of the claimants, negotiators and their counsels interviewed between 2015 and 2020 responded that the Tribunal had been helpful.

55 Waitangi Tribunal *The Hauraki Settlement Overlapping Claims Inquiry Report* (Wai 2840, 2020) at xvii; Ani Mikaere "Three (Million) Strikes and Still Not Out: The Crown as the Consummate Recidivist" in *Colonising Myths, Māori Realities* (Huia, Wellington, 2011) at 147–178; Mutu et al. *Ngāti Kahu: Portrait of a Sovereign Nation* above n 18, at 191, 297.

56 Waitangi Tribunal *The Te Arawa Settlement Process Reports* (Legislation Direct, Wellington, 2007) at 221; McDowell "Screaming from the Shadows" above n 28, at 35–37.

57 Carwyn Jones "Whakatōhea mandate inquiry report – recognising a mandate to negotiate a settlement" (May 2018) MLR.

58 Interview with advisor for many claimants (Tiopira McDowell and the author, Naenae, 7 September 2015). Claimant negotiators who are government servants have serious conflicts of interest that the Crown ignores, despite efforts of claimant communities to remove the conflicts (Mutu et al. *Ngāti Kahu: Portrait of a Sovereign Nation* above n 18, at 286, 293).

59 Miriama Jordan Cribb and Jason Paul Mika "The Design and Operation of Post-Settlement Governance Entities" (2023) 12(2) MAI Journal 111 at 116, 118.

60 Waitangi Tribunal *The Fisheries Settlement Report* (Wai 307, 1992) at 17.

61 This featured strongly in the Ngāpuhi mandate inquiry (Waitangi Tribunal *The Ngāpuhi Mandate Inquiry Report* (Wai 2490, 2015)); Birdling "Healing the Past or Harming the Future?" above n 15.

62 Waitangi Tribunal *The Fisheries Settlement Report* above n 60, at 158–9.

63 Linda Te Aho "Contemporary Issues in Māori Law and Society: The Tangled Web of Treaty Settlements Emissions Trading, Central North Island Forests, and the Waikato River" (2008)16 WLR 229 at 233.

64 M. Hudson "Māori hold a third of NZ's fishing interests, but as the Ocean warms and fish migrate, these rights don't move with them" The Conversation (New Zealand, online ed, 7 July 2022).

65 Waitangi Tribunal *The Tāmaki Makaurau Settlement* above n 48, at 1.

66 Waitangi Tribunal *The East Coast Settlement Report* (Wai 2190, 2010) at 39.

67 Waitangi Tribunal *The Te Aroha Maunga Settlement Process Report – Pre-Publication Report* (Wai 663, 2014) at 8; Interview with negotiator (the author, by phone, Auckland, 13 June 2017).

68 Waitangi Tribunal *The Priority Report on the Whakatōhea Settlement Process – Pre-publication Version* (Wai 1750, 2021).

69 New Zealand Government, Whakatōhea Claims Settlement Act 2024, s 14; Māori Television Service *Te Karere* "Te Whakatōhea iwi settlement signed, but not all agree" (video, 29 May 2023) YouTube https://www.youtube.com/watch?v=Zcxt7lPovZ0.

70 Waitangi Tribunal *The Turangi Township Remedies Report* (Wai 84, 1998) at 33, 85; Waitangi Tribunal, *The Muriwhenua Land Report* above n 51, at 405–406.

71 Waitangi Tribunal "Decision on an Application Concerning Proposed Government Property Services Limited Share Float" (Wai 145, 1998) (August 1998) Māori Law Review at 2–3; Paul Hamer "A Quarter-century of the Waitangi Tribunal" in Janine Hayward and Nicola Wheen (eds) *The Waitangi Tribunal* (Bridget Williams Books, Wellington, 2004) 3 at 7. The Waitangi Tribunal has had its powers reduced many times. Legislation for each settlement removes the Tribunal's powers in respect of the claims being extinguished. From 1993, it could no longer make recommendations in relation to private lands (with the exception of ex-state-owned enterprise and Crown forest lands). From 2008, it could no longer accept historical claims.

72 Waitangi Tribunal *Muriwhenua Land Report* above n 51, at 404.

73 The author is a claimant and the chief negotiator for Ngāti Kahu and was told this directly by Doug Graham and Margaret Wilson.

74 Many interviewees.

75 Mutu et al. *Ngāti Kahu: Portrait of a Sovereign Nation* above n 18, at 291, 296–297. In 2017, Ngāti Kahu returned to the Tribunal seeking binding recommendations for a third time.

76 Waitangi Tribunal *The Ngāti Kahu Remedies Report* (Wai 45, 2013) at xii; Waitangi Tribunal, *The Mangatū Remedies Report* (Wai 814, 2014) at xiii–xv.

77 *Attorney-General v Haronga* [2016] NZCA 626 at [65] and [92].

78 Waitangi Tribunal *The Mangatū Remedies Report 2021* (Wai 814, 2021) at xvi.

79 Personal communication, Te Aitanga a Mahaki lead negotiator, Hastings, 30 October 2024.

80 New Zealand Government, Ngāti Tūrangitukua Claims Settlement Act 1999.

81 Waitangi Tribunal *Te Whanganui-a-Orotu Report on Remedies* (Wai 55, 1998) at vii.

82 *Attorney-General v Haronga* [2016] NZCA 626 at [65] and [92].

[83] United Nations Special Rapporteurs *Mandate* above n 24.

[84] Waitangi Tribunal "Determinations of the Tribunal Preliminary to Interim Recommendations under Sections 8A and 8HC of the Treaty of Waitangi Act 1975" 24 March 2020 at [215].

[85] Waitangi Tribunal *The Wairarapa ki Tararua Report*, Vol. 3 (Wai 863, 2010) at 1056–1059.

[86] Waitangi Tribunal "Decision of the Tribunal in Smiler et al" (18 November 2021) https://forms.justice.govt.nz/search/Documents/WT/wt_DOC_179436738/Tribunal%20Decision.pdf at 2.

[87] At 52.

[88] *Wairarapa Moana ki Pouākani Incorporation v Mercury NZ Limited* [2022] NZSC 142 https://www.courtsofnz.govt.nz/assets/cases/2022/2022-NZSC-142.pdf.

[89] In her memorandum-directions, Judge CM Wainwright observed "if the Ngāti Kahungunu ki Wairarapa Tāmaki nui-ā-Rua Claims Settlement Bill were not passed into law tomorrow, the Tribunal would pursue the path outlined for it in *Wairarapa Moana ki Pouākani v Mercury NZ Ltd* [2022] NZSC 142. This might have the effect of returning significant hydro assets to the Wairarapa Moana ki Pouākani Incorporation or another appropriate entity."

[90] Human Rights Commission "UN Called on to Keep Government On-task with Indigenous Rights, Human Rights Commission" (21 April 2023) Te Kāhui Tika Tangata https://tikatangata.org.nz/news/un-called-on-to-keep-government-on-task-with-indigenous-rights.

[91] United Nations Special Rapporteurs *Mandate* above n 24.

[92] P Goldsmith and T Pōtaka "Response to Joint Communication", 30 August 2024 https://spcommreports.ohchr.org/TMResultsBase/DownLoadFile?gId=38715.

[93] Wairarapa Moana "Wai85 Update: Crown forces settlement on Wairarapa Moana owners" *Mailer* (online ed, New Zealand, March 2023) https://www.wairarapamoana.org.nz/issue-69-march-2023-2/ at 4–6; Goldsmith and Pōtaka "Response to Joint Communication" above n 92, at 16.

[94] Claire Charters, Kayla Kingdon-Bebb, Tamati Olsen, Waimirirangi Ormsby, Emily Owen, Judith Pryor, Jacinta Ruru, Naomi Solomon and Gary Williams *He Puapua: Report of the Working Group on a Plan to Realise the UN Declaration on the Rights of Indigenous Peoples in Aotearoa/New Zealand* (Ministry of Māori Development, Wellington, 2020).

[95] Jo Moir "Jackson Not 'Comfortable' with Co-governance Draft" *Newsroom* (online ed, New Zealand, 29 June 2022) https://newsroom.co.nz/2022/06/29/jackson-not-comfortable-with-co-governance-draft/.

[96] New Zealand National Party and ACT New Zealand *Coalition Agreement* (2023) at 8–10; New Zealand National Party and New Zealand First *Coalition Agreement* (2023) at 8–9, 11.

[97] National–NZ First *Coalition Agreement* at 10.

[98] Waitangi Tribunal 2024 urgent inquiry pre-publication reports: *Ngā Mātāpono/The Principles; Ngā Mātāpono/The Principles Part II; The Oranga Tamariki (Section 7AA); The Oranga Tamariki(Section 7AA) 10 May 2024; The Māori Wards and Constituencies; The Takutai Moana Act 2011 Stage 1.*

[99] Glenn McConnell "The day Wellington was draped in tino rangatiratanga flags" *Stuff* (online ed, New Zealand, 19 November 2024).

[100] National Iwi Chairs Forum "Agenda papers 30 October–1 November 2024" at 238–255.

[101] Waitangi Tribunal *Annual Report Matariki 2023–24* (Wellington, Waitangi Tribunal, 2024) at 30.

[102] Justin Munro "The Treaty of Waitangi and the Sealord deal" (1994) 24 VUWLR 389 at 410.

[103] Rodolfo Stavenhagen *Report of the Special Rapporteur on the Situation of Human Rights and Fundamental Freedoms of Indigenous People. Mission to New Zealand.* e/cn.4/2006/78/Add.3. March 13, 2006 (United Nations Human Rights Commission, Geneva, 2006) at [22]–[42]; James Anaya *The Situation of Māori People in New Zealand* (United Nations Human Rights Council, Geneva, 2011) at [35]–[45]; United Nations General Assembly *Report of the Working Group on the Universal Periodic Review: New Zealand (United Nations General Assembly, New York, 2014).*

[104] *The Te Arawa Settlement Process Reports* (Wai 1353, 2007) at 221.

[105] Dr Michael Cullen.

Chapter 10 | Taonga

*The author thanks Piripi Walker for his comments on a draft, and Samuel Turner O'Keefe, Kaythi Finn, Gulliver MacDonald and Charlie Matthews for their research assistance. Any errors are my own.

1 See, for example, Jayden Houghton "Wai 262 Response: A Whole-of-Government Approach?" (2024) 4 Legalities 196 at 203.

2 See, generally, Janine Hayward and Nicola R. Wheen (eds) *The Waitangi Tribunal: Te Roopu Whakamana i te Tiriti o Waitangi* (Bridget Williams Books, Wellington, 2004); and Nicola Wheen and Janine Hayward (eds) *Treaty of Waitangi Settlements* (Bridget Williams Books, Wellington, 2012).

3 See Jayden Houghton "Tikanga Māori Processes and Procedures" in *Tikanga Māori and State Law* (Thomson Reuters, Wellington, 2025) at [3.5].

4 See, for example, Jayden Houghton "A Tort of Misappropriation of Culture" (2024) 29 Torts Law Journal 215, which proposes a new tort for the protection of taonga works; and Jayden Houghton "Public outrage is not enough: NZ needs to develop a legal remedy for cultural misappropriation" (6 August 2024) The Conversation https://theconversation.com, which raised the profile of the tort to around 25,000 readers.

5 Te Tiriti o Waitangi and tikanga Māori are taught throughout the Bachelor of Laws (LLB) programmes at all New Zealand law schools, such that law graduates are entering the profession with greater awareness of Māori rights and interests and the Crown's obligations to work in partnership with Māori to actively protect them. Take Auckland Law School, for example – in addition to teaching tikanga Māori and te Tiriti in the compulsory courses, specialised courses are offered on the protection of taonga, including the undergraduate elective "Cultural Property and Indigenous Intellectual Property" and the Honours seminar "Mātauranga Māori and Taonga".

6 See, for example, Sabine Lucy Keenan "Beyond Wai 262: Who Are and Can Be Kaitiaki?" (2022) 28 Auckland University Law Review 17, which won the MinterEllisonRuddWatts Prize for Legal Writing. See also the student scholarship in Jayden Houghton and David V. Williams (eds) *Protecting Indigenous Knowledge: Perspectives from Aotearoa New Zealand* (Auckland University Press, Auckland, 2026).

7 Waitangi Tribunal *Report of the Waitangi Tribunal on the Te Reo Māori Claim* (Wai 11, 1986) at [3.4.1].

8 At [3.4.1].

9 At [2].

10 Manatū Taonga – Ministry for Culture and Heritage "Te Wiki o Te Reo Māori - Māori Language Week: Page 6 – Waitangi Tribunal Claim" New Zealand History www.nzhistory.govt.nz.

11 Manatū Taonga – Ministry for Culture and Heritage, above n 10.

12 *Te Reo Māori Claim*, above n 7, at [1] and [4.2.1]. See Manatū Taonga – Ministry for Culture and Heritage, above n 10.

13 *Te Reo Māori Claim*, above n 7, at [4.2.3].

14 At [4.2.7].

15 At [3.2.12].

16 At [4.2.2].

17 At [6.2.8] and [9.1.5].

18 At [1].

19 At [8.1.6] and [8.1.7].

20 Waitangi Tribunal *Ko Aotearoa Tēnei: A Report into Claims Concerning New Zealand Law and Policy Affecting Māori Culture and Identity – Te Taumata Tuarua* (Wai 262, 2011) at [5.7].

21 At [5.7].

22 At [5.8].

23 Waitangi Tribunal *Matua Rautia: The Report on the Kōhanga Reo Claim* (Wai 2336, 2013) at [1.2.3].

24 At [11.6] and [11.9].

25 Haim Mazar *Radio Spectrum Management: Policies, Regulations and Techniques* (John Wiley & Sons, West Sussex, 2016) at [1.3].

26 At [1.1].

27 Constitution and Convention of the International Telecommunication Union 1825 UNTS 331 (concluded 22 December 1992) at preamble; and Radio Spectrum Management "Our role in the international community" www.rsm.govt.nz.

28 Brian Pauling "Radio" (22 October 2014) Te Ara – The Encyclopedia of New Zealand www.teara.govt.nz.

29 Deborah Edmunds "The commercial reports"

in Janine Hayward and Nicola Wheen (eds) *The Waitangi Tribunal: Te Roopu Whakamana i te Tiriti o Waitangi* (Bridget Williams Books, Wellington, 2015) 113 at 121.

30 Radio Spectrum Management "About spectrum auctions" www.rsm.govt.nz.

31 Waitangi Tribunal *The Radio Spectrum Management and Development Final Report* (Wai 776, 1999) at [4.3].

32 *Te Reo Māori Claim*, above n 7, at [7.2.3] and [7.3.8].

33 Waitangi Tribunal *Report of the Waitangi Tribunal on Claims Concerning the Allocation of Radio Frequencies* (Wai 26/150, 1990) at [4.1]–[4.2].

34 Appendix 2 "Statement of Claim: Wai 150" at [1.1].

35 Appendix 2 "Statement of Claim: Wai 150" at [5.1].

36 At [4.2]. The claimant in Wai 26, Ngā Kaiwhakapūmau i te Reo (Inc), primarily objected to the introduction of legislation on te reo Māori before the Crown had an opportunity to consider the Tribunal's Wai 11 report, although it also asserted that "[t]he claim by Maoridom for a channel and resources in television, and radio frequencies, is being denied". Appendix 1 "Statement of Claim: Wai 26".

37 At [4.1].

38 At [8.2]. See at [8.1].

39 See, for example, Christian A Herter Jr "The Electromagnetic Spectrum: A Critical Natural Resource" (1985) 25 Nat Resources J 651 at 663.

40 Waitangi Tribunal *Radio Frequencies Report*, above n 33, at [8.2].

41 At [8.2].

42 At [1].

43 At [8.3].

44 At [1].

45 At [1] and [7.4].

46 At [8.3] and [8.4].

47 At [8.4].

48 Waitangi Tribunal *Radio Spectrum Final Report*, above n 31, at [1.1].

49 At [1.1] and [4.1].

50 At [1.1].

51 At [1.3]. See Waitangi Tribunal *Radio Spectrum Management and Development Interim Report* (Wai 776, 1999) at 17.

52 *Te Runanga o Muriwhenua Inc v Attorney-General* [1990] 2 NZLR 641 at 656 per Cooke P. See Waitangi Tribunal *Radio Spectrum Interim Report*, above n 51, at 6.

53 Waitangi Tribunal *Radio Spectrum Final Report*, above n 31, Part II at [1.3.1].

54 At [1.3.1].

55 At [1.3.1].

56 At [1.3.1].

57 At [1.5].

58 At [1.3.2].

59 *First Amended Statement of Claim* (Wai 262, 10 September 1997) at [1.1].

60 At [4.1]–[4.2].

61 At [4.1]–[4.2].

62 At [4.1]–[4.2].

63 At [5.1], [6] and [12].

64 Waitangi Tribunal *Ko Aotearoa Tēnei*, above n 20.

65 At [2.8].

66 At [2.8.3].

67 At [2.9.1]–[2.9.3].

68 At [IN.1].

69 At [1.9].

70 At [1.9].

71 *Statement of Issues* (Wai 262, 6 July 2006) at [1.2.3].

72 Waitangi Tribunal *Ko Aotearoa Tēnei: A Report into Claims Concerning New Zealand Law and Policy Affecting Māori Culture and Identity – Te Taumata Tuarua* (Wai 262, 2011) at [1.9].

73 At [1.9].

74 At [1.9]. For explorations of the functions, see Jayden Houghton "Spheres Model to Facilitate Rangatiratanga as Far as Possible before Constitutional Transformation" in Jayden Houghton and David V. Williams (eds) *Protecting Indigenous Knowledge: Perspectives from Aotearoa New Zealand* (Auckland University Press, Auckland, 2026); and Khylee Quince and Jayden Houghton "Privacy and Māori Concepts" in Nikki Chamberlain and Stephen Penk (eds) *Privacy Law in New Zealand* (3rd ed, Thomson Reuters, Wellington, 2023) 43 at 125–126, n 505.

75 The Māori Language Bill 1986 (20-1) was introduced and the Tribunal's Wai 11 report was dated and signed on the same day. See (29 April 1986) 674 NZPD 1450; and *Te Reo Māori Claim*, above n 7, at [10].

[76] Māori Language Act 1987, s 5.
[77] *Te Reo Māori Claim*, above n 7, at [10.1].
[78] At [10.2]. See at [8.2.12].
[79] New Zealand Government "Te Taura Whiri i te Reo Māori: Māori Language Commission" (10 September 2020) www.govt.nz.
[80] Manatū Taonga – Ministry for Culture and Heritage, above n 10.
[81] *Te Reo Māori Claim*, above n 7, at [10.3].
[82] At [10.4] and [10.5].
[83] Jayden Houghton "Wai 262 Response: Prioritising the Treaty Relationship to Design a Reconciliatory Procedural Framework" (2024) 31 NZULR 83 at 83.
[84] At 84.
[85] Houghton "Prioritising the Treaty Relationship", above n 83, at 84.
[86] Jayden Houghton "Wai 262 Response: Government Strategy for Māori Engagement" (2023) 18 Otago L Rev 109 at 110.
[87] See at 122.
[88] "Kahu Aronui" Wai 262: Kia Whakapūmau www.wai262.nz.
[89] Jayden Houghton "The New Zealand Government's Response to the Wai 262 Report: The First Ten Years" (2021) 25(5) International Journal of Human Rights 870 at 881.
[90] See, for example, "Te Pae Tawhiti: Wai 262" (17 October 2024) Te Puni Kōkiri | Ministry of Māori Development www.tpk.govt.nz, which describes "[t]he whole-of-government response to the Wai 262 claim".
[91] Houghton "Prioritising the Treaty Relationship", above n 83, at 84.
[92] At 110.
[93] Waitangi Tribunal *Radio Frequencies Report*, above n 33, at [1] and [8.3].
[94] At [8.2].
[95] At [4.3].
[96] Waitangi Tribunal *Radio Spectrum Final Report*, above n 31. See Edmunds, above n 29, at 121.
[97] Waitangi Tribunal *Radio Spectrum Final Report*, above n 31, at [3.2].
[98] See at [2.3] and [3.2].
[99] At [1.3].
[100] Maurice Williamson "Radio Spectrum Auction Date Announced" (press release, 18 October 1999).
[101] See, for example, David Seymour "School kids should not be pushed into political activity" (press release, 15 November 2024).
[102] Waitangi Tribunal *Ko Aotearoa Tēnei*, above n 20, at [5.5.8] and [5.8].
[103] See Shannon Haunui-Thompson "Celebration as Māori language bill passed" (15 April 2016) Radio New Zealand www.rnz.co.nz.
[104] Waitangi Tribunal *Matua Rautia*, above n 23, at [1.2.3], [11.6] and [11.9].
[105] Tama Potaka *The Section 8I Report: A report on the progress made on implementation of Waitangi Tribunal recommendations to the Crown – For the period 1 July 2022 to 30 June 2023* (New Zealand Government, 2023) at 73.
[106] Jayden Houghton "A Kaitiaki Relationships Framework for Trade Marks" [2024] NZ L Rev 311 at 317–318. Compare at 324.
[107] Waitangi Tribunal *Ko Aotearoa Tēnei*, above n 72, at [2.8.1(3)].
[108] At [2.8.1(3)].
[109] At [9.2.4] and [9.2.11].
[110] "Background to the Plant Variety Rights Act review" (26 May 2022) Ministry of Business, Innovation & Employment www.mbie.govt.nz.
[111] Cabinet Legislation Committee "Plant Variety Rights Bill: Approval for Introduction" (6 May 2021) LEG-21-MIN-0051; and Plant Variety Rights Bill 2021.
[112] Houghton "A Kaitiaki Relationships Framework for Trade Marks", above n 106, at 313.
[113] See generally Waitangi Tribunal *Ko Aotearoa Tēnei*, above n 20, Appendix 1.
[114] Houghton "Government Strategy", above n 86, at 109.
[115] Piripi Walker "The spectrum — the battle to reclaim a taonga" (20 February 2022) E-Tangata www.e-tangata.co.nz.
[116] Walker, above n 115.
[117] Andrew Robb "What is spectrum, and why should Māori care?" (20 February 2022) E-Tangata www.e-tangata.co.nz.
[118] Māori Television Service Act 2003; and Tainui Stephens "Māori and television – whakataa" (22 October 2014) Te Ara – The Encyclopedia of New Zealand www.teara.govt.nz.
[119] Te Puni Kōkiri "Strengthening Māori aspirations in radio spectrum" (23 June 2023) www.tpk.govt.nz.
[120] Walker, above n 115.

[121] See Robb, above n 117.

[122] Robb, above n 117.

[123] If Māori are empowered to lead a response, it is more likely to be consistent with te Tiriti and the principles of the Treaty. See Carwyn Jones "Co-governance and the Case for Shared Decision Making" (2023) 19(2) Policy Quarterly 3. But see Jayden Houghton "Co-governance Design and Implementation: Lessons from *Norman v Tūpuna Maunga o Tāmaki Makaurau Authority*" (2024) 31 New Zealand Universities Law Review 263 at 279–283. If Māori are not empowered to lead a response, rangatiratanga is compromised and the potential that the Crown will dominate it increases. See Houghton "Government Strategy", above n 86, at 134–135.

[124] "Raraunga Reo o ngā Ringatoi Māori: Voices of 100 Māori Creatives – On the Misappropriation and Protection of Māori Creative Works" Tiaki Taonga www.tiakitaonga.com.

[125] "Kahu Aronui", above n 88.

[126] "Raraunga Reo", above n 124.

[127] "Raraunga Reo", above n 124. See "Tiaki Taonga: The Tangi of the Pūkāea that Calls Kaitiaki Taonga" Tiaki Taonga www.tiakitaonga.com.

[128] Jamie Tahana "Māori language 'at risk' as a result of government policies, commissioner says" (23 September 2024) The Guardian www.theguardian.com.

[129] Houghton "Government Strategy", above n 86, at 110.

[130] At 120 and 123.

[131] At 119 and 134.

[132] At 132–134.

[133] At 126, 130, 132 and 135.

[134] Houghton "The First Ten Years", above n 89, at 881.

[135] *Te Reo Māori Claim*, above n 7, at [3.1.1]. See New Zealand Government "Te Taura Whiri i te Reo Māori: Māori Language Commission" (10 September 2020) www.govt.nz.

[136] Houghton "Government Strategy", above n 86, at 136.

[137] *Wellbeing Budget 2022: A Secure Future* (Te Kāwanatanga o Aotearoa | New Zealand Government, Wellington, 2022) at 135.

[138] See generally Nicola Willis *Budget 2024: Summary of Initiatives* (New Zealand Government, 2024).

Chapter 12 | Toiora

*The authors would like to thank Claire Neilson for her research assistance.

[1] Waitangi Tribunal *Matua Rautia: The Report on the Kōhanga Reo Claim* (Wai 2336, 2013).

[2] Waitangi Tribunal *Kei Ahotea Te Aho Matua – Pre-publication Version* (Wai 1718, 2024).

[3] Waitangi Tribunal *The Wānanga Capital Establishment Report* (Wai 718, 1999); Waitangi Tribunal *The Report on the Aotearoa Institute Claim Concerning Te Wānanga o Aotearoa* (Wai 1298, 2005).

[4] Waitangi Tribunal *Tū Mai te Rangi! Report on the Crown and Disproportionate Reoffending Rates* (Wai 2540, 2017).

[5] Waitangi Tribunal *He Aha i Pērā ai? The Māori Prisoners' Voting Report* (Wai 2870, 2020).

[6] Waitangi Tribunal *The Offender Assessment Policies Report* (Wai 1024, 2005).

[7] Waitangi Tribunal *Te Whanau o Waipareira Report* (Wai 414, 1998).

[8] *Te Whanau o Waipareira Report*, above n 7, at 33.

[9] *Te Whanau o Waipareira Report*, above n 7, at xxiii.

[10] *Te Whanau o Waipareira Report*, above n 7, at 214.

[11] *Te Whanau o Waipareira Report*, above n 7, at 214.

[12] *Te Whanau o Waipareira Report*, above n 7, at 215.

[13] *Te Whanau o Waipareira Report*, above n 7, at 215.

[14] *Te Whanau o Waipareira Report*, above n 7, at 216.

[15] *Te Whanau o Waipareira Report*, above n 7, at 219.

[16] *Te Whanau o Waipareira Report*, above n 7, at 235.

[17] Waitangi Tribunal *Hauora: Report on Stage One of the Health Services and Outcomes Kaupapa Inquiry* (Wai 2575, 2023).

[18] Waitangi Tribunal *Haumaru: The COVID-19 Priority Report* (Wai 2575, 2023).

[19] Waitangi Tribunal *Hautupua: Te Aka Whai Ora (Māori Health Authority) Priority Report, Part 1 – Pre-publication Version* (Wai 2575, 2024).

[20] *Hauora*, above n 17, at xv.

[21] *Hauora*, above n 17, at 79–97.

[22] *Hauora*, above n 17, at 92–97.

[23] *Hauora*, above n 17, at 96.

[24] *Hauora*, above n 17, at 160.

[25] *Hauora*, above n 17, at 162–163.

[26] *Hauora*, above n 17, at 163–164.

[27] *Hauora*, above n 17, at 164.

[28] *Hauora*, above n 17, at 164.

[29] *Hauora*, above n 17, at 165.

[30] Health and Disability System Review *Health and Disability System Review – Final Report Pūrongo Whakamutunga* (Wellington, 2020) at 245.

[31] Health and Disability System Review, 2020; Waitangi Tribunal, pre-publication version of *Hauora*, 2019.

[32] *Hautupua*, above n 19, at 69–70.

[33] Waitangi Tribunal *Kāinga Kore: The Stage One Report of the Housing Policy and Services Kaupapa Inquiry on Māori Homelessness* (Wai 2750, 2024).

[34] *Kāinga Kore*, above n 33, at 194.

[35] Ministry of Business, Innovation and Employment *He Whare Āhuru He Oranga Tāngata – The Māori Housing Strategy: Directions 2014 to 2025* (New Zealand Government, Wellington, 2014).

[36] *Kāinga Kore*, above n 33, at 48.

[37] *Kāinga Kore*, above n 33, at 51–52.

[38] *Kāinga Kore*, above n 33, at 144.

[39] *Kāinga Kore*, above n 33, at 117.

[40] *Kāinga Kore*, above n 33, at 176.

[41] *Kāinga Kore*, above n 33, at 185.

[42] *He Pāharakeke, He Rito Whakakīkīnga Whāruarua – Oranga Tamariki Urgent Inquiry* (Wai 2915, 2021).

[43] Due to the procedural issues that arose in the Wai 3350 inquiry, the Tribunal initially issued an interim report, *The Oranga Tamariki (Section 7AA) Urgent Inquiry 10 May 2024 Report* (Wai 3350, 2024), before its final report, *The Oranga Tamariki (Section 7AA) Urgent Inquiry 10 May 2024 Report* (Wai 3350, 2024).

[44] There were a number of other public and independent inquiries running at the time that would address different aspects of the claimants' concerns. The Whānau Ora Commissioning Agency, the Office of the Children's Commissioner, and the Ombudsman had all launched their own inquiries, and the broader Royal Commission of Inquiry was being undertaken.

[45] *He Pāharakeke*, above n 42, at 2.

[46] *He Pāharakeke*, above n 42, at 3–4.

[47] *He Pāharakeke*, above n 42, at 5.

[48] *He Pāharakeke*, above n 42, at 11.

[49] *He Pāharakeke*, above n 42, at 14.

[50] *He Pāharakeke*, above n 42, at 12.

[51] *He Pāharakeke*, above n 42, at 94.

[52] *He Pāharakeke*, above n 42, at 97.

[53] *He Pāharakeke*, above n 42, at 98.

[54] *He Pāharakeke*, above n 42, at 178.

[55] *He Pāharakeke*, above n 42, at 189.

[56] See above.

[57] *Oranga Tamariki (Section 7AA) Urgent Inquiry 10 May 2024* (Wai 3350, 2024), at 27.

[58] *Oranga Tamariki (Section 7AA) Urgent Inquiry,* above n 57, at 15.

Chapter 13 | Mana Wāhine

[1] Moana Jackson "Brief of Evidence of Dr Moana Jackson" in the Waitangi Tribunal's *Mana Wāhine Kaupapa Inquiry* – Wai 2700, (2022) at 6.

[2] D Henare "Carrying the Burden of Arguing the Treaty" in W Ihimaera (ed) *Kaupapa New Zealand: Vision Aotearoa* (Bridget Williams Books, Wellington, 1994) 126 at 126.

[3] Evans, R, "Brief of Evidence of Ripeka Evans" in the Waitangi Tribunal's *Mana Wāhine Kaupapa Inquiry* – Wai 2700, (2021) at 6.

[4] M Szaszy in A Rogers and M Simpson (eds) *Te Tīmatatanga Tātau Tātau: Early Stories from Founding Members of the Māori Women's Welfare League* (Bridget Williams Books, Wellington, 1993) at 222.

[5] *Te Tīmatatanga*, at 225.

[6] *Te Tīmatatanga*, at 227.

[7] "Women appeal to tribunal – Call to halt top appointments until leadership role recognised" *Waikato Times* (New Zealand, 11 September 1993).

[8] As claimant Ripeka Evans put it, the claim was "the first of its kind", going "where no claim has gone before": R. Evans "The Negation of Powerlessness: Maori Feminism, a Perspective" (1994) 20 Hecate Special Aotearoa/New Zealand at 64. Note that this paper was initially delivered on 10 August 1993 in the Auckland University Winter Lecture Series.

[9] Evans "The Negation of Powerlessness",

above n 8, at 65; Jackson "Brief of Evidence of Dr Moana Jackson", above n 1, at 25; and L. Pihama "Brief of Evidence of Leonie Pihama" in the Waitangi Tribunal's *Mana Wāhine Kaupapa Inquiry* – Wai 2700, (2021) at 44.

[10] K. Walker "The Chief Historian's Pre-Casebook Discussion Paper for the Mana Wāhine Inquiry" in theWaitangi Tribunal's *Mana Wāhine Kaupapa Inquiry* – Wai 2700, (2020) at 4.

[11] As then president of the Māori Women's Welfare League Prue Kapua commented in 2022, waiting all that time to be heard had been "pretty frustrating": "'Slow progress' and frustration on Mana Wāhine Tribunal Claim" *1News* (online ed, New Zealand, 31 July 2022).

https://www.1news.co.nz/2022/07/31/slow-progress-and-frustration-on-mana-wahine-waitangi-claim/.

[12] Evans "The Negation of Powerlessness", above n 8, at 64.

[13] On 1 April 2015 the Tribunal's kaupapa inquiry programme was initiated, providing a pathway for "claims outside of the district inquiries which raise nationally significant issues affecting Maori as a whole or a section of Maori in similar ways, and which have not previously been fully heard, reported on or settled". Kaupapa inquiries that are currently underway or that have been reported on include those for the Military Veterans, Health Services and Outcomes, Takutai Moana, Mana Wāhine, Housing Policy and Services, The Justice System, Constitutional (including the constitution, self-government and the electoral system) and Education Services and Outcomes: "Appendix B: the Kaupapa inquiry programme" (January 2024) Waitangi Tribunal https://www.waitangitribunal.govt.nz/assets/DOCUMENTS/Kaupapa-inquiry-programme-App-B-updated-Jan-2024.pdf.

[14] A graphic illustration of how things have got worse for Māori women over the past three decades is the dramatic increase in their imprisonment rates: Moana Jackson points out that the number of Māori women in prison has increased by over 150 per cent since 2002, with Māori women now making up nearly 60 per cent of the female prison population. See Jackson "Brief of Evidence of Dr Moana Jackson", above n 1, at 28.

[15] D. Awatere "Brief of Evidence of Donna Awatere-Huata" in the Waitangi Tribunal's *Mana Wāhine Kaupapa Inquiry* – Wai 2700, (2021) at 2.

[16] M. Jackson "Hui Reflections: The Power in our Truth, the Truth of our Power" in A. Mikaere and J. Hutchings (eds) *Changing Worlds, Changing Tikanga—Educating History and the Future, Kei Tua o te Pae Hui Proceedings* (Te Wānanga o Raukawa and NZCER, Ōtaki and Wellington, 2013) 87 at 92.

[17] M. Durie *Ngā Kāhui Pou: Launching Māori Futures* (Huia Publishers, Wellington, 2003) at 33.

[18] Although it is likely that matters such as constitutional status, housing, health, education and so on will be defined by the Crown as mere citizenship rights, shrouded in the rhetoric of "equality" with Pākehā rather than being rooted in the te Tiriti relationship.

[19] Manatū Wāhine Ministry for Women "Mana Wāhine claim progressing" (4 July 2019) https://www.women.govt.nz/news/mana-wahine-claim-progressing.

[20] Prue Kapua "On mana and misogyny: a message for Shane Jones from the Māori Women's Welfare League President" *The Spinoff* (online ed, New Zealand, 28 January 2020).

[21] Māni Dunlop "Mana Wāhine Inquiry: Original claimant Ripeka Evans gives evidence" *RNZ* (online ed, New Zealand, (3 February 2021).

[22] As explained by Judge Reeves during the online launch of Te Kete Pūputu, 6 May 2024.

[23] A. Te One "Wāhine Rangatira me te Kāwanatanga: Wāhine Māori Access to Decision-Making Roles in the Public Sector from 1990 to 2020" in the Waitangi Tribunal's *Mana Wāhine Kaupapa Inquiry* – Wai 2700, (2024); H. Potter and S. Simmonds "Takapou Whāriki: Diverse Experiences of Māori Women" in the Waitangi Tribunal's *Mana Wāhine Kaupapa Inquiry* – Wai 2700, (2024); S. Douglas and L. Greaves "Mana Wāhine i Te Ao Hurihuri: Equity and Disparities in Wellbeing for Wāhine Māori from the 1950s to 2000" in the Waitangi Tribunal's *Mana Wāhine Kaupapa Inquiry* – Wai 2700, (2024); H. Rattray "Ngā Wero a te Mana Wāhine:

Wāhine Māori justice and equity wellbeing, 1990–2020" in the Waitangi Tribunal's *Mana Wāhine Kaupapa Inquiry* – Wai 2700, (2024); T. Wolfgramm "He Wāhine, he Ōhanga; he Ōhanga, he Wāhine: Through Wāhine, Economic Development; by Wāhine, our Economy. The Socio-economic Status and Wellbeing of Wāhine Māori from 1990–2020" in the Waitangi Tribunal's *Mana Wāhine Kaupapa Inquiry* – Wai 2700, (2024); H. Tomlins-Jahnke "Toitū te Mana Wāhine Contemporary Employment and Education Issues for Wāhine Māori: Equity and Disparities from 1990" in the Waitangi Tribunal's *Mana Wāhine Kaupapa Inquiry* – Wai 2700, (2024); R. Wolfgramm "Mana Wāhine Māori i Ngā Wā o Mua: The impacts of Crown legislation, policy and practices on the rangatiratanga, status and roles of wāhine Māori c.1840–1950" in the Waitangi Tribunal's *Mana Wāhine Kaupapa Inquiry* – Wai 2700, (2024).

[24] These include a Mana Wāhine definitional report, a Remedies report, and Ngā Pou Hine reports, covering Land and climate, Family, Leadership, and Economy.

[25] Waitangi Tribunal *Wai 2700 Mana Wāhine Kaupapa Inquiry Joint Research Committee Terms of Reference* (Wai 2700 #3.1.273(b), 2020) at 2.

[26] An amount of $400,000 was allocated for this purpose as noted in above n 25, at 1.

[27] J. Paxman *Empire* (Penguin Books, London, 2011), at 242.

[28] A. Nandy *The Intimate Enemy: Loss and Recovery of Self Under Colonialism* (Oxford University Press, Delhi, 1983), at 10.

[29] By way of example, the three iwi of the ART Confederation (Te Āti Awa, Ngāti Raukawa and Ngāti Toa Rangatira) found themselves at this point by the mid-1970s. They have spent the last fifty years striving to undo the damage unleashed on them by wholesale land removal and environmental despoliation, implementing Whakatupuranga Rua Mano, an iwi planning strategy that sought to revitalise te reo Māori, restore relationships, look after the people and regain rangatiratanga.

[30] A. Smith *Conquest: Sexual Violence and America Indian Genocide* (South End Press, Cambridge, 2005) at 23.

[31] Awatere "Brief of Evidence of Donna Awatere-Huata", above n 15, at 5.

[32] Nandy "The Intimate Enemy", above n 28, at 11.

[33] H. Potter and S. Simonds "Takapou Whāriki: Diverse Experiences of Mana Wāhine" in the Waitangi Tribunal's Mana Wāhine Kaupapa Inquiry – Wai 2700, (2024).

[34] At 343.

[35] At 343.

[36] At 347.

[37] At 349.

[38] At 348.

[39] Tuakoi Ohia in above n 33, at 375; Kim McBreen put it succinctly: "I would hope that as a result of the claim we can stop talking about it", in above n 33, at 368.

[40] Kim McBreen quoted in above n 33, at 368.

[41] Veronica Tawhai quoted in above n 33, at 367.

[42] Kassie Hartendorp quoted in above n 33, at 366.

[43] Above n 33, at 371.

[44] K. Irwin "Towards Theories of Māori Feminisms" in R. Du Plessis (ed) *Feminist Voices: Women's Studies Texts for Aotearoa/New Zealand* (Oxford University Press, Auckland, 1992), 1 at 19.

[45] And by some Māori men – it should be noted that a small number of men gave evidence during the tūāpapa hearings.

[46] Tina Ngata "New Zealand's Māori women have more to contend with than ordinary sexism" *The Guardian* (online ed, New Zealand, 5 February 2021).

[47] Dr Tania Wolfgramm, "He Wāhine, he Ōhanga; he Ōhanga, he Wāhine: Through Wāhine, Economic Development; by Wāhine, our Economy. The Socio-economic Status and Wellbeing of Wāhine Māori from 1990–2020" in the Waitangi Tribunal's Mana Wāhine Kaupapa Inquiry – Wai 2700, (2024) at 78.

[48] Prue Kapua "On mana and misogyny: a message for Shane Jones from the Māori Women's Welfare League president" *The Spinoff* (online ed, New Zealand, 28 January 2020).

[49] L. Smith "Maori Women: Discourses, Projects and Mana Wahine" in S. Middleton and A. Jones (eds) *Women and Education in Aotearoa* (2nd ed, Bridget Williams Books, Wellington, 1992), at 47.

Chapter 14 | Rangatiratanga

1 I wish to acknowledge the work of my research assistant, Kate Hatley, in completing the groundwork on which this chapter is based.
2 The focus of this chapter is on te Tiriti o Waitangi, the te reo Māori language document that was debated and signed by rangatira.
3 Waitangi Tribunal *Whaia te Mana Motuhake In Pursuit of Mana Motuhake: Report on the Māori Community Development Act Claim* (Wai 2417, 2015).
4 Waitangi Tribunal *Report on the Trans-Pacific Partnership Agreement* (Wai 2522, 2016).
5 Waitangi Tribunal *Ngā Mātāpono The Principles: The Interim Report of the Tomokia Ngā Tatau o Matangireia – the Constitutional Kaupapa Inquiry Panel on the Crown's Treaty Principles Bill and Treaty Clause Review Policies* (Wai 3300, 2024) and Waitangi Tribunal *Ngā Mātāpono The Principles: Part II of the Interim Report of the Tomokia Ngā Tatau o Matangireia – the Constitutional Kaupapa Inquiry Panel on the Crown's Treaty Principles Bill and Treaty Clause Review Policies* (Wai 3300, 2024).
6 Margaret Mutu "Constitutional Intentions: The Treaty of Waitangi Texts" in Malcom Mulholland and Veronica Tawhai (eds) *Weeping Waters, The Treaty of Waitangi and Constitutional Change* (Huia Publishers, Wellington, 2010) at 24.
7 Maori Community Development Act 1962, s 18.
8 Above n 7, ss 9, 12 and 15.
9 Above n 7, s 7.
10 Above n 3, at 2.
11 Above n 3, at 27.
12 Above n 3, at 1 and 50.
13 Above n 3, at 49.
14 Above n 3, at 5.
15 Above n 3, at 267.
16 Above n 3, at 348.
17 Above n 3, at 348.
18 Above n 3, at 284 and 387.
19 Above n 3, at 26.
20 Above n 3, at 346 and 392.
21 Above n 3, at 27.
22 Above n 3, at 34.
23 Above n 3, at 38.
24 Above n 3, at 41.
25 Above n 3, at 40.
26 Waitangi Tribunal Memorandum 2.5.9, pp 15–16.
27 Above n 4, at 3.
28 Waitangi Tribunal *He Whakaputanga me te Tiriti The Declaration and the Treaty, The Report on Stage 1 of the Te Paparahi o Te Raki Inquiry* (Wai 1040, 2014).
29 Above n 4, at 5.
30 Above n 4, at 39.
31 Above n 4, at 38.
32 Above n 4, at 1.
33 Above n 4, at 4.
34 Above n 4, at 2 and 34.
35 Above n 4, at 39.
36 Above n 4, at 40.
37 Waitangi Tribunal *Ko Aotearoa Tēnei, A Report into Claims Concerning New Zealand Law and Policy Affecting Māori Culture and Identity* (Wai 262, 2011).
38 Above n 37, at 236–237.
39 Above n 3, at 8.
40 Waitangi Tribunal *The Report on the Comprehensive and Progressive Agreement for Trans-Pacific Partnership* (Wai 2522, 2023) at 20.
41 Ngā Toki Whakarururanga https://ngatoki.nz/.
42 Research Services Team, Waitangi Tribunal *Report Three: Research Reports Concerning Constitutional Issues Review of existing research in relation to constitutional matters for the start-up phase of the Waitangi Tribunal's Constitutional Kaupapa Inquiry (Wai 3300)* (Wai 3300, #6.2.1, 14 December 2023) at 8.
43 Memorandum – Directions of the Chief Judge Dr C.L. Fox, 17 April 2023 (Wai 3300 #2.3.1) at [7].
44 Memorandum – Directions of the Chief Judge Dr C.L. Fox commencing wānanga ā-rohe phase, 1 October 2024 (Wai 3300 #2.6.019) at [9].
45 Memorandum – Directions of the Chief Judge Dr C.L. Fox prior to first inquiry planning wānanga, 19 January 2024 (Wai 3300 #2.5.5) at [12], [14] and [18].
46 Memorandum – Directions of the Chief Judge Dr C.L. Fox regarding the second wānanga ā-rohe and forward planning for future wānanga, 19 February 2025 (Wai 3300 #2.6.46) at [5] and [16].

[47] Above n 5, Part 1 at 68.
[48] Above n 5, at 69.
[49] Above n 5, Part 1 at xvii.
[50] Above n 5, at 32.
[51] Above n 5, Part 2 at 109.
[52] Above n 5, Part 1 at 116 and Part 2 at 107–108.
[53] Above n 5, Part 2 at xvi and xv.
[54] Above n 5, Part 1 at 164.
[55] Above n 5, Part 1 at 174–175.
[56] Above n 5, Part 1 at 181.
[57] Above n 5, Part 1 at 137.
[58] Above n 5, Part 1 at 138.
[59] Above n 5, Part 1 at 139–140.
[60] Above n 5, Part 1 at 76.
[61] Above n 5, Part 1 at 79.
[62] Waitangi Tribunal, *Te Mana Whatu Ahuru: Report on Te Rohe Pōtae Claims* (Wai 898, 2023) vol 1 at 38–45.
[63] At 25.
[64] Above n 5, Part 1 at 109.
[65] At 25.
[66] Above n 5, Part 1 at 135.
[67] Above n 5, Part 2 at 103.
[68] Above n 5, Part 2 at 112.
[69] 1News "Waitangi Tribunal slams proposed new Treaty Bill" (Televised report, 16 August 2024) Waitangi Tribunal slams proposed new Treaty Bill | 1News on TVNZ+.
[70] Horizon Research *Human rights and Te Tiriti/ Treaty issues Prepared for Te Kāhui Tika Tangata Human Rights Commission* (November 2023) at 5 and 17.

Chapter 15 | Whakamana i te Tiriti

[1] Treaty of Waitangi Act 1975.
[2] Such as the proposed Regulatory Standards Bill and the Treaty Principles Clauses Review.

Notes on Contributors

Tai Ahu (Waikato-Tainui, Te Paatu, Ngāti Kahu) is a lawyer at Whāia Legal, Co-Tumuaki of Te Hunga Rōia Māori o Aotearoa and teaches law and tikanga at Te Herenga Waka, Victoria University of Wellington and Te Whare Wānanga o Awanuiārangi. Tai is a translator and interpreter, has two tamariki and lives in Ōtaki.

Maria Bargh (Te Arawa, Ngāti Awa) is Professor of Politics and Māori Studies at Te Herenga Waka, Victoria University of Wellington. She researches and teaches in the areas of Māori politics, te taiao, and diverse economies. She has led multi-year research projects and served on a number of governance boards.

Hon Justice Sir Edward Taihākurei Durie (Rangitāne, Ngāti Kauwhata, Ngāti Raukawa) was appointed a judge of the Māori Land Court in 1974. He has served as Chief Judge of the Māori Land Court (1980–1998), Chair of the Waitangi Tribunal (1980–2004), a judge of the High Court of New Zealand (1998–2004) and a member of the New Zealand Law Commission (2000–2010). He is a former Chair and a current Pou of the New Zealand Māori Council.

Chief Judge Dr Caren Fox (Ngāti Porou, Rongowhakaata) is the Chief Judge of the Māori Land Court and Chairperson of the Waitangi Tribunal and holds a PhD from Te Whare Wānanga o Awanuiārangi. She was first appointed to the Māori Land Court in 2000 and served as Deputy Chief Judge from 2010–2023. She was sworn in as the Chief Judge of the Māori Land Court in August 2023, the first women to hold this role in the Court's history.

Jayden Houghton (Rereahu Maniapoto) is a Senior Lecturer and Assistant Dean at the Faculty of Law, University of Auckland. He is the author of *Tikanga Māori and State Law* (Thomson Reuters, Wellington, 2025) as well as various articles and chapters on te Tiriti o Waitangi and tikanga Māori.

Horiana Irwin-Easthope is a Ngāti Porou, Rakaipaaka, Ngāti Kahungunu and Dharug woman. Horiana is a Tumuaki at Whāia Legal specialising in public law. Horiana has an LLB/BA (Majoring in Maori Resource Management) from Te Herenga Waka, Victoria University of Wellington and a LLM from Harvard Law School.

Judge Wilson Isaac (Ngāti Porou, Ngāi Tūhoe, Ngāti Kahungunu) was appointed to the Māori Land Court bench on 20 December 1993. He was appointed as Chief Judge of the Māori Land Court and chairperson of the Waitangi Tribunal in 2009, positions he held until his retirement in 2023. He currently retains an acting warrant as a Māori Land Court judge and continues to sit as a Waitangi Tribunal Presiding Officer. Judge Isaac was also appointed as a judge of the High Court of Niue in 2007 and of the High Court of the Cook Islands in 2010.

Carwyn Jones (Ngāti Kahungunu ki Te Wairoa) is a Kaihautū of Te Whare Whakatupu Mātauranga at Te Wānanga o Raukawa and teaches in the Ahunga Tikanga (Māori Laws and Philosophy) programme there. He is an Honorary Adjunct Professor at Te Kawa a Māui – the School of Māori Studies, at Te Herenga Waka, Victoria University of Wellington.

Rhiannon Jones (Ngāti Kahungunu ki Te Wairoa) is a māmā, teacher and researcher with Te Rōpū Rangahau Hauora a Eru Pōmare and the Department of Public Health, University of Otago, Wellington. Her work is underpinned by values of anti-racism, decolonisation and equity in health for whānau Māori. She is a registered dietitian.

Peter Meihana (Rangitāne, Ngāti Kuia, Ngāti Apa, Ngāi Tahu ki Mangamaunu) is Senior Lecturer in History at Te Kunenga ki Pūrehuroa, Massey University. He is a member of Te Rūnanga a Rangitāne o Wairau, a past member of Te Rūnanga o Ngāti Kuia, and sits on committees for Ngāti Apa. He researches and writes on the notion of Māori 'privilege', and on the histories of the Kurahaupō people of the northern South Island.

Ani Mikaere (Ngāti Raukawa (Ngāti Pareraukawa, Ngāti Huia), Ngāti Porou). As Pou Whakatupu Mātauranga at Te Wānanga o Raukawa, Ani is responsible for leading and promoting activity that nurtures and grows the mātauranga continuum—the constantly evolving body of knowledge that has been produced by successive generations of Māori theorists and practitioners.

Margaret Mutu (Ngāti Kahu, Te Rarawa, Ngāti Whātua) is the Professor of Māori Studies at Waipapa Taumata Rau, The University of Auckland and teaches courses on Māori language and Māori rights. She is also the chair of the representative council of her Ngāti Kahu nation, Te Rūnanga-ā-Iwi o Ngāti Kahu.

Jacqueline Paul (Ngā Puhi, Ngāti Tūwharetoa, Ngāti Kahungunu ki Heretaunga) is a researcher at Pūrangakura Kaupapa Māori Research Centre, specialising in Māori housing research and policy. She is also a doctoral candidate in urban planning at the Massachusetts Institute of Technology, researching treaties and indigenous housing sovereignty.

Jacinta Ruru (Raukawa, Ngāti Ranginui) MNZM, FRSNZ, PhD is Deputy Vice-Chancellor Māori and Distinguished Professor of Law, University of Otago. Jacinta researches how state legal systems should reconcile with their Indigenous peoples, their laws and knowledges, specifically considering how law and policy can be more te Tiriti o Waitangi compliant to better enable Māori to contribute towards caring for, owning, managing and governing lands and waters.

Linda Te Aho (Ngāti Koroki Kahukura, Ngāti Mahuta, Waikato) is an Associate Professor at Te Piringa Faculty of Law, University of Waikato and teaches Tikanga, Māori Land Law, and Indigenous Peoples' Rights. Linda holds senior governance positions for Waikato-Tainui and was an appointed guardian under the landmark settlement for the Waikato River ecosystem.

Metiria Turei (Ngāti Kahungunu ki Wairarapa, Te Āti Haunui a Pāpārangi, Rangitane, Te Ātiawa) joined the Faculty of Law at Ōtākou Whakaihu Waka in 2019. Her teaching includes Mātāpono Māori and Mātauranga Ture, Jurisprudence, Public Law and Tort Law. She was a Member of Parliament for fifteen years.

Tracey Whare (Raukawa, Te Whānau-a-Apanui) is a Pouako Matua of Te Wāhanga Ture at Waipapa Taumata Rau. Tracey currently teaches the first year law course, Law and Society, as well as Contemporary Tiriti issues. Her research focuses on Māori legal issues and Indigenous Peoples' rights in international law.

Hon Justice Sir Joe Williams (Ngāti Pūkenga, Te Arawa (Waitaha, Tapuika)) was appointed a judge of the Supreme Court in May 2019. Prior to this, he was a judge of the Court of Appeal (February 2018), a judge of the High Court (September 2008), Chairperson of the Waitangi Tribunal (2004) and Chief Judge of the Māori Land Court (December 1999). He has an LLB from Victoria University of Wellington and an LLM (Hons) from the University of British Columbia.

Index

aboriginal title *see* customary title
ACT Party 200
Anderson, Robyn 147
Aotearoa Independent Monitoring Mechanism 141
Asher, Bill 47
Awatere, Donna 209, 215

Baragwanath, Sir David 18–19
Bassett, Michael 38
Battersby, John 32
Bazley, Margaret 147
Belgrave, Michael 26, 36–37, 39
Bennett, Bishop Manuhuia 18, 19, 151, 176
binding recommendations 8, 129, 131, 137–40, 143
Binney, Judith 31–32
Birch, Sir William 17
Brash, Don 102
Byrnes, Giselle 26, 36

Cairns, Tamati 65
Cameron, Awhina 216
Cammell, Kathryn 114
casebook method 28, 33, 38
Central North Island forests settlement 129, 142
chairpersons 5–6
see also Durie, Edward Taihākurei; Fox, Caren; Isaac, Wilson; Scott, Ken; Williams, Sir Joseph
Chhour, Karen 200–202
claim kaupapa 156–57, 163–64, 169, 171–72
claimants 150–51, 164, 238, 240
claims criteria 5
Clarke, H.T. 31–32
Clarke, John 176, 179
co-governance and co-management 55–56, 70–71, 75, 77
constitutional issues
kāwanatanga–tino rangatiratanga relationship 81, 141, 171, 224, 230, 238–39, 248
legal fictions and Crown assumptions 45, 51, 88–89, 98, 103, 127, 129, 235
Māori self-governance arrangements 226–28, 237
representation in international fora 229–32, 237
tino rangatiratanga scope 62, 142, 224, 227–28, 235, 237–39
transformation of constitutional arrangements 140–42, 248
Constitutional Kaupapa Inquiry
Ngā Mātāpono reports 224, 234, 235–36
regional wānanga approach 142, 233–34, 238
Treaty Clause Review and 234–35, 238, 249
Treaty Principles Bill and 234–35
constitutional roles
of the courts 247
of executive branch of government 229
of kāwanatanga 228, 231–32
of the Treaty 14, 68, 235, 238, 247–48
of the Tribunal 201–2, 247
contra proferentem 52
Cooke, Sir Robin 18, 161
Cooper, Whina 206
Corban, Brian 20, 147
Couch, Ben Riwai 17
Crown Forestry Rental Trust 21, 147–48
Crown responses to Tribunal reports
claim kaupapa responded to 166, 169, 172, 211
Māori-led responses 170–71, 172, 199
political will and 156–57, 164–65, 166–70, 172, 218
recommendations responded to 66, 167–69, 172, 192
rejection/disregarding of recommendations 75, 133, 137, 166, 199, 231, 237, 240
section 81 reports 80
unwillingness 54, 76, 80–81, 169, 218
Crown settlement policies
averting binding recommendations 128–29, 131, 137–40, 143
Crown control of process 128, 130–32
cultural conflict 128, 132, 135
divide-and-rule tactics 132, 135
impacts on claimants of 101, 131–32, 135, 146
inquiries into 128, 133–37, 146, 175

'large natural groupings' requirement 130, 134, 137
mandating process 128, 134–35, 136, 139
negotiation tactics 131–32, 136
obfuscation of Crown's intent 129–30, 132, 142
see also Treaty settlements
Crown–Māori relationship *see* Māori–Crown relationship
customary fishing rights
in court decisions 111–12, 117, 118–19
in Fisheries Settlement 119–22
in legislation 102, 110–11, 118, 119–21, 123
in regulations 121
Tribunal reports 110, 112–15, 117–19
customary rights, issues 33–34, 67, 112
customary title 54, 87, 89, 97, 103

Dawson, Martin 18
decolonisation 217–18
Delamere, Sir Monita 3, 16, 18, 19
Dennis, Hurimoana 195
Department of Conservation lands 130–31
district inquiry programme 7, 23, 245
District Māori Councils 14, 225–27
Doctrine of Discovery 131, 140, 141
Doogan, Mike 179
Durie, Edward Taihākurei 2–3, 15, 16–18, 27, 148, 151
Durie, Mason 210

Education Act 1989 165
Elias, Dame Sian 18
Ellison, Craig 122
English, Bill 79
Evans, Ripeka 206, 211
Everton, Rangiaho 161

Finlay, Martyn 15–16
fiscal envelope policy 27–28
fisheries
customary title to 110
in English text of the Treaty 45, 46
quota management system (QMS) 116–17, 119–20, 123, 136
traditional practices 48, 102
Tribunal reports 112–15, 117–19
see also customary fishing rights
Fisheries Settlement
1989 Interim Fisheries Settlement 119
1992 Fisheries Settlement 109, 119–20, 134
court decisions 123–24
political context 109–10
rangatiratanga and 108, 120, 122–23
Te Ohu Kai Moana Limited 119–20, 122, 123
Flavell, Te Ururoa 176
Fletcher, Ned 25
Foreshore and Seabed Act 2004 94–96, 103–4, 140
foreshore and seabed inquiry (Wai 1071)
Māori property rights extinguished 86, 94–95, 96, 97
Māori use rights to be defined by Crown 95–96, 102
public access 94, 97
recommendations 100, 103
tikanga evidence 90–93
Tiriti o Waitangi analysis 91, 98–99
foreshore and seabed issues
context of 87–90, 94–96, 100–103
Labour Government proposal 89–90, 94–97
ownership 88–90, 94
political scaremongering 84, 90, 93, 96, 97, 103
protest hikoi 86
public access 94, 97, 103
stakeholders 95
see also Marine and Coastal Area (Takutai Moana) Act 2011
foreshore and seabed urgent inquiriy (Wai 3400) 104–6
Fox, Caren 233
freshwater (wai)
co-management of 55–56, 70–71, 75, 77
degradation and pollution of 44, 52, 55, 57–58, 63
interconnectedness of water systems 55, 56–57, 65
iwi hapū relationship with 42, 43–44, 45, 53–54, 60–65, 67, 74
kaitiakitanga of 44, 57–58, 64–65, 70, 76
mauri of 45–47, 64–65, 67
ownership/rangatiratanga over 50–54, 56, 58–59, 62, 66–71, 72–74, 79–82, 113
as taonga 49, 51, 59, 63, 66–68

Te Mana o te Wai 57, 75, 76, 78, 80
Tribunal recommendations 56, 75–79
well-being of 44, 54, 55–58, 75
see also rivers
freshwater inquiry
customary rights 70–71, 74
Mighty River Power share sale issue 78–80
resource management reform 74–75, 76–77
Stage one Report 65, 68, 70, 72–74, 78
Stage two Report 70–71, 74–75, 76–78, 80
Supreme Court's conclusions 79–80
and tino rangatiratanga 69–71, 72–73
water allocation reform 77–78

Genter, Julie Anne 211
geothermal inquiry 66, 72, 79–80, 179, 180
Gisborne inquiry 146–47
Graham, Douglas 129, 137

Hamer, Paul 147
Hartendorp, Kassie 217
Hauora report 57, 188–92
Hauraki 137
Hayward, Janine 6
He Maunga Rongo report 64, 67–68
He Whakaputanga me te Tiriti report 133, 141, 210, 229, 234, 237
Health and Disability System Review 192
Health Services and Outcomes Kaupapa Inquiry 182, 187–93
see also *Hauora* report; Te Aka Whai Ora (the Māori Health Authority)
Henare, Denese 206
Hingston, Heta Kenneth 20, 88
historical inquiries
casebook method 28, 33, 38
definition of historical claims 6, 23
district inquiry programme 7, 23, 27, 245
loss of land and resources 14–15, 208, 213–14
National Overview Report 27–28
proliferation of claims 23, 148, 183, 208–10
Rangahaua Whānui research programme 27–28, 39, 148, 245
see also Mōhaka ki Ahuriri inquiry; Te Tau Ihu inquiry; Te Urewera inquiry
histories
academic v. Tribunal history 25–26, 30–31, 36–40
conflicting narratives 39
contextualists v. presentists 36–38
historians' analyses of the Treaty 25
oral and written histories 22, 26–27, 31–32
Hoani Waititi Marae 184–85
Horomia, Parekura 176
Horowhenua The Muaūpoko Priority Report, 39–40
housing needs of Māori see *Kāinga Kore* report
Huata, Canon Wi Te Tau 49

Ingram, Sir John 20
Irwin, Kathie 115
Isaac, Wilson 9, 29, 175

Jackson, Moana 205, 209, 250
James, Paul 115
Joe, Ramon 46
Jones, Carwyn 69
Jones, Pei Te Hurinui 24
Jones, Shane 219–20

Kahu Aronui 165, 170–71
Kāinga Kore report 193–97
kaitiakitanga
concept of 53, 64, 69–71, 76, 92
of foreshore and seabed 100
of rivers and water bodies 44, 57–58, 64–65, 70, 76
of taonga species 162, 168
of taonga works 163, 165
Kaituna River 53, 66, 113
Kapua, Prue 219–20
"Karanga Rā" 2–3
kaupapa inquiries
procedural changes for 9, 176, 178
social policy issues 184
Tribunal membership 176–78
see also Constitutional Kaupapa Inquiry; Health Services and Outcomes Kaupapa Inquiry; Mana Wāhine Kaupapa Inquiry (Wai 2700); Oranga Tamariki inquiries; *Te Whānau o Waipareira Report*
Kawharu, Sir Hugh 19–20, 69
Kereopa, Hōhepa 65
Kermadec Ocean Sanctuary 123

Kidd, Sir Doug 177, 207
King, Martin Luther Jr. 250
Kīngitanga 13
Kirkwood, Carmen 18
Kneebone, John 20
Ko Aotearoa Tēnei see Wai 262 inquiry
kōhanga reo 158–59, 168
Kruger, Tamati 30
Kurahaupō-Rangitāne claims 34–35

Lake Taupō 67–68
land tenure 14, 29, 87, 135
Lands (state-owned enterprises) case 17–18, 128–29
Lange, David 2–3
Latimer, Sir Graham 16–17
legal aid 21
Luxon, Christopher 237

MACA Act *see* Marine and Coastal Area (Takutai Moana) Act 2011
mana wāhine claim (Wai 361) 205–9
Mana Wāhine Kaupapa Inquiry (Wai 2700) 178–79, 208, 211–12, 215–18
mana whenua 135
Mangatū Remedies Report 138
Manukau Harbour claim 18, 47, 55
Māori Appellate Court 35–36, 39
Maori Community Development Act 1962 225
Māori Community Development Act claim, report on see *Whaia te Mana Motuhake* report
Māori Health Authority 57–58, 188, 191–92
Māori Land Court 35, 87–88
Māori Land Court judges 5, 15, 20, 87
Maori Language Acts 164–65, 167
Māori Language Commission 165
Māori Plant Varieties Committee (MPVC) 168–69
Māori Television Service 170
Māori Trade Marks Advisory Committee (MTMAC) 168–69
Māori Wardens 225–27
Māori Women's Welfare League 206–7
Māori–Crown relationship 171, 177, 180, 230, 235, 238–39, 250
Marine and Coastal Area (Takutai Moana) Act 2011 104–5
Marlborough Sounds mussel farms 87–89
mātauranga Māori
  Māori world view 55–57, 63–64, 84, 91–93, 205
  traditional knowledge 45, 48, 59, 102, 155, 162–63, 168, 213–14
  see also tikanga
Matike Mai Aotearoa 141–42
McAloon, Jim 26, 36
McGechan, Andrew 36
Mead, Aroha 217
Mead, Hirini 176
Metge, Dame Joan 19
Military Veterans Kaupapa Inquiry 176, 178–79
Milroy, Stephanie 116
Milroy, Wharehuia 147, 176
Minhinnick, Nganeko 18
Mōhaka ki Ahuriri Inquiry (Wai 201) 28–29, 46, 48, 53, 179–80
Moorsom, Richard 147, 175
Morris, Joanne 18, 20
Motunui–Waitara Report 17, 46, 50, 55, 113–14
Muldoon Government 16, 17
Muriwhenua Fishing Report 117–19
Muriwhenua Land Report 138
Mutu, Margaret 178, 224

Nandy, Ashis 213
Napier Hospital inquiry 179
National Iwi Chairs Forum 140–41
National Overview Report 27–28
National Park District Inquiry 180
National Party 103
National-led coalition government (2023–2026)
  ACT party coalition agreement 200
  policies 81, 104–5, 141, 171, 172, 192–93, 199, 249
  reactions to 141–42
Native Land Court 29–30, 87
native title *see* customary title
New Zealand Māori Council 14, 17–18, 128–29, 160, 206, 225
Newton, Pania 219
Ngā Toki Whakarururanga 232
Nga wai hono i te po, Kuīni 59
Ngāi Tahu
  boundary disputes 32–36, 178
  High Court hearing on waterways 54, 81–82
  inquiry (Wai 27) 24, 26–27, 34, 39
Ngai Tahu Sea Fisheries Report 117–18
Ngarimu, Kim 177

Ngata, Apirana 24
Ngata, Sir Henare 14
Ngata, Tina 216, 219
Ngāti Apa 87–89
Ngāti Kahu 138
Ngāti Porou 177
Ngāti Rangi 180
Ngāti Whare 22, 32
Ngāti Whatua 16
Northover, Tuahine 147

Office of Treaty Settlements 129–30, 136–38, 142–43, 147
Oliver, W.H. 25, 26, 36–37
Oranga Tamariki inquiries
    Oranga Tamariki (Section 7AA) inquiry (Wai 3350) 199–202
    structural racism and 198–99
    tamariki Māori in state care inquiry (Wai 2915) 197–99
    Tribunal's power to summons Ministers of the Crown 201–2
Orange, Claudia 25
O'Regan, Rolland 13
O'Regan, Tā Tipene 112
Orr, Gordon 20, 148, 151
ownership
    Crown's assumption of 51, 94
    exclusive ownership v. mana whenua 72, 135
    of freshwater 51–54, 59, 66–68, 73, 80, 113, 180
    not a consequence of sovereignty 89–90
    of takutai moana 87–90, 97, 103
    see also rangatiratanga

Pae Ora (Healthy Futures) Act 2022 192
Parsonson, Ann 147
patriarchy 212–13, 214–15, 218
Paul, Cletus Maanu 65
Paul, Jacqueline 195
Pawson, Eric 115
Petroleum Report Part 1 101–2
Phillipson, Grant 36–38, 147, 175
Poroti Springs 68
post-settlement governance entities 131, 134
protests 13–14, 15–16, 141
Public Health and Disability Act 2000 189–90
radio spectrum
    context of inquiries 159
    Interim Māori Spectrum Commission 170
    Te Huarahi Tika Trust 170
    Wai 26/150 159–60, 166
    Wai 776 160–61, 166
Radiocommunications Act 1989 159, 161
Rangahaua Whānui research programme 27–28, 39, 148, 245
rangatiratanga
    concept of 49–51, 53–54, 58–59, 69, 186, 210, 223, 236
    constitutional sphere 141–42
    in contemporary settings 222, 227
    Crown attempts to redefine 122–23, 235
    Crown recognition of 120–21
    in He Whakaputanga 49
    and the Indigenous Declaration 222, 227–28
    kaitiakitanga and 71
    ownership and 53–54, 66–68, 72–74, 103, 113
    partnership and 71–72, 122
    in te Tiriti 46, 49–51, 62, 68, 81, 114, 160, 198
    tikanga and 224, 236
    tino rangatiratanga of hapū 134, 186, 210
    undermining of 45, 48, 50, 56, 81, 136, 159, 162, 163, 186, 207, 209, 236
    see also customary title; ownership
Rata, Matiu 2–3, 14–15
Raumati, Ngaropi 216
Reeves, Paul 2–3
resource management 55, 57, 70–71, 75–77, 78, 80
Resource Management Act 1991 (RMA) 53, 71, 74–75, 76–77, 80–81, 94
Richardson, Sir Ivor 18
Richmond, James 31
Rigby, Barry 20
rivers
    in English common law 52
    hāngi stones in 49, 50
    kai sovereignty and 47–48, 57–58, 66
    traditional river knowlege and 48, 59
    as tūpuna 52
    see also freshwater (wai); *specific river names*
Ross, Ruth 25
Savage, Patrick 161, 176

Scott, Ken 16
Sealord deal 23, 103, 120, 122
settlements *see* Treaty settlements
Seymour, David 237
Sharples, Pita 176
Sim Commission 15
Simmonds, Naomi 216–17
Sinclair, Douglas 14
Sinclair, Keith 24–25
Smit, Grace 176
Smith, Linda 220
Sorrenson, Keith 19, 28, 179
Southwick, Laurie 16
sovereignty
  authority not ownership 88–90
  fallacy that sovereignty was ceded 30, 133, 140, 229
  legal fiction of indivisibility of 127
State-Owned Enterprises Bill (SOE Bill) 116, 128–29
Stokes, Dame Evelyn 15, 20, 179
structural racism 198–99
Sullivan, Sir Desmond 20
Szaszy, Dame Mira 205–7, 219–20

Tahuparae, John 176
takutai moana *see* foreshore and seabed issues
Takutai Moana Act 2011 Urgent Inquiry Stage 1 (Wai 3400) 104–6
Tangaere, Julie 176
taonga
  creative works 162–63, 165–66, 171
  definitions 46, 49, 155, 161
  flora and fauna species 57–58, 162, 168
  freshwater 71, 73, 78
  mātauranga Māori 155
  radio spectrum 160–61, 166, 170
  rivers 45–46, 49, 51, 59, 63, 65–68
  te reo 158
  Tiriti guarantee of rangatiratanga 46–47, 71, 155, 160–61
Tau, Te Maire 59
Taupō 67–68
Tauranga inquiry 38
Te Aho, Linda 62, 63, 231–32
Te Aka Whai Ora 57–58, 188, 191–92
Te Hāhi Rātana 13, 14
Te Heuheu, Dame Georgina 18, 20
Te Ika Whenua Rivers Report 51, 67
Te Kete Pūputu: The Online Guide to the Mana Wāhine Tūāpapa Evidence 212
Te Kooti 30–31
Te Pae Tawhiti 165–66, 171, 172
Te Paparahi o Te Raki Inquiry, Stage 1 133, 141, 210, 229, 234, 237
Te Pāti Māori 87, 103–4
te reo Māori
  in broadcasting 159–60
  critical state of 158, 214
  in education 159, 165
  Maori Language Acts 164–65, 167
  revitalisation of 160, 167, 171
  Wai 11 158, 164, 167
  Wai 262 158–59, 167
  Wai 2336 159, 167–68
Te Rōpū Whakamana i te Tiriti o Waitangi *see* Waitangi Tribunal
Te Tau Ihu inquiry 33–36, 178
Te Taumata Whakapumau 165, 170
Te Ture Whenua Māori Act 1993 87, 95
Te Urewera inquiry 29–33
Te Weehi case 112, 118
Te Whānau o Waipareira Report 184–87
Temara, Pou 176
Temm, Paul 18
Tiakiawa, Te Irirangi Cairo 53, 66
tikanga
  evidence in inquiries 90–91, 211–12
  gender equality 205
  interconnectedness 55–57, 63–64, 84, 90–93, 213–16
  rangatiratanga and 224, 236
  reciprocity 92
  see also kaitiakitanga; mātauranga Māori; whanaungatanga
Tipping, Andrew 36
Tirikatene, Whetu 13
Tiriti o Waitangi
  as a constitutional document 14, 68, 235, 238, 247–48
  Crown's Article 2 obligations 69, 71, 81, 91, 155, 158, 161, 185–87
  as a living instrument 114, 161
  tino rangatiratanga in 50, 68–69, 70–71, 81, 155, 210
  Tribunal understandings of 30, 46, 98–99, 133, 225
  see also Treaty of Waitangi
Tomokia Ngā Tatau o Matangireia inquiry *see* Constitutional Kaupapa Inquiry
Trans-Pacific Partnership Agreement 10, 229–31

Trans-Pacific Partnership Agreement inquiry (Wai 2522) 224, 228–32, 237–39
Trapski, Sir Peter 20
Treaty of Waitangi
English text compared to te Tiriti 25, 46, 210
fisheries in 45, 46
pre-emption in 98
undisturbed possession in 98, 116, 122
see also Tiriti o Waitangi
Treaty of Waitangi Act 1975 4, 15–16, 25, 248
Treaty of Waitangi Amendment Acts 6, 19, 249
Treaty of Waitangi (Fisheries Claims) Settlement Act 1992 102
Treaty principles
active protection 26, 53, 99, 105, 114, 115, 186, 191, 194–95, 235
ahistorical nature of 26
duty to consult/engage with Māori 180, 192, 194–95, 226, 231, 235
equity 9, 98–99, 189–91, 194, 202
good faith 105, 234
good government 93–94, 105, 194–95, 235
options 99, 191, 199
partnership 70–71, 76, 99, 160–61, 187, 191, 193–95, 199, 234
rangatiratanga 9, 186, 190
reciprocity 99, 236
redress 99–100, 236
in statutes 115
in Tribunal's terms of reference 4
Treaty Principles Bill 234–36, 248–49
Treaty Principles Clauses Review 234–35, 238, 249
Treaty settlements
impacts of 45, 54, 56, 58–59, 101, 128, 142
lands and resources not available for 130–31
see also Crown settlement policies
Tribunal inquiries, processes
boundary disputes and cross-claims 34–35, 178
casebook method 28, 33, 38
commissioning research 27–28, 39, 148
effectiveness of 164, 169, 180
flexibility of 179, 245–46
interim recommendations 246
for kaupapa inquiries 178–79, 211–12
new approach to 146–47
powers to summon Ministers of the Crown 201–2
prioritising claims 176
regional wānanga approach 142, 178, 233, 238
tikanga-informed approach 17, 19, 233
tūāpapa hearings 211–12
venues and 16–17, 48, 178
Western judicial approach 16, 179, 233
Tribunal reports
as sources of information 25, 82, 113, 133, 240, 250
as taonga 43–45, 63
as tools for debate and advocacy 76, 169, 245
tūāpapa hearings 211–12
Tuheitia Potatau Te Wherowhero, Kīngi 59, 105
Tūhoe 29–30
Turangi township reports 47, 138
Turei, Sir John 19, 176, 179
Turia, Dame Tariana 59, 86–87, 103
Tūwharetoa 180

United Nations
Indigenous Declaration 132, 140, 141, 222, 225–28
interventions 140, 142

veterans inquiry *see* Military Veterans Kaupapa Inquiry

wai *see* freshwater (wai)
Wai 262 inquiry
Crown responses to 165–66
kaitiakitanga 64, 69, 71, 76, 163
Māori engagement in decision-making 69, 231
taonga species 58, 162, 168–69
taonga works 162–63, 165–66
Wai 1071 inquiry *see* foreshore and seabed inquiry (Wai 1071)
Waiau Pā Power Station Claim 16, 113
Waikato River 47, 54, 55–56, 58
Waikerepuru, Huirangi 158
Wairarapa Moana ki Pouākani claim 139–40
Waitangi Tribunal

amendment to jurisdiction 183
biculturalism 4, 7, 12, 17, 149–50, 246
establishment 4–5, 16, 140, 247–48
first ten years 6, 63, 183
future directions 82, 152
governance group 147
influence on public opinions 115, 167, 212, 218, 240, 246
members 5–6, 7, 16, 19–21, 149, 246–47
prohibited issues 5, 131
reconciliation and nation-building role 2–4, 7, 45, 58–59, 82–83, 145, 243, 246
statutory role and functions 5, 43–45, 167, 183–84, 247
underfunding of 179, 208
see also chairpersons; historical inquiries; kaupapa inquiries; Tribunal inquiries, processes; Tribunal reports
Walker, Keita 19, 147
Walker, Ranginui 25
Ward, Alan 20, 25, 27, 39
wastewater disposal 55, 57
Wetere, Koro 2–3, 19, 116
Whaia te Mana Motuhake report 225–28, 237
whakapapa 63–64, 84, 91–93, 213–15
Whakatōhea 137
whanaungatanga 64, 134, 200
Whanganui River 52, 56–57, 67
Wheen, Nicola 6
Whiting, Cliff 59
Whitmore, George 31–32
Williams, David 23, 38
Williams, Sir Joseph 8, 64, 145, 150–51
Willis, Max 17
Wilson, Bill 18, 20
Wilson, Margaret 102, 138
Winiata, Whatarangi 13, 17
women's status
according to tikanga 205, 209, 211–12, 218
colonisation and 209, 212–15, 217–18, 219
colonised thinking about 219–20
erosion of 206, 214, 216
female–male disparities 219
injustice of 204, 205–6, 209
Mana Wāhine Joint Research Committee 212
remedies sought 207–8, 215–17
tikanga evidence on Tribunal website 212
see also mana wāhine claim (Wai 361); Mana Wāhine Kaupapa Inquiry (Wai 2700)